THE BEST
MEXICAN
TRAVEL
TIPS

Also by John Whitman

The Best European Travel Tips

THE BEST MEXICAN TRAVEL TIPS

John Whitman

PERENNIAL LIBRARY

HARPER & ROW, PUBLISHERS, New York
Cambridge, Philadelphia, San Francisco, London
Mexico City, São Paulo, Singapore, Sydney

FIRST EDITION

Designer: Judy Allan (THE DESIGNING WOMAN CONCEPTS)

Library of Congress Cataloging-in-Publication Data

Whitman, John
  The best Mexican travel tips.

  "Perennial Library."
  Includes index.
  1. Mexico—Description and travel—1981–   —
Guide-books. I. Title.
F1209.W44   1986   917.89'0453   85-45241
ISBN 0-06-096035-3 (pbk.)

87 88 89 90 MPC 10 9 8 7 6 5 4 3

CONTENTS

INTRODUCTION

Mexico is the land of the good, the bad, and the ugly. Getting what you want (the good), avoiding or dealing with the bad, and accepting the ugly—that's what this book is all about. Below is the good —seventy reasons why over 5 million people from the United States and Canada travel to Mexico each year.

70 REASONS TO GO TO MEXICO

- ☐ Archaeology
- ☐ Art
- ☐ Ballet
- ☐ Beachcombing
- ☐ Beaches
- ☐ Bird watching
- ☐ Boating
- ☐ Body surfing
- ☐ Bullfights
- ☐ Business
- ☐ Camping
- ☐ Churches
- ☐ Clamming
- ☐ Cockfights
- ☐ Diving
- ☐ Drinking
- ☐ Dune buggies
- ☐ Exploration
- ☐ Festivals
- ☐ Fishing
- ☐ Folklore
- ☐ Food
- ☐ Fossil hunting
- ☐ Golf

- ☐ Hang gliding
- ☐ Hiking
- ☐ Horse racing
- ☐ Hunting
- ☐ Indian culture
- ☐ Jai alai
- ☐ Markets
- ☐ Motorcycling
- ☐ Mountain climbing
- ☐ Museums
- ☐ Music
- ☐ Natural wonders
- ☐ Night life
- ☐ Nude bathing
- ☐ Painting
- ☐ Parasailing
- ☐ People
- ☐ Photography
- ☐ Recreational vehicles (RVs)
- ☐ Relaxation
- ☐ Resorts
- ☐ Retirement
- ☐ Riding
- ☐ Rodeo

- ☐ Romance
- ☐ Ruins
- ☐ Sailing
- ☐ Sex
- ☐ Shelling
- ☐ Shopping
- ☐ Sightseeing
- ☐ Snorkeling
- ☐ Soccer
- ☐ Spas
- ☐ Spectacles
- ☐ Study
- ☐ Sun
- ☐ Surfing
- ☐ Swimming
- ☐ Tennis
- ☐ Train rides
- ☐ Water skiing
- ☐ Whale watching
- ☐ White water rafting
- ☐ Wildflowers
- ☐ Wind surfing
- ☐ Yachting

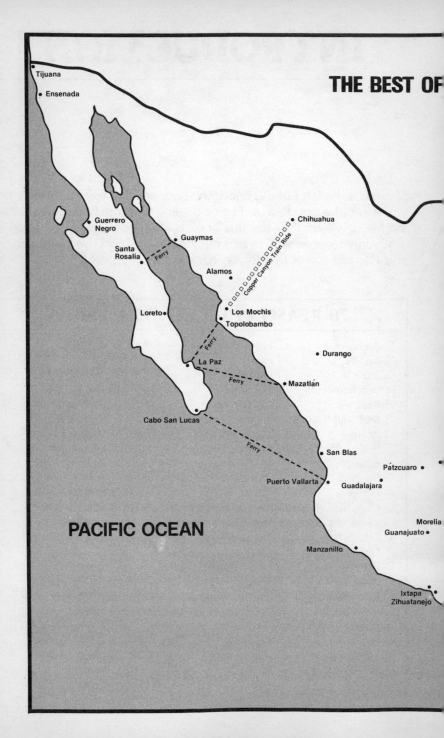

THE BEST OF

PACIFIC OCEAN

- Tijuana
- Ensenada
- Guerrero Negro
- Santa Rosalia
- Guaymas
- Alamos
- Chihuahua
- Loreto
- Los Mochis
- Topolobambo
- La Paz
- Durango
- Mazatlán
- Cabo San Lucas
- San Blas
- Puerto Vallarta
- Guadalajara
- Pátzcuaro
- Morelia
- Guanajuato
- Manzanillo
- Ixtapa Zihuatanejo

Copper Canyon Train Ride

Ferry

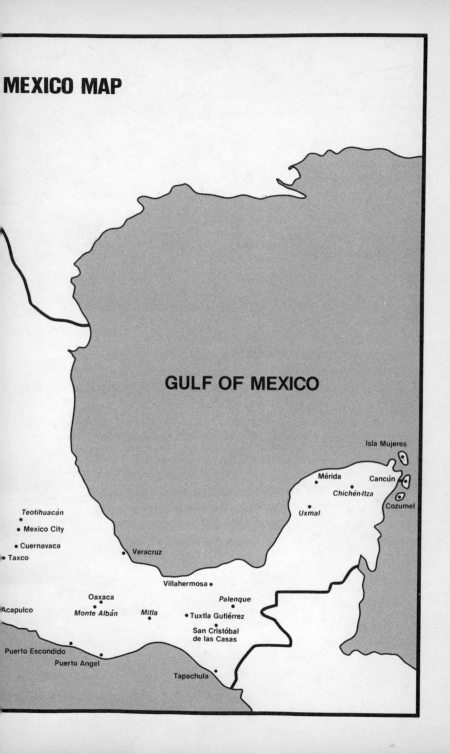

MEXICO MAP

GULF OF MEXICO

Isla Mujeres

Mérida •   Cancún
     • Chichén-Itza
Uxmal •   Cozumel

• Teotihuacán
• Mexico City
• Cuernavaca
• Taxco
    • Veracruz

    Villahermosa •

   Oaxaca •   Palenque
Acapulco
  Monte Albán   Mitla •   • Tuxtla Gutiérrez
          San Cristóbal
          de las Casas
Puerto Escondido •
   Puerto Angel
      Tapachula •

TRAVEL DOCUMENTS

You'll need certain documents to travel freely through Mexico or to avoid potential problems. Here are some tips to make the whole process of getting these documents less costly and more enjoyable.

PASSPORTS

If you are planning a trip to Mexico, it's a good idea, but not required, to obtain a passport. If you already have one, check the expiration date to make sure that your passport will be valid for the entire length of your trip. If it will expire during your stay in Mexico, apply for a new one ahead of time.

Kinds of passports

• If you plan to travel extensively through Central and South America, ask for the special forty-eight page passport when you apply. It costs no more than the standard document and provides added space for the visas you will need (see p. 9).

When to apply for a passport

• If you intend to travel to countries which require visas, apply for a passport as much as six months in advance. This will give you enough time to get visas (Mexico requires visas only for business travelers and students).

● You can pay extra to get a passport in as little as three days. In an emergency you can obtain a passport in one day, at a substantial fee. This service is not available to the jet setter who decides on a whim to get a passport overnight; it is reserved for emergencies only!

Applying for a first passport

● To get your first passport, you must apply in person at the appropriate agency, as must all members of your family who are twelve years of age or older. Younger children need not apply in person.

● The passport agency is listed in your telephone directory under U.S. Government Offices. If there is no passport agency in your town, the service may be handled by a federal, state, or probate courthouse or at a designated post office. Call the listed number for hours.

● Be sure to ask the clerk about the least busy hours to come in and apply for a passport. This can save you an hour or two of waiting in line!

What to bring when you apply

PASSPORT APPLICATION   You will need to fill out a passport application in person at the appropriate passport agency.

PROOF OF U.S. CITIZENSHIP   For proof of U.S. citizenship, come armed with a birth certificate or certified copy (it must have a raised seal to be valid) or with a certificate of naturalization or citizenship. If you don't have any of these, you can get by with certificates of baptism or circumcision; hospital birth records; documentary evidence from census, school, or insurance companies; or affidavits. No proof, no passport!

PROOF OF IDENTITY   If you're known to the clerk or if you have a certificate of naturalization or citizenship, that's all the proof of identity you'll need. Otherwise you must produce a valid driver's license, a government identification card or pass, or a witness. The witness must have valid identification (passport, driver's license, government pass, or certificate of naturalization or citizenship) and must have known you for at least two years. All identification must bear signatures and photos.

TWO PASSPORT PHOTOS You'll need two passport photos, taken within the last six months. Each should be signed on the front, along the left-hand edge. Note that photos taken in a photomat machine will not be acceptable. Passport photos must be 2 inches by 2 inches. They should be clear, front-view shots of your head and shoulders only, taken against a white background. No hats or sunglasses allowed! Prints must be on thin, nonglossy paper. Photos can be either in color or in black and white.

Passport photos

- Agencies no longer allow passports with a dark background, and this has caused some resentment and confusion. Photos must be taken with a white background.

- Many agencies issuing passports now offer a passport photo service as well. Be sure to call ahead to see whether or not such a service is available in your area. Ask what the fee will be and the cost of *extra* prints. Then call several passport photo studios listed under the same title in the yellow pages as well as the local branch of the American Automobile Association (AAA) for cost comparison. A separate trip might save you several dollars if you're on a tight budget.

- You will need two photos for your passport. You should always carry two spares for emergencies. And you will need additional photos for visas (see p. 9).

Passport fees

- You will be charged both a passport fee and an execution fee for each passport. The execution fee varies from one area to the next. Call ahead to see what the total charges will be.

- When you call, ask how the payment should be made. Some offices refuse to take cash and may insist on a bank draft, money order, or check (personal, traveler's, certified, or cashier's). Avoid this situation: "What do you mean you won't take cash?" You've been warned!

Applying if you have had a passport before

• If you have had a passport during the last eight years and don't intend to make a change, apply for you new passport by mail. This will save you a trip and the execution fee.

• Call the nearest passport agency and ask them to send you Passport Office Form DSP-82, "Application for Passport by Mail." When this form arrives in the mail, fill it out, sign, and date it. Attach your old passport, two up-to-date passport photos signed on the front along the left-hand edge, and a check or money order to cover the passport fee.

• If your name has changed, be sure to include the original or a certified copy of your marriage certificate, or of the change-of-name papers, when making an application by mail.

• Be sure to send the passport by registered mail and hold on to the receipt until the new passport arrives.

• **A special note:** If you were under eighteen when you applied for your old passport, you'll have to apply for the new one in person.

• Naturally, you can always apply for a passport in person if you prefer. But in that case you must pay the execution fee.

Protecting yourself and your passport

• When your passport arrives in the mail, check it for correctness before signing it. If there is an error in any of the information, you must return the passport to have it corrected. Fill in the information on the inside (your home address, your foreign address, and a person to contact in case of emergency). This is the only information you can change at a later date without invalidating the document. Never write in, alter, or mutilate any portion of a passport, as this would make it invalid.

• Make two photocopies of the information contained in your

passport. These photocopies will be invaluable if your passport is lost or stolen. File one of the photocopies in a safe place and take the other with you to Mexico. Don't carry it with your passport!

If you lose your passport in the United States or Canada

● If your passport is lost or stolen in the United States, contact the Passport Office, Department of State, Washington, DC 20524 *immediately.* You'll need the information which you've recorded on a photocopy of the original passport.

● Canadian citizens should report lost or stolen passports to the closest Canadian passport office. You'll find one in each province.

VISAS

Visas are special notations and stamps, added to your passport by officials of foreign countries, which allow you to enter and leave these countries. Mexico does not require visas except for long-term study and for business travel.

● Business travelers should get visas well in advance of a trip to Mexico.

● Although a visa is required for any study in Mexico, most schools suggest getting one only if you intend to stay in Mexico for more than 180 days.

● If you plan to travel extensively in Central or South America, check on visa requirements well in advance. Visa information for U.S. citizens is outlined in a government leaflet entitled **Visa Requirements of Foreign Governments** (Passport Office Publication M-264). You can get the leaflet from most passport agencies. This will tell you what countries require visas. You'll then have to write the embassy or consulate of the foreign country to get a visa application form with information on fees and procedure.

- Canadians should contact a travel agency or nearest passport office. Visa information is outlined in the **Travel Information Manual,** which good agents should have.

Special tips on getting visas

- To get visas you'll have to mail your passport along with the appropriate application to a foreign consulate or embassy. Be sure to use registered mail and keep the receipt until your passport has been returned.

- You are expected to include a check for the visa as well as enough money to cover **return postage.** Ask the consulate or embassy to return the passport by registered mail. Make sure you've included enough money to cover the fee for such a service.

- Always apply for visas at the foreign consulate or embassy in your city or the city nearest you. Most embassies and consulates are located in Chicago, New York, San Francisco, and Washington, DC. You'll find the addresses in individual city directories or in the **Congressional Directory,** found in most major libraries.

- In Canada refer to the **Travel Information Manual** previously mentioned, which you'll find at many travel agencies and in a few libraries. If they don't have one, ask them to order it.

Travel Information Manual
P.O. Box 7627
1117 vj Schipol Airport
The Netherlands

- If you intend to travel to areas requiring visas, allow an extra three to six weeks for each necessary visa. Obtaining visas can be a long—disturbingly long—process. You may want to start the process months ahead of your planned trip!

Tourist card *(tarjeta de turista)*

In order to travel in Mexico you need a tourist card, an official document that you must carry with you at all times and present on request.

The tourist card is really just a small piece of paper given to you by the Mexican government allowing you to travel in Mexico for ninety days (it can be extended for another ninety days in Mexico).

The tourist card allows you into, out of, and through the country. Don't let it get wet or mutilated. Nor should you lose it. Without it you will not be able to leave Mexico, since it must be surrendered to Mexican immigration *(migración)* officials as you leave the country.

There are two **types** of tourist cards—single-entry and multiple-entry.

SINGLE-ENTRY TOURIST CARDS Most tourists need the single-entry tourist card, since they're only entering the country once.

• The single-entry tourist card is valid for stays up to ninety days, but it can be extended for another ninety days.

• It is free.

• It is available from Mexican government tourist offices, airlines, travel agencies, Mexican consulates, and border officials.

• Each person, regardless of age, must have a tourist card.

MULTIPLE-ENTRY TOURIST CARDS Multiple-entry tourist cards are needed by people going in and out of the country frequently. This would include travelers on business, people traveling by cruise ships, yachters, and others crossing the border into neighboring countries with the intention of returning off and on to Mexico.

• You'll need two passport photos to get a multiple-entry tourist card, which is issued by Mexican consulates. If you want the address of the nearest Mexican consulate, call your local library or contact the following:

Mexican Consulate
1019 19th Street Northwest, Suite
   1020
Washington, DC 20036
tel.: (202) 293-1710

Embassy of Mexico
130 Albert Street, Suite 206
Ottawa, Ontario K1P 5G4
tel.: (613) 233-8988

● These cards are valid for 180 days.

WHAT YOU NEED TO GET A TOURIST CARD

● To get a tourist card you need proof of citizenship. The best proof of citizenship is a passport.

● An original birth certificate or a copy with a seal *imprinted* (raised) on it, or naturalization papers are also valid proof of citizenship—a driver's license is *not*.

● Any document presented as proof of citizenship in obtaining a tourist card must be taken with you into Mexico. However, it does not have to be on your person at all times—you can leave it in a hotel safe, for example.

PHOTOCOPY YOUR TOURIST CARD

In Mexico you're required to carry your tourist card with you at all times. However, if you lose it, it's a tremendous hassle to replace it. So wily travelers make a photocopy *(fotocopia)* of the tourist card and carry this as identification—the original is left in the hotel safe.

● The photocopy can also help you get a new tourist card much more quickly if you should lose the original.

TRAVEL WITH MINORS

Any parent who wants to take a minor into Mexico must have the other parent's permission. Mexican consulates have a form "Permission for a Minor to Travel in Mexico." Write for this and have your mate sign it.

● Note that officials often don't even ask for this form, but they can.

MINORS TRAVELING ALONE

If you're under eighteen and want to travel in Mexico without your parents along, you must have two copies of a notarized letter stating that this is okay. It must be signed by both parents.

- You must also have a passport.

INSURANCE

If you carry any insurance at all, it will probably cover part of your trip. Exceptions to this general rule, and additional information on the subject, are detailed below.

Accident insurance

- Check to see whether your policy is valid in Mexico.

Baggage insurance

- Read your homeowner's policy. In most instances it will cover your baggage up to a specific value. But don't assume this. Ask your agent to be sure.

- If you intend to bring valuables into Mexico, ask about a **personal articles floater.** This is the safest overall protection and will include cameras.

- Find out whether your policy will cover new purchases made in Mexico for a specified grace period.

- If you don't have a homeowner's policy, buy special baggage insurance, which is available from most insurance companies and can be obtained directly from the airline at check-in time.

- Do some comparison shopping over the phone to come up with the least expensive coverage. Don't assume the costs will be comparable.

- To protect yourself, keep a list of all the clothes and personal belongings packed in each bag. Also note the value of each article.

- Note that if your bags are lost or damaged during a flight, the airline will reimburse you up to a specified limit. However, all items will be depreciated, and you may have to produce receipts.

● Lost baggage in Mexico is barely covered by insurance.

● If you travel light and with very few valuables, all of this worry and expense is eliminated!

Car insurance

● Your car insurance is invalid in Mexico. See p. 95 for full details on Mexican insurance.

Health insurance

● **Medicare** and **Medicaid** don't cover you in Mexico. Check to see whether the law has changed recently, however.

● If you've got a serious health problem but still plan to travel, ask about **medical evacuation insurance**—it could save your life.

● Most health policies do cover you worldwide, but you must ask to be sure. Generally, you'll have to pay for all expenses in Mexico and be reimbursed when you return home.

● Carry your insurance card, your agent's telephone number, and your insurance company's telephone number when you travel. This way you can always get in touch with them for advice in an emergency.

● Note that costs for medical treatment in Mexico are a fraction of comparable costs in the United States.

Home insurance

● Since your home may not be covered if you are away for more than thirty days, check with your agent for advice if you plan an extended trip.

Life insurance

● If you already carry a reasonable amount of life insurance, you won't need any extra for the vacation. Flight insurance is basically a rip-off.

- Flying is—statistically—incredibly safe.

- Some policies are written with a double-indemnity clause for accidental death.

- If you belong to a travel or auto club, they often provide life and accident insurance to members. Check on the most recent offerings.

- Many credit card companies now offer *free* flight insurance if you charge the flight to the card.

- Some travel agencies offer *free* flight insurance to their customers.

Trip cancellation insurance

- Some airline tickets (charter and special fares) have a rigid and steep penalty for cancellation. If this is the case with yours, consider taking out trip cancellation insurance.

- Many companies and airlines offer this to their customers. You pay a set fee per $100 coverage.

DOCUMENTS FOR A TRUSTED FRIEND

Following is a list of things you should leave with a trusted friend or relative. Although your trip may go without a hitch, this simple precaution could save you an incredible amount of trouble and time.

- **Itinerary:** Come as close to places and dates as possible. Leave exact mailing addresses (see advice on mail, p. 299).

- **List of traveler's check numbers:** You should carry a list of these numbers, but it's a very good idea to leave a duplicate list at home—just in case you lose everything, including the list of traveler's check numbers.

● **Numbers of credit cards:** Photocopy all your credit cards as a way of keeping accurate records of pertinent information. Leave one copy with a friend.

● **Number, date, and place of issue of passport:** Photocopy this information and leave it with a friend. If you ever lose your passport, it will be invaluable.

● **Airline ticket numbers, date and place of issue:** If you want to get reimbursed for lost or stolen airline tickets, have these numbers readily available—it will really help.

TRAVEL DOCUMENT CHECKLIST

Official
  Customs registration slip
  Passport or birth certificate
  Tourist card
  Visas

Medical
  International certificates of
    vaccination
  Prescriptions for narcotics

Driving
  International driver's license (not
    required)
  Car permit
  Trailer permit
  CB permit

Special permits
  Gun permit
  Fishing permit

Traveling with minors
  Notarized permission

Students
  International student
    identification card
  International youth hostel card

Money
  Credit cards
  Traveler's checks

Photocopies
  Passport
  Tourist card
  Credit cards

2

ITINERARIES

This chapter provides useful information on planning an itinerary for Mexico, a step that can be almost as fun as the trip itself.

WHERE TO GO

You have the perfect Mexican vacation mapped out in your personality—try to match your destination with what you want most from the trip.

Basic personalities

- Most travelers to Mexico fall into two general personality groups: One which wants nothing more than to find a resort and stay put for a week or more, the other planning to travel more extensively with the idea of getting to know something about a particular area or series of sights and towns.

The gringo trail

- Most of the roamers end up on the "gringo trail," a whimsical title for an amalgam of popular tourist attractions that more or less fall along a defined route. While there are excursions off the trail, it's so well traveled that the name seems totally appropriate.

Basic considerations

● If you and any potential travel partner can't agree on where to go or how to travel, plan to travel independently. You can still arrange to meet to do the things that you *can* agree on during the trip.

● If money is a major consideration, then try to match one of the more economical resorts to your pocket book (see p. 207). If you plan to travel extensively, then study the appropriate sections of this book carefully to pick up hundreds of tips on cutting costs in hotels, restaurants, and public transportation.

● If time is a problem, plan your trip carefully. Try to get a flight directly to the resort you've chosen. If you're going to roam, keep movement limited and choose just the sights or towns you most want to visit. Consider each day of movement from one place to the next as wasted.

● And if you're energy is limited, save it by joining a tour or staying in one area most suited to your life-style and finances.

HOW LONG TO STAY

The length of your trip may be predetermined by the time you have available for your vacation, so that you feel you have little leeway in this regard. However, if it's at all possible, try to make a trip to Mexico last at least ten days. This will give you time to enjoy and savor the scene.

● Subtract two days of the overall trip as wasted—the first and the last. If you're traveling for a week, that leaves only five days of vacation.

HOW FAR AND HOW FAST

Do you fall into the group of travelers who wants to get to "know"

Mexico? If so, you'll be tempted to travel far and fast, to give yourself a sneak preview of trips to come. It is totally natural to want to do this, and high-speed travel can be exhilarating. The trouble is, it's also exhausting and relatively expensive. Just remember in planning your trip that distances in Mexico are staggering, and that the pace "on paper" won't match reality—give yourself lots of "extra" time.

Planning trip mileage

• To help you enjoy your trip more fully, use mileage charts and a map to plan your itinerary. Decide which cities you'd like to see. You might trace your route in red with a felt-tipped pen. Now add up the mileage to see just how far you plan to go.

• Divide the total mileage by the number of days you'll be in Mexico. (Don't count the first and the last).

• If you are traveling by bus, train, or car, don't plan to cover more than 150 miles per day. The same rule applies to a tour. Naturally, you will sometimes wind up having traveled farther than the average distance. If you consistently cover much more than 150 miles per day, however, your trip will turn out to have been too time consuming, as well as too tiring.

• If you will be flying between two points, ignore the mileage between them—and simply write off one full day. Do this for each plane trip you'll be taking. Subtract these days from the total number of days you'll be in Mexico (minus the first and last days). This will give you a good idea of how many days you'll have left to enjoy Mexico.

• If you find that you'll be traveling too far in too short a period, admit it. Here are some options: Cut down on the number of cities and sights to be seen, extend your trip to make your travel time more enjoyable, or plan a second trip for a later date. With the possible exception of a few volcanoes, Mexican tourist attractions will still be there in years to come.

Structuring short trips

The shorter the trip, the more organized it must be! Every

phase of the trip should be planned to help you avoid waits (you'll still have some anyway). You should have reservations for plane flights, all reservations for hotel rooms, and reservations for fancier restaurants made well in advance of arrival. If you plan to attend festivals, musical events, the ballet, or any popular tourist attractions which could be sold out—get reservations in advance if possible.

● In planning sightseeing, watch your schedule very carefully. Certain events take place on certain days (like the bullfights and *ballet folklórico*) and many museums are closed on Mondays. Certain markets are open or best on certain days. So if you're on a tight schedule, work out even smaller details in advance. The section on what to do in Mexico on p. 310 will give you insight in this area. Read it *before* you go to Mexico.

● Limit yourself to one carry-on bag to cut baggage claim time.

● Note that you'll often pay a little more for a structured trip, but it will be worth every extra peso!

Structuring long trips

If you've got three weeks or more to play around with, you might want to follow a much looser program. Some people get by without any reservations at all—for anything. They allow themselves extra time to find a room, obtain tickets for popular attractions, and so on. Their attitude is relaxed and easygoing, a sign that they are more experienced travelers.

● Note that the big advantage of this style of travel is that you have a choice: You're never bound by a prearranged schedule, you can shift travel plans daily (and often do), you can move out of a hotel you don't like, you can seek out typical restaurants on your own—in short, you can do just about anything at whim.

● Loosely structured trips appeal greatly to younger and older travelers with lots of time to spare. But this kind of trip is gaining popularity with others as well, because it has another great advantage over structured travel: it's less expensive.

When you get through with this book, you'll discover how easy it is to cut costs if you begin to "think Mexican."

WHEN TO GO

A great deal of fiction has been written about Mexico, but the statements about the weather are true. No country offers more reliable winter sun than Mexico, and it's this consistency that draws millions of sun worshippers each year.

Temperature guidelines

- The farther south you go, the hotter you get.
- The higher in altitude you go, the cooler you get.

About rainfall

- The charts on pp. 24–25 give you *exact* information on rainfall in major tourist destinations, but in general winter is dry, summer is wet.

Humidity

- The farther south you go, the more humid it gets.
- Many coastal areas are hot and sticky (even in winter).

Wind

- Wind is usually pleasant relief in much of Mexico, but breezes bordering on gusts can become irritating—bring a wind jacket and ask about wind conditions for any resort when making a reservation.

Storms

Two areas in Mexico are prone to storms:

- **Baja:** *chubascos* (violent storms) are most common from July to October.

● **Yucatán:** Late fall and early winter are the least favorable times to travel in the Yucatán.

WEATHER TIPS BY REGION

Each general region has its own peculiarities which may influence your decision on when to travel.

The Baja

● The **north:** Much of northern Baja can be cool and frequently wet in winter (especially around Tijuana). Summers are hot to very hot, while deserts in the summer are torrid in the day and cool to cold at night. Mountainous areas are best visited in spring and fall, since winters are very cold and summers are like a blast furnace.

● The **south:** From La Paz south you'll find mild winters, although the best weather is in spring and fall. Summers are very hot. It's cool in the desert areas at night, however. As in the north, the mountainous areas are cold in the winter and torrid in the summer. In the season of storms stretching from July to October, some resorts close down. These storms do *not* come through every year, but when they do, they can be violent.

Inland Triangle (Guadalajara, Mexico City, and Oaxaca)

● In the inland area you'll find mild winter weather with occasional cool to cold spells at the higher altitudes including Mexico City. Summers tend to be hot and wet, with two-hour showers in the afternoon. Weather from October to December is tops. January and February are cool but dry. It gets windy in February and March. By April it's getting hot with rains lasting through September. August is frequently the rainiest month despite what the rainfall chart indicates.

The Pacific Coast

• Much of the Pacific Coast tends to be windy in the winter with very mild temperatures and lots of sun. The most dependable heat can be found in the area from Puerto Vallarta south. Winter and early spring are the "in" seasons here. During fall and winter it's possible to have five or six months without rain, although there's usually a short (two-week) period in late December or early January when the weather is "iffy." Summers are hot to very hot, and you'll need a room with air-conditioning or with a hilltop location for breezes. From June 15 to October it can be sticky.

The Yucatán

• The Yucatán has two seasons—hot and hotter. The inland areas of the peninsula are usually 10 degrees (Fahrenheit) hotter than the coast. May is extremely hot. In the summer, the dry areas are torrid, the wetter areas steamy. The Gulf Coast is very unpredictable, and storms appear sporadically. Or, as the natives put it, hurricanes have no rudder. The *nortes* (north winds) sweep in from late fall to early winter, but from late winter to early spring the weather is ideal—the perfect time to visit the region.

This chart gives you a good idea of an area's weather with its breakdown of average temperature (in degrees Fahrenheit) and rainfall (in inches) on a month-to-month basis. Naturally, temperatures drop by 10 degrees or so in the evening to rise again by 10 degrees or more over the average at midday—so take these overall averages with a grain of salt. Nevertheless, the chart does provide a good, accurate idea of what to expect in the way of weather in Mexico at any given time—and might influence your decision as to when to travel to different areas of Mexico.

AVERAGE MONTHLY RAINFALL (IN INCHES)

City or Town	Altitude	J	F	M	A	M	J	J	A	S	O	N	D
Acapulco	sea level	.4	0	0	0	12	17	8.6	9.8	14	6.7	1.2	.4
Aguascalientes	6,130	.5	.2	.1	.1	.7	4.8	5.8	4.1	3.6	1.3	.7	.6
Campeche	80	.7	.4	.5	.2	1.7	6.1	7.0	6.7	5.7	3.4	1.2	1.2
Cancún	sea level	3.5	2.2	1.6	1.7	4.6	7.0	4.3	6.0	9.0	8.6	3.8	4.4
Chetumal	10	3.0	.9	1.1	1.2	5.5	7.0	5.1	4.2	5.5	8.4	3.4	3.7
Chihuahua	4,670	.1	.2	.3	.3	.4	1.0	3.1	3.7	3.7	1.4	.3	.8
Ciudad Obregon	230	.3	.2	.1	0	0	.1	.3	1.8	1.7	.6	1.7	.5
Ciudad Victoria	2,000	1.4	1.0	.8	1.5	5.0	4.8	4.1	2.7	7.9	4.3	1.7	.6
Cozumel	sea level	3.5	2.2	1.6	1.7	4.6	7.0	4.3	6.0	9.0	8.6	3.8	4.4
Cuernavaca	5,050	.1	.2	.3	.3	2.1	7.8	8.6	8.7	9.7	3.1	.3	.1
Durango	6,200	.5	.4	0	.1	.5	2.4	4.9	3.6	4.0	1.2	.6	.7
Fortín de las Flores	3,330	1.9	1.5	1.6	2.1	5.0	14.0	15.0	16.0	18.0	8.5	3.5	2.4
Guadalajara	5,210	.7	.2	.1	0	.7	7.6	10.0	7.9	7.0	2.1	.8	.8
Guanajuato	6,680	.5	.3	.2	.2	1.1	5.4	6.6	5.5	6.0	2.0	.7	.6
Guaymas	140	.3	.2	.2	.1	.1	0	1.8	3.0	2.1	.4	.4	1.1
Hermosillo	690	.1	.6	.2	.1	.1	.1	2.8	3.3	2.5	1.6	.2	1.0
Isla Mujeres	sea level	3.5	2.2	1.6	1.7	4.6	7.0	4.3	6.0	9.0	8.6	3.8	4.4
Ixtapa/Zihuatanejo	sea level	.6	.1	0	.2	1.1	7.1	9.7	9.1	7.1	3.4	.4	.1
La Paz	sea level	.1	.5	0	0	0	0	.3	1.6	2	.4	.5	1.3
Manzanillo	sea level	.9	.5	0	0	.1	4.0	5.4	7.4	15.0	5.0	.7	2.1
Mazatlán	sea level	.5	.4	.1	0	0	1.1	6.6	9.6	10.0	2.4	.5	1.7

24

AVERAGE MONTHLY RAINFALL (IN INCHES)

City or Town	Altitude	J	F	M	A	M	J	J	A	S	O	N	D
Mérida	30	1.2	.6	.8	1.0	3.2	5.9	5.5	5.1	6.0	4.0	1.2	1.2
Mexico City	7,350	.2	.3	.4	.5	.2	4.2	4.9	4.1	4.6	1.3	.6	.3
Monterrey	1,770	.8	.9	.6	1.1	1.7	3.3	2.9	2.5	8.1	4.3	1.0	.9
Morelia	6,300	.5	.3	.3	.3	1.7	5.2	6.8	6.4	6.2	2.3	.8	.2
Oaxaca	5,070	.1	.1	.4	1.0	2.4	4.9	3.7	4.1	6.7	1.6	.3	.4
Pátzcuaro	7,250	.8	.5	.3	.2	1.5	7.9	9.8	9.5	8.5	3.1	1.0	.9
Puebla	7,050	.2	.2	.5	.5	2.9	6.2	5.4	5.8	7.4	2.2	.8	.3
Puerto Vallarta	sea level	.8	.4	.3	.3	.2	9.1	14.1	13.3	13.3	5.5	.4	.5
Querétaro	6,040	.4	.1	.2	.5	1.1	3.7	4.1	3.4	4.8	1.3	.4	.5
San Cristóbal	7,090	.3	0	.4	1.4	5.1	10.0	5.6	6.3	9.9	6.0	.9	.6
San Luis Potosí	6,160	.5	.2	.4	.2	1.2	2.8	2.3	1.7	3.4	.7	.4	.6
San Miguel de Allende	6,400	.4	.2	.1	.7	1.4	4.2	3.5	3.4	3.4	1.5	.3	.3
Tampico	sea level	2.1	.9	.5	.4	2.0	7.9	5.8	5.9	13.0	7.0	2.2	1.7
Taxco	5,760	0	.2	.4	.9	3.0	10.0	12.0	14.0	13.0	3.5	.2	.1
Tepic	3,000	1.2	.8	0	0	.1	6.8	14.0	12.0	8.1	8.0	.3	2.1
Toluca	8,740	.4	.4	.4	1.1	2.0	5.3	3.6	5.7	6.0	1.9	.8	.3
Tuxtla Gutiérrez	1,760	0	.2	.4	.2	3.0	9.2	7.0	6.1	8.0	3.2	.2	.2
Veracruz	sea level	.8	.6	.8	.6	2.5	10.6	15.1	11.7	13.8	6.8	2.4	1.1
Villahermosa	30	5.5	3.9	1.8	1.8	3.5	8.0	7.6	7.6	10.0	11.0	5.6	7.1

AVERAGE MONTHLY TEMPERATURE (IN DEGREES FAHRENHEIT)

City or Town	Altitude	J	F	M	A	M	J	J	A	S	O	N	D
Acapulco	sea level	78	78	81	81	83	84	84	84	82	81	81	79
Aguascalientes	6,130	55	58	63	68	72	70	69	67	67	66	64	56
Campeche	80	72	74	77	79	81	81	80	81	81	80	76	74
Cancún	sea level	77	78	78	82	82	84	84	85	82	82	81	76
Chetumal	10	73	75	77	80	81	82	82	82	81	79	75	75
Chihuahua	4,670	49	52	63	65	74	81	77	75	73	65	56	50
Ciudad Obregon	230	65	68	72	77	81	90	93	93	91	85	75	67
Ciudad Victoria	2,000	60	64	70	76	79	81	81	82	79	74	67	60
Cozumel	sea level	77	78	78	82	82	84	84	85	82	82	81	76
Cuernavaca	5,050	65	67	73	73	74	70	68	68	68	68	67	66
Durango	6,200	53	56	63	65	69	69	68	69	66	64	58	55
Fortín de las Flores	3,330	61	64	67	70	72	71	71	70	70	69	64	62
Guadalajara	5,210	58	61	66	70	72	73	69	68	68	65	61	59
Guanajuato	6,680	57	60	66	68	71	68	67	66	66	63	60	59
Guaymas	140	64	66	70	73	73	82	87	87	86	81	72	64
Hermosillo	690	60	63	68	73	79	88	90	88	87	79	70	60
Isla Mujeres	sea level	77	78	78	82	82	84	84	85	82	82	81	76
Ixtapa/Zihuatanejo	sea level	75	75	82	86	90	86	82	81	81	81	79	79
La Paz	sea level	64	68	72	74	79	82	88	88	85	80	72	60
Manzanillo	sea level	75	74	74	76	79	81	83	83	81	81	79	77
Mazatlán	sea level	67	67	70	70	75	81	81	81	81	79	74	70

AVERAGE MONTHLY TEMPERATURE (IN DEGREES FAHRENHEIT)

City or Town	Altitude	J	F	M	A	M	J	J	A	S	O	N	D
Mérida	30	73	74	79	81	82	81	81	81	81	79	75	73
Mexico City	7,350	54	56	61	63	63	63	61	60	60	59	58	55
Monterrey	1,770	59	62	72	74	78	82	82	82	75	72	63	57
Morelia	6,300	57	60	64	67	69	68	65	64	64	63	60	57
Oaxaca	5,070	63	66	72	72	73	68	70	69	68	67	65	64
Pátzcuaro	7,250	57	56	63	64	68	68	63	63	63	61	58	54
Puebla	7,050	54	60	66	66	66	64	63	63	63	61	58	57
Puerto Vallarta	sea level	73	73	73	77	81	82	84	84	82	82	79	74
Querétaro	6,040	57	60	66	68	70	70	67	67	66	63	61	59
San Cristóbal	7,090	54	55	57	60	60	60	60	60	60	59	55	55
San Luis Potosí	6,160	55	59	66	69	70	68	67	67	66	63	59	55
San Miguel de Allende	6,400	63	65	67	74	77	75	73	73	71	69	66	62
Tampico	sea level	65	68	73	77	80	82	82	82	81	78	72	66
Taxco	5,760	66	69	75	75	76	72	70	70	70	69	68	68
Tepic	3,000	63	63	65	70	71	74	74	74	74	73	73	64
Toluca	8,740	49	52	55	57	59	57	56	56	55	54	52	50
Tuxtla Gutiérrez	1,760	71	73	77	80	81	79	78	78	77	76	73	70
Veracruz	sea level	71	72	75	76	79	82	82	82	81	79	75	72
Villahermosa	30	72	75	77	80	83	85	85	85	85	80	76	66

AGENTS AND AGENCIES

Good agents can find super trips and super bargains amidst the garble of airlines and tour brochures. Still, it's really a customer's responsibility to do reading and research before going to a travel agent. This will make your relationship more beneficial.

● You may well save more money by planning and arranging for your trip by yourself if you're a free spirit, if you're aggressive and resourceful, and if you're ready to study up on alternatives in transportation, food, and lodging.

● Even if you fit that description, an agent may know of tour packages that are so reasonably priced that you can't afford *not* to take advantage of them. So never rule out travel agencies before checking to see what they have to offer.

● If you don't want to plan or arrange for your trip yourself, a well-chosen agent can be a fine resource.

● In short, shop around. Compare what an agent can do with what you can do, balance the benefits and costs, and act accordingly.

What good agents can do

● They can find the cheapest airfare from A to B without making you go through the hassle.

● They can get you on a cruise or tour which matches your personality. You pay nothing extra for their service.

● They can make appropriate reservations for hotels, car rental, and sporting activities. None of these services should involve a charge.

What agents can't do

● Travel agents can't read minds. Be as specific as possible in telling an agent what you really want. The more specific, the better the chance of getting it.

Picking an agency

- Larger agencies tend to have more clout than smaller ones. It may be more personal and more convenient to go to a neighborhood agent, but what happens if something goes wrong?

- Ask the agency what kind of travel it specializes in. If it doesn't match your travel plans, ask the agency to refer you to another agency specializing in what you want. Most agents are glad to do this.

- In special cases, you may want to work with agents in other cities. If the best agency for Baja tours happens to be in Los Angeles, carry on your business through the mail.

Recognizing a good agent

Good travel agents are harder to find than the American Society of Travel Agents would like to admit. Unfortunately, many of them are in the business more to get low-cost travel for themselves than to help their clients.

On the other hand, some agents are outstanding. Most of the good ones specialize in some way: low-cost tours, luxury travel, study groups, incentive travel, business, etc.

- Most travel agents are members of the American Society of Travel Agents (ASTA), so be wary of those who are not. ASTA maintains a file of complaints. You can write or call them:

ASTA
4400 MacArthur Boulevard NW
Washington, DC 20007
tel: (202) 965-7520

- Look for the initials CTC—for Certified Travel Consultant—after an agent's name. This designation signifies that the person has a good reputation and has been through a specialized course.

- Find out whether someone in the agency is familiar with the specific area you plan to visit. If you find such a person, you can learn a great deal—and in addition he will be able to reserve flights, make reservations, and book tours as part of his general assistance to you.

INFORMATION AVAILABLE WHILE IN THE UNITED STATES AND CANADA

Mexico is a huge country with something for just about everyone. The more information you have before going there, the more your trip will match your personality.

Fine-tuning your choices

● Go to the library to browse in travel books and magazines, so you have an idea of the possibilities. No single book can do it all, but each has its own value.

● Read thoroughly at least one guide which matches your budget and personality. Start to pick out places you most want to visit and the names of hotels which intrigue you.

● The more you know, the better you'll plan; the better you plan, the more likely you are to get what you want.

Recommended magazines

● *Gourmet, Travel Holiday,* and *Travel & Leisure* are three major magazines that often have information on travel in Mexico.

Baja travel

● *The Baja Book II* by Tom Miller and Elmar Baxter is your best bet.

Mexico West Travel Club, Inc.
2424 Newport Boulevard, Suite 91
Costa Mesa, CA 92627
tel.: (714) 662-7616

Travel reports

• If you like to travel in style, check into *Passport*. If you're more interested in budget or business travel, check into the reports put out by *Travel Smart*.

Passport
20 North Wacker Drive
Chicago, IL 60606
tel.: (312) 332-3574

Travel Smart
Communications House
40 Beechdale Road
Dobbs Ferry, NY 10522
tel.: (914) 693-8300

• To find out which of these reports suits your personality, write to each of them asking for a sample copy.

Books for the travel trade

• Plan your own itinerary (if you are so inclined) using specialized books familiar to most travel agents: *Official Airline Guide, Official Hotel and Resort Guide,* and *World Travel Directory.*

• These are extremely expensive volumes used in the travel industry. You can find them in the travel section of a few major libraries.

• Also very good, if quite expensive, are the reports put out by:

STAR (Sloane Travel Agency
   Reports)
P.O. Box 15619
Fort Lauderdale, FL 33318
tel.: (305) 472-8794

Mexico City Tourist Bureau

• The Mexico City Tourist Bureau puts out a guide each year which you'll find in many better hotels. You can contact them for information about getting a guide before you go (note you can pick up one from the tourist office in the Mexico City airport).

Mexico City Tourist Bureau
Calzada Mexico—Tacuba 235, 4th
   Floor
Mexico City, D.F.
tel.: 541-3367

Mexico City Tourist Bureau
5901 North 10th Street
McAllen, TX 78504
tel.: (512) 630-4507

AAA guides

• The American Automobile Association (AAA) puts out guides on Mexico which are free to members. These guides contain information on sights, restaurants, and hotels (note many fine hotels are not included).

• There is a special *Baja California Guide* and a separate *Accommodation and Camping Guide* for the Baja which must be added to make the Mexico information complete. These are most readily available from:

Auto Club of Southern California
2601 South Figueroa Street
Los Angeles, CA 90007
tel.: (213) 741-3111

• The AAA also produces maps for mainland Mexico and the Baja which are free to members. They're fine for general travel.

Dan Sanborn's travelog

• If you're traveling to Mexico by car or recreational vehicle (RV) and if you buy your insurance from Sanborn's, you'll be given an extremely detailed travelog to match the route and areas you'll be visiting.

• Try to buy your insurance far ahead of time so that you can get the travelog weeks or even months ahead of your planned trip. This is one of the finest freebies available to motorists!

General travel guides

● Most of the general travel guides on Mexico are very inaccurate, because much of the material supplied to the writers is inaccurate.

● Since information in Mexico is nearly impossible to verify, take what is said in guides with sympathetic skepticism (the ferry hours from Cancún to Isla Mujeres changed four different times in 2½ months).

● Read guides before going to Mexico and take the general information with you in simple notes. Rip out any sections which you think will be useful. Lugging bulky and heavy books to Mexico makes no sense at all.

Mexican Government Tourist Offices

● For adequate general background information and some helpful tips, write to the Mexican Government Tourist Office closest to you. You can ask for *general* hotel and restaurant information; sightseeing suggestions; pamphlets on ruins, museums, and tourist sights; travel maps; and so on.

● Note that any tourist office will shy away from questions of comparison ("Is one hotel better than another?" "Should we go here instead of there?"). The more specific your question, the more difficult it may be for a tourist office to answer. You may get general information instead.

● Be sure to include a self-addressed, stamped envelope in your letter. It is not required, but it is basic courtesy. And it speeds up the reply!

● Write the office well ahead of your planned departure (preferably several months in advance), and allow as much time as possible for a reply.

● Probably the single most valuable item in any tourist office is a good map—free for the asking.

- Following are the addresses of Mexican Government Tourist Offices in the United States and Canada:

UNITED STATES

Chicago

Mexican Government Tourist Office
233 North Michigan Avenue, Suite 1413
Chicago, IL 60601
tel.: (312) 565-2785

Los Angeles

Mexican Government Tourist Office
10100 Santa Monica Boulevard, Suite 224
Los Angeles, CA 90067
tel.: (213) 203-8151

Houston

Mexican Government Tourist Office
2707 North Loop West, Suite 450
Houston, TX 77008
tel.: (713) 880-5153

New York

Mexican Government Tourist Office
405 Park Avenue, Suite 1203
New York, NY 10022
tel.: (212) 755-7212

CANADA

Montreal

Mexican Government Tourist Office
One Place Ville Marie, Suite 2409
Montreal, P.Q. H3B 3M9
tel.: (514) 871-1052

Toronto

Mexican Government Tourist Office
181 University Avenue, Suite 1112
Toronto, Ontario M5H 3M7
tel.: (416) 364-2455

State tourist offices

There are thirty-one states or *estados* in Mexico plus the Federal District (*Distrito Federal—D.F.*), which encompasses Mexico City and the immediate area. Each state has its own tourist office.

- In each state the federal government also runs a tourist office. And most cities have tourist offices. These are best visited *in person* for any information. Note that many of them close for lunch—and for any other appropriate excuse, including whim.

Travel clubs

Every club broadcasts its benefits, some of which can be valuable. Check into the following clubs to see whether or not you think the benefits match the cost:

National Travel Club
51 Atlantic Avenue
Travel Building
Floral Park, NY 11001
tel.: (516) 352-9700

Mexico West Travel Club (for the Baja)
2424 Newport Boulevard, Suite 91
Costa Mesa, CA 92627
tel.: (714) 662-7616

The Good Sam Club (for RVs)
Customer Service
P.O. Box 500
Agoura, CA 91301
tel.: (800) 423-5061

AUTO CLUBS

You should comparison shop when looking for an automobile club. The main things to compare are membership fees, emergency road services, emergency travel expenses, accidental death and dismemberment payoff amounts, arrest and bail bond, legal defense fees, and routing maps.

- Some clubs promise a lot and deliver a little.

- Read the fine print. There may be a limit to the miles that a car will be towed or a limit to the expense that will be covered.

ALA Auto and Travel Club
888 Worcester Street
Wellesley, MA 02181
tel.: (617) 237-5200

Allstate Motor Club
34 Allstate Plaza
Northbrook, IL 60062
tel.: (800) 323-6282

American Automobile Club (AAA)
8111 Gatehouse Road
Falls Church, VA 22047
tel.: (703) 222-6000

Amoco Motor Club
P.O. Box 9049
Des Moines, IO 50369
tel.: (800) 334-3300

Chevron Travel Club
P.O. Box P
Concord, CA 94524
tel.: (415) 827-6000

Exxon Travel Club
P.O. Box 3633
Houston, TX 77253
tel.: (713) 680-5723

Gulf Auto Club
P.O. Box 105287
Atlanta, GA 30348
tel.: (800) 422-2582

Shell Motorist Club
P.O. Box 60199
Chicago, IL 60660
tel.: (800) 621-8663

Montgomery Ward Auto Club
200 North Martingale Road
Schaumburg, IL 60194
tel.: (800) 621-5151
    (800) 572-5577 (Illinois)

United States Auto Club Motoring
    Division
P.O. Box 660460
Dallas, TX 75266
tel.: (219) 236-3700

MAPS

Good maps appropriate to the kind of traveling you'll be doing can make a trip far less frustrating and more enjoyable. For most travel you can get *free* maps, which are adequate for your purposes. Detailed maps are expensive, but essential for off-road travel.

Good general maps (free)

• **Mexican government tourist offices:** Request a free *Mapa Turístico de Carreteras* (road map) from the Mexican government tourist office nearest you.

• **Travel agents:** Ask any agent you deal with to provide a *free* map for your travels.

• **AAA and other auto clubs:** If you belong to any auto or travel club, have them give you a *free* map to Mexico. These clubs should also provide route maps and related services. Request these as far in advance as possible!

• **Insurance companies:** If you'll be traveling by car, get your insurance in advance and have the company send you *free* maps. Sanborn's city maps with his travelog are very helpful.

• **A special note:** Every person in your party should have a map. It makes travel more exciting, makes kids feel special, and divides the responsibility—and it costs nothing!

Good detailed maps (not free)

The San Diego Map Center stocks a wide variety of maps on Mexico, including the fine *Carta Turística* maps. The U.S. Department of Commerce puts out aeronautical charts for Mexico, which are quite detailed.

World Aeronautical Charts
U.S. Department of Commerce
National Oceanic & Atmospheric
  Administration
6501 Lafayette Avenue
Riverdale, MD 20840
tel.: (301) 436-6990

San Diego Map Center
2611 University Avenue
San Diego, CA 92104
tel.: (619) 291-3830

INFORMATION IN MEXICO

Getting good information in Mexico can be tough, so here are a few tips to help you out:

● If you're going to Mexico City by plane, stop at the Mexico City Tourist Information Booth *(Información Turística de la Ciudad de México)* in the airport.

● Ask for the book **Mexico City in Your Hands—Tourist Directory.** If you don't ask for it, you won't get it. It has lots of helpful general and specific information, and it's free!

● The booth also has a free, but poor, map of the city—good enough to get you to your hotel, but that's about it. It also has an airport guide if you want to find the location of all services, including the transportation booths selling tickets for buses into town.

● Also in Mexico City there are two locations of the Central Tourist Office *(Secretaría de Turismo).* The main office on Avenida Presidente Mazaryk can book a room for you, if you need such a service. These offices have lots of general information on the city and adequate maps.

Secretaría de Turismo
Avenida Presidente Mazaryk 172
Colonia Polanco
Mexico City, D.F. 11587
tel: 250-8555
    250-0123 (tourist information)
    545-4613 (tourist assistance)
    254-1954 (tourist assistance)
    250-4618 (tourist complaints)

● To get to this office take a taxi or if you're on a budget, take the metro to the Sevilla stop. Then get in a **pesero** (jitney cab) and share a ride to Mazaryk. Just tell the driver *turismo;* he'll understand.

Mexican Government Tourist Office
Avenida Juárez 94
Mexico City

● To get to the Juárez branch office (often out of maps) take the subway to either the Hidalgo or Juárez metro stops and walk from there. Direct all *telephone* calls to the Mazaryk office.

Map sources in Mexico

● **DETENAL** produces a wide variety of maps which will interest travelers looking for highly detailed profiles. The organization has a booth in the Mexico City airport and in other locations listed below. At present, it has maps of the following states:

Aguascalientes	Morelos
Baja California	Nayarit
Coahuila	Nuevo León
Colima	Tamaulipas
Guanajuato	Tlaxcala
Jalisco	Zacatecas
México	

DETENAL LOCATIONS

Durango

DETENAL
Avenida Felipe Pescador No. 706
   Oriente
Entre Laureano Roncal y Voladores
C.P. 34000 Durango, Durango
México
Tel.: 22 825

Hermosillo

DETENAL
Carretera a Bahía Kino, Km. 0.5
Hermosillo, Sonora
C.P. 83000 México
tel.: 91 621

Mérida

DETENAL
Calle 21 No. 93 G-H por Av.
Alemán
Col. Itzimná
Mérida, Yucatán
C.P. 97100 México
tel.: 91 992

Mexico City

DETENAL
Balderas No. 71, P.B.
Centro
C.P. 06040 Mexico City, D.F.
tel.: 521-4251

DETENAL
Insurgentes Sur No. 795, P.B.
Col. Nápoles
C.P. 03810 Mexico City, D.F.
tel.: 687-4691

DETENAL
Centeno No. 670, 3er. piso
Col. Granjas Mexico
C.P. 08400 Mexico City, D.F.
tel.: 657-8944 ext. 214

Monterrey

DETENAL
Eugenio Garza Sada No. 1702 Sur
Col. Nuevo Repueblo
Monterrey, Nuevo León
C.P. 64700 México
tel.: 91 83 43

Oaxaca

DETENAL
Calzada Porfirio Díaz No. 317
Esq. Demetrio Mayoral Pardo
Col. Reforma
Oaxaco, Oaxaca
C.P. 68050 México
tel.: 91 951

Puebla

DETENAL
19 Sur No. 1102 Esq. 11 Poniente
Col. San Matías
Puebla, Puebla
C.P. 74400 México
tel.: 91 22 41

San Luis Potosí

DETENAL
Independencia No. 1025
Centro
San Luis Potosí, San Luis Potosí
C.P. 78000 México
tel.: 91 481

Toluca

DETENAL
Hidalgo Ote. 1227
Centro
Toluca, Edo. de México
C.P. 50000 México
tel.: 91 721

Zapopan

DETENAL
Mariano Otero No. 2347
Zapopan, Jalisco
C.P. 45000 México
tel.: 91 36 22

Mexico City maps

- One of the best **Mexico City maps** is produced by

Guía Roja, SA
Calle República de Colombia 23
Mexico City, México 06020
tel: 522-6040

TRAVEL PARTNERS AND TOURS

Should you make a trip by yourself, with a friend or spouse, with a group of people you like, or as part of a tour group? Should you take the kids or a baby? There's no easy answer, although the answer's often taken for granted—especially in the case of couples. The hints in this chapter should be helpful to you, not only in making your decision, but also in living with it!

SOLO TRAVEL

There are many advantages to traveling alone: you can do as you damn well please, when you damn well please, at your own pace, with or without someone else along, as you choose. In short, you have total freedom.

On the other hand, you pay for such freedom. If you go on a tour, you may be socked with a single surcharge. If you're totally on your own, you will have no way of sharing expenses at mealtimes, in the hotel, and for personal transportation (mainly a car). It's all out of your pocket and only your pocket.

You may also be lonely—but loneliness can be converted into an advantage, as it will force you to get to know Mexicans and other travelers.

Traveling alone and liking it

• As a loner, take advantage of short and inexpensive tours to popular tourist sights. You'll not only meet people, but also keep your costs down.

• Be willing to share the cost of a room. In Mexico a single only costs a dollar or two less than a double. If you are concerned about sharing a room with a stranger, put anything of value in the hotel safe.

• When faced with the prospect of eating alone, bring a newspaper, a book, or writing paper with you to the restaurant. If you meet someone interesting, fine; if not, you'll catch up on your reading or write a few letters.

• Go a little before or after the peak dinner hours, to avoid running into poor treatment at the hands of waiters, as solo travelers sometimes do.

Women traveling alone

• Most women advise other women not to travel alone in Mexico.

• If you do, you must cope with the aggressive behavior of Mexican men, which includes hissing, whistling, and lewd comments.

• Women traveling alone are often considered sexually permissive, because they're breaking a social taboo against this behavior. The older you get, the more this taboo seems to break down.

• Be sure to read the section on personal safety (p. 161) before deciding to travel alone.

Single but looking for company

• Cruises are a natural for someone looking for a travel partner, but they're not as reliable as some television programs would have you believe.

• Probably better are resorts and tours aimed at single travelers:

Club Med (Head Office)
40 West 57th Street
New York, NY 10019
tel.: (800) 528-3100
    (212) 750-1670

Gramercy Singleworld
444 Madison Avenue
New York, NY 10022
tel.: (800) 223-6490
    (212) 758-2433

Mesa Travel Singles Registry
P.O. Box 2235
Costa Mesa, CA 92628
tel.: (714) 546-8181

Society of Single Travelers
3000 Ocean Park Boulevard, Suite
    1004
Santa Monica, CA 90405
tel.: (213) 450-8510

Travel Companion Exchange
P.O. Box 833
Amityville, NY 11701
tel.: (516) 454-0880

Travel Mates International, Inc.
49 West 44th Street
New York, NY 10036
tel.: (212) 221-6565

TWOSOME AND FAMILY TRAVEL

The big advantage of staying together are shared company and shared costs. A room for a couple or traveling partners may only be a few dollars more than it would be for a solo traveler. In short, it costs far less for two people to travel together than to go independently. But savings mean nothing unless you're both doing what you really want to do.

Traveling as a twosome

● If you and your partner cannot agree on the purpose of a trip, consider traveling independently. You may prefer completely different destinations in Mexico, so why not go separate ways?

● Meet again in places you'd both like to visit.

● Carry your own bags, unless you're willing to pay someone else to do it. It is unfair to ask a partner to carry your luggage.

● Share all responsibilities with your partner. Anyone who has to make all the decisions shoulders the burden for any mistakes made. That burden should be equally divided.

- Iron out all money matters before you start. Good reckoning makes good friends.

- Each person of a married couple should have control of part of the money, including "mad money" for special occasions. Each person should be responsible for handling part of the payment for everyday expenses.

Family travel

The more people involved in a trip, the more complex the planning is going to be. You can't expect to suit all tastes at all times when working with a group.

- Make sure each person has his own personal Mexican map. Kids especially enjoy keeping a log by marking a trip route.

- Gear the pace of the trip to that of the youngest member of the group.

- Agree that the responsibilities shall be shared.

- Since each person will carry his own luggage, make sure that the size of the bag matches the size of the person.

- If children are along, allow time for numerous breaks in the itinerary: for a trip to the beach, a hike through a park, a pause for a cold drink.

- If your kids like cameras or radios, encourage them to bring one along. The portable radios can be traded for any number of Mexican items (kids love to bargain and trade).

- Note that younger children can appreciate cathedrals, markets, and museums—in small doses. Children tend to be activity-oriented, which means that they'd rather go swimming than to the ruins at Palenque—or would rather combine the two, preferably in a period of twenty minutes (at Palenque they can).

- Allow for the option of splitting up a party from time to time, so that those primarily interested in cultural attractions or shopping can have adequate time to enjoy them.

- Note that Mexicans like children and treat traveling families accordingly.

Traveling with a baby

- When making reservations for air travel, try to schedule departure and arrival times so that they do not coincide with the baby's feedings. This is not easy every time, just try to do it as often as you can.

- Contact any airline well in advance if you wish to reserve a bassinet.

- Most airlines now offer preboarding privileges to anyone traveling with children as a matter of course.

- Be sure to have something for the baby to drink during takeoff and landing: the sucking will help relieve the pressure that builds up in the baby's ears.

- Bring a towel to cover you during feeding and to place under the baby at changing time.

- Bring a small blanket, plastic bags for disposable diapers, small toys for the baby to play with, and a folding (umbrella) stroller—the latter is a big help.

- An organization devoted solely to traveling with young children:

TWYCH—Travel With Your Children
80 Eighth Avenue
New York, NY 10011
tel.: (212) 206-0688

FOR OLDER PEOPLE

The following organizations have lots of information for older travelers. Elderhostel offers courses worldwide for people over sixty and keeps the price manageable.

American Association for Retired Persons
1909 K Street Northwest
Washington, DC 20049
tel.: (202) 872-4700

Elderhostel
80 Boylston Street, Suite 400
Boston, MA 02116
tel.: (617) 426-7788

Grand Circle Travel
555 Madison Avenue
New York, NY 10022
tel.: 1 (800) 221-2610

YOUNGER TRAVELERS

Generally, the young have more time, less money, and more energy than other travelers—a potent combination in Mexico.

● Take more money than you think you're going to need. It's cheap, but not *that* cheap.

● Pick up an **International Student Identification Card** available from:

Council on International Education
   and Exchange (CIEE)
205 East 42nd Street
New York, NY 10017
tel.: (212) 661-1414

● **Don't hitch**—take inexpensive public transportation instead. It'll get you anywhere for next to nothing.

● Try to have a vague itinerary for friends and relatives who can get in touch with you in an emergency through:

Citizens Emergency Center
U.S. Department of State
Washington, DC 20520
tel.: (202) 632-5225

● No itinerary? Then register with consulates as you make your vagabond way through Mexico (it goes against everyone's grain).

HANDICAPPED TRAVEL

Mexico is not geared for handicapped travel, but the following organizations may have a way of making it available to you despite *its* handicaps:

Evergreen Travel Service
19505M 44th Avenue West
Lynnwood, WA 98036
tel.: (206) 776-1184

Mobility International/USA
P.O. Box 3551
Eugene, OR 97403
tel.: (503) 343-1284

Flying Wheels Travel
P.O. Box 382
143 West Bridge Street
Owatonna, MN 55060
tel.: (507) 451-5005

Whole Person Tours
P.O. Box 1084
Bayonne, NJ 07002
tel.: (201) 858-3400

TRAVELING WITH PETS

You're allowed to take one dog, one cat, and four canaries into Mexico, but why would you want to? Mexicans thoroughly dislike pets, and very few hotels allow them.

If you insist

Mexico has strict regulations regarding pets brought into the country:

- You have to take the pet to the vet within seventy-two hours of entering Mexico and get a signed health certificate claiming that the animal is in good health.

- You must have a vaccination certificate for rabies, hepatitis, pip, and leptospirosis.

- And you'll have to pay a fee for a permit allowing you to cross the border with Bowser.

- **A special tip:** Don't let animals roam freely in Mexico. Not only because they're not liked, but also because they can get into rodent poison (especially common in ports).

TOURS

Tours can be the answers to travelers' prayers or forms of temporary damnation. The most important question for you to ask yourself, then, is whether or not you are a good prospect for a tour. Loners should not take tours. Most people who are impatient standing in lines will not like tours. Impulsive, free-spirited people often regret traveling on tours.

On the other hand, people who dislike unplanned weekends, who are not very aggressive, who lead scheduled lives, and who don't speak Spanish find tours an excellent way to travel. For those in poor health, joining a tour may be more attractive than traveling alone. In short, it's a question of personality. If you do decide to join a tour, be sure its goals and your own goals match.

Advantages of tours

- Tours can save you money, lots of it in some cases. You're joining a group that buys everything as a block, which ensures substantial price reductions across the board.

- Tours can be prepaid, allowing you to know in advance how much the trip is going to cost. You can also put off payment by financing the trip.

- Tour packages, which cover all major expenses, allow you to pay in dollars. In this way you avoid the hassle of currency exchange.

- Tours can be found that are tailored to individual needs or interests, from fishing to whale watching.

- Tours offer companionship and frequently humor for travelers prone to loneliness.

- Tours help less aggressive travelers to cope with the language barrier and avoid embarrassing situations.

- Tours have clout, the ability to get you into a hotel or restaurant in peak tourist seasons. And to get the most that place has to give!

- Tours save you time and energy by preventing potential hassles and knowing how to avoid others.

- Tours are organized by experts who know the most interesting sights to see. They generally hire competent travel guides in each city to help you understand its beauty, history, and tradition.

Disadvantages of tours

• Tours herd people together. To find out how you react to this experience, go on a local tour in your home town; perhaps, to a museum or art gallery. If it's enjoyable you may find a Mexican tour enjoyable as well. If it turns you off, then skip longer tours altogether!

• Tours can be hurried, impersonal, and flavorless affairs. Throughout the trip you will be bound to follow a prearranged schedule, oriented to a group and its needs. It may take the travail out of travel, but it can also wring the lust out of wanderlust.

• The normal mode of transportation for tour groups in Mexico is the bus. It's convenient and usually comfortable, but it can be equally boring and confining.

• You pay for a tour sight unseen, which is something like marrying the same way. You don't know what you've got until it's in the boat. There's no real chance for a refund if things go awry.

• Tours are groups of people, people whom you may or may not like. Whatever your feelings, you're stuck with them all the way.

• The words in tour brochures are just that—words. A "first-class" hotel may end up being, well, second-rate, even in Saltillo.

• Most tour contracts squirm with loopholes and catches, which rarely protect you.

• If you don't like the hotels chosen for you or the restaurant's bland fare, your complaints may fall on deaf ears.

• In some cases, you could do much better from a financial standpoint by not taking a tour. Some of the luxury tours are a good example—Jason could have picked up a bucketful of golden fleece sheared from wealthy tour goers!

TOUR PACKAGE CHECKLIST

If you take the trouble to consult tour brochures or agents and find answers to the following questions, you will be in a much better position to judge the quality of any tour package you're considering.

- ☐ Is the tour operator a member of the United States Tour Operators' Association? (Most of these operators are reliable.)
- ☐ How much will the tour cost altogether?
- ☐ Will a service charge be added on? If so, how much will it be? Often you'll find that there is a service charge outlined in very fine print at the end of the brochure. Words like "extra," "optional," and "bonus" should also be red flags to you.
- ☐ What extra or supplemental charges will apply to you? What will optional packages cost you? How much is the advance deposit?
- ☐ What are the penalties for cancellation?
- ☐ Are substitutions allowed on the passenger list?
- ☐ Can the dates of the tour be changed arbitrarily?
- ☐ Can the schedule or itinerary be rearranged for any reason?
- ☐ Can the tour be canceled? How much notice must be given?
- ☐ Does the tour include transportation to and from the airport? Most tours don't.
- ☐ Does the tour cost include the full price of airfare to and from Mexico? What are the dates and times of flights? Are the flights nonstop?
- ☐ Does the tour price cover all airport departure taxes?
- ☐ What kind of transportation is provided for in Mexico?
- ☐ Does it include all transfers from airports and train stations? Does it include the cost of transportation to meals and night life?
- ☐ What kind of intercity transportation is provided: bus, train, air?
- ☐ If it's a bus, is it air-conditioned, or "air-cooled" (a tour brochure expression meaning that the windows can be opened)?
- ☐ If it's a plane or a train, what class will you be in?
- ☐ How many nights' accommodation is included in the tour price? Are there any nights where the cost of a room has been left out?
- ☐ Is there a supplemental charge if you want a room to yourself? How much?
- ☐ Which hotels will you be staying in? Get the names.
- ☐ Can other hotels be substituted arbitrarily? If so, get the names.
- ☐ What's included in the room? Bath or shower? Two beds? Get details.
- ☐ Where are the hotels located? Tell them to show you on a map.
- ☐ Are all tips and taxes included in the room price?
- ☐ Is there any charge whatsoever that's not included?
- ☐ Are all meals included in the price of the tour? Is any meal not included? If not, why not? Or if not, where not?

TOUR PACKAGE CHECKLIST

☐ Where will you be eating? In the hotel? In a restaurant? What restaurants?

☐ What's included with the meal? Is wine included? Is coffee included? Is dessert included? Is anything excluded? If so, how much will it cost?

☐ Do you have a choice from the menu at each meal? Can you make substitutions at no extra charge?

☐ Are all tips and service charges for meals included in the tour price?

☐ Who pays the entrance fee to museums, galleries, and events?

☐ What is the pace of the tour? Does it leave you any free time?

☐ Does the tour spend enough time in each city to let you get anything out of the visit?

☐ Will the tour have an escort? Will the same escort be with the tour for the whole time? If so, that's an added value.

☐ Will the tour have travel guides for each city?

☐ Does the tour include insurance for accidents, health, baggage, etc.? If so, how much? Any deductible? Any exclusions?

☐ Who takes care of the baggage? Is there any extra cost? How many bags are *free*? Are all tips to porters included in the cost of the hotel room?

The Tour Payment Protection Plan

Following are tour companies that are a part of ASTA's (American Society of Travel Agents) Tour Protection Agreement that protects customers from any hanky-panky. New companies join this group, so check with ASTA for updated information:

ASTA
American Society of Travel Agents
4400 MacArthur Boulevard, N.W.
Washington, DC 20007
tel.: (202) 965-7520

● Companies Offering the Plan include:

American Leisure, Inc.
9800 Centre Parkway, Suite 800
Houston, TX 77036
tel.: (800) 392-2380 (TX)
        (713) 988-5777

Apple Tours
606 East Baltimore Pike
Media, PA 19063
tel.: (800) 662-5184 (PA)
       (800) 523-7555 (East Coast)
       (215) 565-7550

Cartan Tours, Inc.
One Crossroads of Commerce
Rolling Meadows, IL 60008
tel.: (800) 323-7888

Four Winds
175 Fifth Avenue
New York, NY 10010
tel.: (800) 248-4444

Friendly Holidays, Inc.
118–21 Queens Boulevard, #310
Forest Hills, NY 11375
tel.: (800) 257-3500

Gem Tours
P.O. Box 81
Verona, NJ 07044
tel.: (800) 432-9150
       (201) 484-2220

Holland America Westours, Inc.
300 Elliott Avenue West
Seattle, WA 98119
tel.: (800) 426-0327

Nielson Tours
One West Main Street
P.O. Box N
Mesa, AZ 85201
tel.: (800) 543-0890

Talmage Tours, Inc.
1223 Walnut Street
Philadelphia, PA 19107
tel.: (215) 923-7100

Tours to the Baja

The following company specializes in varied tours to the Baja. If this area intrigues you, contact:

Baja Adventures
16000 Ventura Boulevard, Suite 200
Encino, CA 91436
tel.: (800) 543-2252
       (800) 345-2252 (California)

For women only

Womantour organizes both group and individual tours for women alone:

Womantour
5314 North Figueroa Street
Los Angeles, CA 90042
tel.: (213) 255-1115

STAYING HEALTHY

Certain health problems come up frequently when people travel to Mexico, so frequently that they become standard jokes. However, for the person suffering the indignities of diarrhea, nothing seems amusing. The hints in this chapter can help you avoid health problems and deal with others.

RISK AREAS

Some areas of Mexico involve greater health risk than others. The tourist traveling to a major resort will probably have few health problems, but the traveler on a two-month sojourn covering much of Mexico will run the gamut of health hazards—which are very real indeed.

Poor sanitation

At best, areas in Mexico are adequate in sanitation, at worst, appalling. Refuse everywhere along the road, open burning of garbage, sewage running through trenches or gutters in streets, flies—these all represent a better than even chance of causing illness.

What can you do when traveling in areas of poor sanitation? Not as much as some people would have you believe! In fact, even the most scrupulous traveler following *all* the standard travel advice can easily get sick.

• **When you travel to Mexico, especially to inland and remote areas, you run a risk of illness which is much greater than you'd run in more developed countries.** This is what any informed traveler should expect. You have to decide whether it's worth it.

Tips on preventing major illness

The innoculations suggested in this chapter will help you prevent the most serious illnesses in Mexico, but they are not foolproof. If you behave like a fool, you can still end up getting the very diseases you've tried to prevent.

• Wash your hands frequently. You don't want to contaminate yourself.

• Don't go barefoot. Wear sandals or shoes to avoid cuts, abrasions, and parasites.

• Carry food and water with you wherever you go. This way when you're thirsty or hungry, you won't be forced to eat or drink whatever's handy at the time.

• Drink lots of fluids in hot climates to prevent dehydration.

• Drink only purified or bottled water. None available? Buy a soft drink—they're sold everywhere in Mexico.

• Make sure ice is of purified water.

• Dirty or wet bottle? Use a straw.

• Avoid leafy vegetables, such as lettuce.

• Most dairy products sold in major stores are safe, but avoid them in rural areas—the cheeses may be made from unpasteurized milk.

• Unless seafood is freshly caught, it can make you very sick. To be completely safe avoid **all raw shellfish** (more and more doctors agree).

• Avoid cold foods that were once hot—leftovers, snacks, anything.

• Be suspicious of mayonnaise and egg-based custards unless they're refrigerated (they rarely are).

• Don't use Mexican ceramics for cooking or serving food unless you're certain they're lead-free. Watch out for glazed pottery with the color green.

• Purify all fresh vegetables and fruits by soaking them in appropriate solutions (information follows). The fact that you can peel them (the usual advice) is totally meaningless. You can contaminate what you eat in the peeling process.

Purifying water, fruits, and vegetables

• The safest way to purify water is to boil it for thirty minutes at sea level, for forty-five minutes at higher altitudes. Cooked vegetables and fruits are usually safe to eat. Boiling water kills **giardia,** the other methods of purification do not.

• Water purification tablets *(pastillas para purificar agua)* will kill most bacteria if left to soak for thirty minutes. You can buy these in the United States. They're very expensive, and it takes many of them to purify each quart of water. Use them only in emergencies. Your pharmacist will recognize the name **Halazone.**

• Liquid bleach *(blanqueador)* will kill most bacteria. If it's a 1 percent solution, add ten drops to each quart of water. If it's a 4 to 6 percent solution, add two to four drops per quart. Let the chlorine do its work for thirty minutes. Iodine *(yodo)* can be substituted for bleach in this process.

• Purify fruits and vegetables by letting them soak in any of these solutions for thirty minutes or longer. Now they are safe to peel and eat.

Mexican purification

• Mexicans believe that lime juice kills bacteria. Limes are served with just about everything. In theory, if you squeeze the juice of a lime over a salad and let it sit for thirty minutes, the bacteria should be dead. My limes must have been old or tired.

INNOCULATIONS

No two doctors agree on the shots that travelers should have before going to Mexico. However, you should follow commonsense guidelines. The longer you travel and the more remote your destination, the more you need protection.

- Many innoculations are given free of charge or for a token charge at public clinics.

- Start shots well ahead of your trip. Some must be given in series over weeks or even months.

- Some have side effects which could affect your trip if you wait until the last minute!

Cholera

- A vaccination against cholera is needed *only if* you're traveling to an area known to have it. This is rarely the case.

- Cholera shots are not totally reliable in preventing the disease and have a relatively short-term value.

Gamma globulin

- Gamma (immune) globulin can be effective in preventing hepatitis A. If you're planning a long trip, then the dosage must be larger.

- Since the shot provides only short-term protection, get it only if you'll be traveling to more remote areas with poor sanitation. Backpackers and explorer types should get it.

Hepatitis B

- Hepatitis B serum is roughly 96 percent effective against hepatitis B, which can be debilitating at best, deadly at worst.

- Unfortunately, hepatitis B is becoming more common, although only 5 to 10 percent of the population in the United States has been exposed to it. In other countries the rate is much higher.

● Hepatitis B serum is given in three doses over a 6-month period. It is also very expensive.

● If you plan to travel extensively in developing countries, the cost is worth it. It is doubly important if you have frequent sexual contact.

● Some doctors recommend a blood test before giving you the serum. If the cost of the blood test is low, then you might save yourself a great deal of money if the test shows that you have already been exposed to hepatitis B. However, if the test is expensive, skip it. According to the laboratory which makes it, there are no adverse reactions to the serum even if you have already been exposed to hepatitis B earlier.

Polio

● All doctors agree that this is essential. You may need a booster.

Tetanus/diphtheria

● Doctors agree on this one, too. You may be due for a booster.

Typhoid

● Typhoid shots are somewhat controversial. Their value can only be related to risk, which in most areas is low. Again, if you'll be traveling to remote areas, it may well be worth the cost of this "insurance."

● Initially, you'll get two typhoid shots. After that, boosters are effective.

● Some people have a reaction to typhoid shots, but most have soreness only. Try to have these shots two or more months ahead of your trip.

Yellow fever

- Yellow fever shots are not required for travel to Mexico. However, if you plan to travel to Central America or South America, check on recommendations for the areas you plan to visit.

Malaria

During the last five years there have been seventy-two cases of malaria reported by U.S. travelers to Mexico. The chance of getting malaria in major tourist areas is remote, but not absent.

- **The risk areas** include the following states of Mexico: Campeche, Chiapas, Chihuahua (May to October), Durango, Guerrero, Jalisco (May to October), Michoacán, Morelos (May to October), Nayarit, Oaxaca, Puebla (May to October), Quintana Roo, Sinaloa (May to October), Sonora (May to October), Tabasco, Veracruz, and the Yucatán.

- As you can see, that's quite a chunk of Mexico, but some areas are only dangerous in the rainy season from May to October.

Preventing malaria

- The simplest way to protect yourself from malaria is to protect yourself from mosquitos (see p. 74).

- Since that's not quite as simple as it sounds, your backup is the medication called *chloroquine phosphate*. These white pills are roughly the size of aspirin and are usually effective against the strain of malaria found in Mexico.

- You have to take two pills a week, starting the treatment one week before the trip and continuing it for six weeks after.

- Diarrhea and headache can be two side effects of the medication.

MEDICAL INFORMATION

Never ask travel agents for medical information, since they're usually behind the times on health problems.

In the United States

Check with a **public health office,** the best being state head-quarters where bulletins are kept up to date on disease outbreaks worldwide.

- For useful, current bulletins on disease, contact:

The Centers for Disease Control
Atlanta, GA 30333
tel.: (404) 329-3311

In Canada

The **Travel Information Offices of Health and Welfare** in Canada can give you current information and health bulletins on Mexico. You'll find these offices in Edmonton, Gander, Halifax, Montreal, Ottawa, Prince George, Prince Rupert, Regina, Saint John, Saint John's, Sydney, Thunder Bay, Toronto, Vancouver, Victoria, and Winnipeg.

INTERNATIONAL CERTIFICATES OF VACCINATION

At one time every international traveler was required to show proof of smallpox vaccination. Since smallpox has been officially eradicated, such proof is no longer necessary. The proof consisted of a doctor's signature and official stamp in a **"yellow card."** These cards are still available and are technically called **International Certificates of Vaccination.**

Although yellow cards are no longer necessary for travel to Mexico, it doesn't hurt to have one. By having all of your immunizations listed in this official document, you have an accurate record of them. In the case of an unusual outbreak of a specific disease you can be immunized abroad and have that noted in the yellow card. This will allow you to cross the border into and out of a "disease zone." Such an occurrence is rare, but it does happen—particularly in the case of cholera.

Most passport agencies, health service offices, and medical clinics have copies of the yellow card, which is given out free of charge.

GETTING SET TO GO

A few routine steps can help take the worry out of travel if you have a medical problem of any kind. Here are some suggestions.

Medical preparations for travel

● Before going on a trip, see both a doctor and a dentist for a quick checkup.

● Have your doctor fill out the yellow card with a complete history of your immunizations.

● Get the immunizations suggested for the kind of travel you'll be doing.

● Get a prescription for a good drug to combat diarrhea as well as one for malaria pills if you'll be traveling in a possibly infectious area.

Chronic health problems

● If you have a chronic health problem, take with you all the drugs you'll need for the entire trip and include enough to cover a week or two extra in case of an unexpected, extended stay.

● If you're pregnant, you'll want to get suggestions from your doctor before going to Mexico.

● If you have heart or respiratory problems, be wary of Cuernavaca, Guadalajara, and Mexico City. These all have a severe air pollution problem, and Mexico City is at a high altitude which compounds the danger.

Diabetics

● Consider signing up with one of the organizations in this chapter that provides help in Mexico and identification.

● Carry urine-testing equipment, regular and long-lasting insulin, oral drugs or syringes, extra carbohydrates (your schedule will get fouled up), and a doctor's note stating that you are a diabetic. This note helps you explain syringes when you cross the border into and out of Mexico.

● Becton-Dickinson does have disposable syringes in Mexican pharmacies.

● If you buy insulin in Mexico, learn about the variations in strengths and how to deal with them before going.

USEFUL MEDICAL ORGANIZATIONS

If you have a chronic illness or medical problem, you may be interested in contacting the following organizations for information on their services.

Assist-Card International
347 Fifth Avenue
New York, NY 10016
tel.: (800) 221-4564
      (212) 686-1288

Intermedic, Inc.
777 Third Avenue
New York, NY 10017
tel.: (212) 486-8900

International Association of Medical
   Assistance to Travelers (IAMAT)
736 Center Street
Lewiston, NY 14092
tel.: (716) 754-4883

International Health Care Service
440 East 69th Street
New York, NY 10021
tel.: (212) 472-4284

International SOS Assistance, Inc.
   (mailing address)
P.O. Box 11568
Philadelphia, PA 19116
tel.: (800) 523-8930
      (215) 244-1500

International SOS Assistance
One Neshaminy Interplex, Suite 310
Trevose, PA 19047
tel.: (800) 523-8930
      (215) 244-1500

Medic Alert Foundation
P.O. Box 1009
Turlock, CA 95381
tel.: 1-800-344-3226

PRESCRIPTION ITEMS

Drugs

● Be sure to bring fresh drugs with you. If you're not sure about the value of older medications, call your pharmacist.

• Make sure that you're carrying enough of any prescription to last a week or two beyond your expected stay, just in case you get delayed for some unforseen reason.

• Always keep all prescription drugs in the original containers. Some of these containers are huge, so ask the pharmacist to divide the amount into two smaller containers, both clearly labeled. These are easier to carry, and you can throw them away as they're used up.

• If your drugs contain narcotics, then carry your doctor's prescription with you.

• Ask your doctor or pharmacist for the generic name of any drug you're using. Write it down. This name will probably be familiar to a Mexican druggist if you lose or run out of pills.

• Never put drugs into luggage that will be checked on a plane. Always carry it with you.

Eyeglasses

• Either bring a spare pair of glasses with you in a hard case or the prescription itself. Note that a lens can be duplicated from the pieces of a broken pair of glasses (in case you forget to bring a prescription).

MEDICAL EVACUATION

Medical evacuation is a relatively rare occurrence, but consider it if you'll be doing high-risk activities in Mexico or have a serious health condition. You can take out medical evacuation insurance. Following are companies specializing in this procedure.

Air Evac International, Inc.
8665 Gibbs Drive, Suite 202
San Diego, CA 92123
tel.: (619) 292-5557

Critical Air Medicine, Inc.
4141 Kearney Villa Road
San Diego, CA 92123
tel.: (619) 571-8944

Life Flight
1203 Ross Sterling
Herman Hospital, Texas Medical
  Center
Houston, TX 77030
tel.: (800) 231-4357
      (800) 392-4357 (TX)
      (713) 797-3950

Schaefer's Ambulance, Inc.
4627 Beverly
Los Angeles, CA 90004
tel.: (213) 469-1473

WARNING

Go to a doctor if after a trip to Mexico you have any of the following symptoms: fever, diarrhea that lasts over a week, fatigue, reoccurring diarrhea, recurrent itching skin, an asthma-like cough, or undue weight loss.

HEALTH CARE IN MEXICO

Health care in Mexico can be good, but you have to know the ropes to take advantage of the good and to avoid the bad.

Doctors

- If you need a doctor for a minor illness, you can trust someone in your hotel to come up with a name.

- If you feel that language will be a barrier and you're in a larger city, call the U.S. or Canadian consulate and ask for the name of a doctor specializing in your condition or illness.

- Most doctors will come to your hotel if you request or need it.

- The advantage of a local doctor is that he's familiar with the local illnesses and can usually treat your problem effectively.

- Mexican doctors charge relatively low fees.

Drugs

- Most drugs in Mexico are incredibly cheap in comparison

to drugs in the United States and Canada. Pick up your Lomotil in Mexico!

● Many drugs that are restricted in the United States and Canada are available over the counter in Mexico.

● If you purchase drugs in Mexico, they must legally be declared coming back into the United States or Canada.

Pharmacies

● Pharmacies sell drugs in Mexico that are outlawed in the United States.

● All drugs have the maximum legal price listed right on the package.

● When filling a prescription *(receta),* make sure that you get the drug prescribed.

● Pharmacists are allowed to administer shots in Mexico. If you need an antibiotic, you can get it here, but buy a new syringe (some pharmacists reuse them).

● Late-night pharmacies are listed in the yellow pages of the phone book as *farmacias—servicio de 24 horas, farmacias de turno, farmacia de la guardia,* or *farmacia de la vigilancia.*

Hospitals

● Avoid public hospitals unless the situation is critical. If you can, get to Mexico City. The American British Cowdray Hospital has a staff of 480 doctors, all who speak good English.

The American British Cowdray Hospital
Sur 136 Esq. Observatoria
Colonia América
01120 Mexico, D.F.
tel.: 277-5000 or 515-8359 (emergencies)

GENERAL HEALTH PROBLEMS

Certain health problems crop up frequently in Mexico. Here are a few tips to help you deal with them.

Altitude sickness

In Mexico City and other cities in higher altitudes you may experience loss of appetite, nausea, mental confusion, fatigue, and shortness of breath—that's altitude sickness.

- The simple, but somewhat drastic solution is to go to a place at lower altitude.

- **Diamox,** a medication, can relieve its symptoms.

- Slow down the pace. Relax and let your body get used to the lack of oxygen.

- Avoid alcohol, its effect being tripled at high altitudes.

- Drink lots of liquids—fruit juices, water, colas.

- Eat less and eat your main meal in the middle of the day.

- Sleep more. Here's the perfect excuse for a nap after a tiring trip.

Amoebic dysentery

You can't do much to prevent getting this disease. If you do get it, it's just bad luck. There are a number of drugs which will kill amoeba, and they're available both in Mexico and the United States.

- You may have to submit a stool sample to know for sure that you've got amoeba. However, a negative stool sample does *not* mean that you don't have amoeba. Some doctors say that stool samples are negative so frequently that they may be a waste of money. They treat for amoeba without them.

Anxiety

Some travelers feel out of their element in Mexico and experience anxiety.

- Slow down the pace, don't feel compulsive about tours and sightseeing, get plenty of rest, and eat well.

- Beer is a natural tranquilizer. So is the Mexican fruit *zapote*.

- Get physical. Exercise relieves stress. It's hard to be uptight after two hours of snorkeling in the Caribbean.

Bee stings

Any person who has ever had an allergic reaction to a bee sting, should carry along antihistamines. Get someone to a doctor if he shows signs of severe swelling, difficulty breathing, or a rash.

Bleeding

If you're bleeding internally, get to a doctor *immediately*. Apply pressure to any external bleeding until it stops—it can sometimes take a long time.

Blisters

Nothing can ruin sightseeing or hiking faster than a blister.

- Wear comfortable walking shoes that you've used at home before your trip. Don't worry about how they look. No one else gives a damn. Comfort and convenience should always come ahead of fashion while traveling.

- The minute you feel a blister forming—stop! Try to cover the tender spot with a Band-Aid or some Mole skin. If you don't stop, a blister will form.

- If you do get a blister, clean it with soap and pure water. Rub your foot with alcohol if possible. Keep the blister covered with a Band-Aid until it heals.

Broken bones

The rough surf in Mexico can do a lot of damage in seconds. Be wary of it. Never get in front of a boat coming into a beach. A wave can smash it into you.

- If someone has a broken bone, don't try to set it. Immobilize the area as best you can. Get the person to a doctor.

Burns

Someone in a group of campers always manages to get a burn.

- Clean the area with soap and purified water.
- If ice is available, apply it to the burn.
- Rub vitamin E oil or cream on the burn.
- Cover it with a sterile bandage.
- If you've got a burn, drink lots of liquids.

Cactus spines

Watch where you sit and don't walk around Mexico in bare feet.

- If you have a tweezer, you may be able to remove some cactus spines. Don't count on it.
- A better method is to cover the area with melted wax (try not to burn yourself doing this). Let the wax harden and then pull it off—the spines will come with it.

Coconuts

Watch for coconut bombs! Don't walk, stand, camp, or park your car under coconut palm trees. This is not a joke.

Colds

Cold remedies can be hard to find in Mexico. If you're prone to colds, bring medication with you. Popular Mexican cold remedies include honey and lime juice, hot tea, warm salt water, garlic, and vitamin C—not really so different from U.S. remedies.

Constipation

Mineral water is a natural laxative and so is lots of exercise.

- If you're prone to constipation, bring medication with you.

Coral

Unless you're familiar with coral, keep your hands off it.

- If you do get stung, clean the area with warm salt water and apply cortisone cream.

Cramps

Climbing ruins can easily bring on a case of cramps. The best solution is usually a steaming hot bath. Let muscles rest to work out the lactic acid.

Dengue fever

Dengue fever is an illness found in Mexico which causes high fever and aches in your joints. The only prevention is to avoid mosquito bites. The only cure is rest and a good diet. It is not a common disease, but it is reported every year. If you don't feel well, go to a doctor!

Diarrhea

This is the number one problem for travelers in Mexico. It is not funny, because it can ruin a vacation.

HOW TO PREVENT DIARRHEA

- Do not premedicate for diarrhea. This will kill off helpful bacteria in your system. However, you might want to take freeze-dried *acidophilus* tablets, made up of the same kind of bacteria found in kefir and yogurt.

- These tablets are quite expensive and should be kept cool. For a short trip, they make sense. But for longer trips, forget it! Many travelers swear by them.

- Coffee often causes diarrhea. If you're a coffee drinker, switch to tea.

- Sewage runs directly into the sea in some Mexican resorts. If you're a mile away from the outlet, you're probably okay. But if you're not, you may pick up a bug.

- Many Mexican foods are very spicy, and these can cause diarrhea. Watch what you eat!

HOW TO TREAT DIARRHEA

- If you have to travel, go ahead and take something like

Lomotil. It locks in infections, but you don't have much choice.

● As soon as you can, lay off the Lomotil (don't take it for more than three days). Switch over to something milder. Your doctor will suggest a prescription. We found **Imodium** effective.

● In Mexico, diarrhea can become a reoccurring problem— you keep reinfecting yourself. If this happens, go to a local doctor and get fixed up.

● The main danger of diarrhea is **dehydration.** So here's a diarrhea potion: In one glass put 8 ounces of fruit juice, ½ teaspoon of sugar, and a pinch of salt. Fill another glass with 8 ounces of purified water and a ¼ teaspoon of soda. Alternate swallows from each glass until both glasses are empty. Yum!

● Or pour salt and soda into a bottle of coke and swill that.

Drowning

● Many people drown in Mexico, most from carelessness. Always ask whether an area is safe for swimming.

● The secret to saving a drowning person is speed. Begin artificial respiration from the moment you make contact, that usually means in the water. Get air into the person's lungs as *quickly* as possible. Don't wait for the perfect moment or ideal conditions.

Ear problems

● If your ears begin to hurt during the landing of a plane, try to yawn. This should release some of the pressure.

● If you'll be flying on your trip and have a stuffy head, use a decongestant before landing. This will make it easier to relieve the pressure.

● Babies should be given a bottle to suck on during a landing.

● Sometimes your ears get plugged with water after a swim. If you've tried everything from dancing on one foot to shaking your head like a madman and nothing works, have someone pour warm (not hot) water into the ear. Let it sit there for a minute and then roll over. This often works.

- Bug in your ear? Use a flashlight to draw it out.

Exhaustion

Travel, more tiring and stressful than everyday living, may catch you off balance. Exhaustion can lead to more serious health problems as your resistance is lowered. Listen to your body, which speaks in sign language. It will always tell you what pace to keep.

- If you're traveling with people who want to move at a faster pace, split up and plan to meet them at a later date.

- If you're caught on a whirlwind tour, skip part of it. Don't worry about missing something you've paid for—a trip is for fun.

- Match your style of travel to your energy level. If you don't feel well, pamper yourself with a nicer hotel or a more comfortable mode of transportation. Consider making your trip short but sweet.

Eye (something in it)

Nothing is more frustrating than getting something in your eye and being unable to get it out. Here's the secret:

- Pull your upper eyelid out and down as far as you can. Let go. The irritant will often come off on the first try.

- If that doesn't work, have someone else look for the spot. Have them touch it gently with the end of a tissue. The piece of grit will usually adhere to the tissue and be out of your eye in an instant.

Eyestrain

More than likely the cause of eyestrain in Mexico is bright sun. Cure the problem with a good pair of sunglasses.

Fever

For mild fever take aspirin, drink lots of liquids, and keep cool. A high fever signals a trip to the doctor.

Fish poisoning

Fish poisoning *(ciguatera)* causes a tingling in the mouth, nausea, and diarrhea. Mexican fish that sometimes cause it are barracuda (usually ones over 2 feet), jacks, moray eels, parrot fish, and snappers. It is not a major concern, but something that travelers should know about.

Fleas

Fleas, very common in more casual accommodations, can be discouraged with eucalyptus leaves.

Food poisoning

Headache, nausea, vomiting, and diarrhea (often all at once) —these are the signs of food poisoning, which can only be described as the next worst thing to death.

- See a doctor. Some food poisoning can be fatal. Note that there is little that can be done for most cases except to ride it out.

Giardia

Giardia is spreading and causing problems in water worldwide. The only thing that knocks it dead is boiling. Be wary of contaminated water.

- Diarrhea and pain are two symptoms. Doctors can prescribe antibiotics to knock it out.

Hangovers

Mexicans like to drink and drink hard. Prevent some of the effect of a hangover by drinking lots of water during a night of hard drinking. This helps prevent dehydration. Mexican say that dog tea *(té de perro)* diminishes the effects of a hangover. A little tea of the dog that bit you.

Heartburn

Carry some antacid with you—heartburn is inevitable. Experts say not to eat too fast, not to eat too much, to avoid spicy foods, to loosen your belt, to avoid big late-night meals—how many of those experts have traveled in Mexico? Bring lots of antacid!

Heat prostration/sunstroke

The Mexican sun can cause a lot of damage. Mexicans don't take siestas for nothing. If you're going to be out in the sun for long periods of time, never underestimate its effect.

• Wear light-colored, lightweight, and loose clothing.

• Never travel without a wide-brimmed hat. They're very cheap in Mexico and absolutely essential.

• Drink lots of fluids—constantly be drinking. Carry soft drinks and bottled waters with you.

• Put more salt on your foods than you normally would. And if you'll be hiking, carry salt tablets.

• If you know you're getting too hot, get out of the sun into any available shade.

• Lie down and rest.

• Anyone who gets flushed, hot and dry skin, and runs a rapid pulse should get to a doctor immediately. If ice is available, get into an ice bath until your temperature drops to 102 degrees Fahrenheit. Sunstroke can be fatal.

Hepatitis

Hepatitis is spread by food and drink as well as sexual contact with an infected person. You can prevent most forms of hepatitis with hepatitis B serum and gamma globulin (see p. 56).

• If you get hepatitis, a good diet and rest is the only cure. No booze or cigarettes will be allowed.

Hoarseness

The low humidity in the higher areas of Mexico can cause temporary hoarseness. It's generally just an irritant.

Hypothermia

It doesn't have to be freezing outside to get hypothermia. Campers and hikers should be wary of this condition.

• Stay dry. Be prepared for sudden rains with a good poncho.

• Keep your head, neck, and hands covered to prevent heat loss.

• Wet clothes lose 90 percent of their insulating value and drain heat from the body 240 times faster than dry clothes! So change clothes.

• Drink something warm and eat high-energy foods. Do not drink alcohol which leads to heat loss.

• Get warm. Crawl into a sleeping bag, preferably with another person (no joke).

• Rest. And watch for danger signals: uncontrollable shivering, difficulty talking, confusion, puffy face, or unconsciousness. *This person needs help.*

Infections

All infections should be taken seriously, even if they seem minor.

• Clean them frequently, preferably with alcohol and treat them with an antibiotic ointment.

Insomnia

• Exercise, lots of liquids, and a good diet high in protein will help you avoid insomnia.

• Certain foods contain sleep-inducing substances. Drink a little beer to take advantage of its lupulin (a product of hops). Eat a light snack with milk. It contains both L-tryptophan and calcium—both cause drowsiness.

• Take a warm bath just before going to bed. This helps relax muscle tension.

• If noise bothers you, carry earplugs. Try Flents, which can be molded to your ear and block out most noise. They're found in pharmacies throughout the United States.

• Keep the room dark by pulling down the shades. If that's not enough, use a mask.

• Follow a routine at home and during travel that sets up or triggers sleep. For many people this is reading a book or magazine.

● Certain things cause insomnia: heavy drinking, late meals (the norm in Mexico); spicy foods (also very common); chocolate and colas, which contain caffeine; and afternoon naps.

● Sleep-inducing drugs work, but they can cause sleep disturbances and other side effects that may do more harm than good. No one ever died of insomnia.

Jellyfish

If you find yourself surrounded by jellyfish, dive down and try to swim under them. If you're already in the tentacles, dive down to get out of them.

● Here are a few things that might take away the sting: Benadryl *(jarabe)*, cortisone cream, mild ammonia, Windex, papaya juice, warm salt water.

Jet lag

Since the time differences are minimal from most U.S. and Canadian cities to Mexico, jet lag tends to be a minor problem. It's much more serious when crossing many time zones.

Malaria

Malaria is a very serious illness. Its prevention is covered in detail on p. 58.

Mosquitos

Mexico remains a prime breeding ground for some of the world's most prolific mosquitos.

● Get an insect repellant with a high degree of diethyloluamide in it. The higher the better. The kind that comes in stick form like deodorant is easiest for travelers.

● If you can't stand the smell of these repellants, try Avon's Skin So Soft. Some readers claim it really repels them.

● Stay in a protected area, especially in the evening when the breed of mosquitos carrying malaria comes out.

- Always carry mosquito netting *(pabellon)* for camping or staying in smaller hotels without good screens on the windows. You can buy it in Mexico if you forget to bring it with you. *It's absolutely essential in some areas.*

- A strong breeze will often keep mosquitos away. If you're camped in a low area, consider moving up into the wind or closer to the sea shore.

- Di-Delamine and Camfo-Fenicol can be purchased in Mexico and will give you relief from bites.

- Never scratch insect bites. If they're itching, push down on them with your finger tip. This will give some relief.

Motion sickness

You're either susceptible to this, or you're not. And you know very quickly whether or not you are. If you don't want to take the chance, there are many medications available such as Benadryl, Bonine, Dramamine, Marezine, Phenergan, and Scopolamine (Transderm-V). The latter consists of a little pad placed behind your ear.

- These drugs may have side effects, and some of them must be prescribed by a doctor.

- If you forget to get pills in the United States, ask for *pastillas para mareo* at a pharmacy in Mexico.

- If you forget to take pills, here are a few suggestions: eat frequent, but light snacks during the voyage. Skip alcohol altogether.

- Lie down away from annoying smells or noise. The diesel smell of a motor is enough to make you sick even if you're not prone to seasickness. The smell of food or tobacco can also be nauseating.

- If you're in a car, ask to drive. Drivers rarely get motion sickness.

Nausea

Try camomile or dog teas to overcome the sensation of nausea. Both are available in most areas of Mexico.

Pain

Since pain is only a symptom of a medical problem, see a doctor. In the meantime aspirin works for minor aches and pains— just like they say in the commercial. And for more major pain you can use Mecoten or Prodolina, available in pharmacies *(farmacias)*.

Parasites (intestinal)

Folk remedies include fresh garlic, chopped cloves, and lime juice. You can give these a try for temporary relief and see a doctor in Mexico or on your return home for a permanent cure.

Poisoning

Many Mexicans buy inexpensive alcohol. Make sure that it's the kind that can be drunk before you drink it. If you have to siphon gasoline from a tank, don't swallow any of the gas. A good reason to carry a spare tank.

Rabies

If you're traveling with small children, tell them not to play with stray animals. Rabies is quite common in Mexico.

Scorpions

Roughly 250,000 scorpion stings are reported each year in Mexico. They are very common, especially in Colima, Durango, Jalisco, Michoacan, and Nayarit. They can be deadly if they sting small children or an adult on the head, but they rarely cause more than pain. Here are some tips:

● Scorpions come out at night. Never walk around in bare feet and carry a flashlight to see where you're going.

● Scorpions like to hide in things, anything from dry brush to your shoes. Shake everything out before going to bed and when you get up in the morning.

● If you get stung by a scorpion, lie down and relax. The calmer you are, the less severe the reaction, usually no worse than a bee sting.

● If you have an antihistamine, take it.

- Antiscorpion serum is sold in pharmacies as *Antialacran.* But you must be tested to see whether you're allergic to it. If you are, you'll immediately be given adrenalin. It is said that more people die from the serum each year than from scorpion stings.

- If ice is handy, put it on the sting. Also good remedies are crushed garlic and lime juice.

- Drink anything loaded with vitamin C, such as lime juice.

- Don't take opiates or morphine derivatives, which means *no codeine, Darvon, Demorol, or paregoric.*

- Don't eat or drink dairy products, don't smoke, and don't drink alcohol. Stick to fruit juices.

Sea urchin spines

If you step on a sea urchin or get pushed into one by a wave, you will get pricked by one of the sharp spines which may lodge in your skin.

- Pull it out with a tweezers or use a needle to get it out. Get the wound to bleed slightly.

- Squeeze lime juice on the wound or dab it with cortisone cream.

Smog

If you've got respiratory or heart problems, consider the smog problem in Mexico's major cities. Areas with a real problem include Cuernavaca, Guadalajara, and Mexico City.

Snakes

Rattlesnakes, fer de lances, and pit vipers are three common poisonous snakes in Mexico. Very rarely is a tourist bitten by one. If you are, remain calm and still. Ask to be carried to a doctor.

- You'll find some coral snakes in Mexico. They have extremely small mouths and rarely bite people. There is no cure for a coral snakebite.

Spiders

The bird spider and black widow are the two poisonous spiders that can cause trouble in Mexico. The average tourist will see neither.

Stingrays *(rayas)*

Stingrays like to rest in the sand along the shoreline. When you walk into the sea, shuffle your feet instead of taking big steps. The rays scurry off, more afraid of you than you are of them.

Sunburn

The sun and diarrhea are the two big health problems in Mexico. The dangerous rays come through even on cloudy days. Doctors insist that *no* sun is best—but who listens?

• If you haven't been in the sun recently, you're the one most vulnerable to it.

• If you have light and dry skin, you're the most prone to trouble.

• However, even with a dark base, you can still get blisters and serious skin damage near the tropics. I've seen it happen!

• The sun is extremely intense from 11 A.M. to 3 P.M., one reason why Mexicans are eating lunch or taking a siesta at this time. Consider following their lead.

• If you use a sunscreen, you can stay out longer in the sun. You may want to begin with maximum protection products. Following are companies that put these out: Clinique, Eclipse Total, Elizabeth Arden, Estée Lauder, Lancôme, Orlane, Pabanol, Piz Buin Exclusive, Pre-Sun, Solbar Plus, and Supershade.

• Sunscreens contain PABA. The higher percentage of this, the more protection. The number on the container will indicate the power of the sunscreen and runs from low protection of 1 up to 15 for best protection.

• Do not use products containing 5-methoxypsoralerv (5-MOP). These are believed to be dangerous, although many Europeans use them.

● Many products promote tanning, but they provide no protection from the sun. Coconut oil is one.

● Don't fall asleep in the sun.

● Wear a t-shirt when snorkeling since the sun's rays easily penetrate water.

● Cotton clothing has a tight weave that offers good sun protection. It breathes nicely in hot climates.

● Put on all sunscreens at least forty-five minutes before going out into the sun. Although some sunscreens claim to be good after swimming, apply them again anyway.

● Wear a sombrero and good sunglasses to protect your head and eyes.

● Drink lots of water when you're out in the sun.

● Remember that certain drugs can make you sun-sensitive including tetracyclene, diabetic medications, sulfa drugs, and tranquilizers. If you're taking medications, ask the doctor about sun sensitivity.

● If you begin to get red, get out of the sun. To test your skin push down on any spot with your finger for a few seconds. Lift up. If the spot remains white for more than a second or two, you've got trouble.

● The time to use tanning oils such as coconut oil *(aceite de coco)* is after you've been in the sun. Apply them liberally after you've taken a shower or bath to prevent peeling.

● If you do get burned, these things may help: Solarcaine, Neosporin, vinegar, lime juice, aloe vera, or papaya.

● Also, if you get burned, drink lots of liquids with a good dose of salt. Lots of fresh lime juice should be added to the drinks. But do not drink alcohol.

● Use water-based moisturizer on your skin to help it heal.

● For serious burns apply an antibiotic ointment.

● *Note:* Sun damage is believed to be cumulative. More and

more skin specialists are warning people to stay out of the sun. Since Mexico is close to the equator, the sun is particularly strong. The same is true in areas of high altitude where there is less protection from the sun.

Tarantulas

Yes, they do exist in Mexico, but they are not poisonous—just very ugly and frightening.

Ticks

Use oil, kerosene, or fingernail polish to smother the little buggers. Then wash the area with soap and water.

Toothache

Until you can get to a doctor, try clove oil *(aceite de clavo)* or whole cloves. You may need antibiotics to clear up an infection.

Vomiting

The only danger of vomiting is dehydration. Try to drink liquids as soon as humanly possible. Since it is a sign of a more serious illness, see a doctor.

5

PLANE TRAVEL

Plane travel is the fastest and most convenient way to get to and around Mexico. Prices today are also remarkably reasonable because of competition within the United States and Canada. You'll find generally low fares in Mexico as well.

BASIC CONSIDERATIONS

Following is a brief description of the pluses and minuses of plane travel.

Advantages of plane travel

- Plane travel is much less tiring than car, bus, and train travel.
- For trips of 300 miles or more, plane travel is the fastest way.
- It's the only way to get to some places, including remote ruins and fishing camps.
- For a solo traveler covering great distances, it can be quite economical.

• You waste less time covering the vast distances of Mexico.

• It's safe—popular misconceptions aside.

Disadvantages of plane travel

• Plane travel is more expensive than bus or train travel.

• Plane trips are oriented to travel between major cities.

• Plane travel can actually be slower than train or bus travel for short trips.

• Flights can be canceled.

• You've got to spend time and money on transfers from the airport into town. In some cases, this can be very expensive.

• You can be locked in by bad weather (rare in Mexico).

• You pass over, not through the countryside.

FLIGHTS TO MEXICO—SAVING MONEY

For many people flying to Mexico is the only practical way of getting there. Yet, on every flight, some passengers wind up paying as much as three or four times what some others pay. Smart travelers know this and learn strategies to keep costs down.

Comparison shopping—scheduled airlines

• Call Aeroméxico and Mexicana to get up-to-date price quotes on airfare to Mexico. These lines often offer low fares from major U.S. and Canadian cities to a wide variety of destinations in Mexico.

• Note that the distance of the flights often seems irrelevant in the price structure of these two airlines. In short, fares to all destinations within Mexico are almost the same. Structure your trip to take advantage of this.

• Spend some time on the telephone getting different quotes on comparable flights from other airlines. Since the market has opened up competitively, prices do vary along identical routes.

● Watch for introductory fares or special coupon offers. As airlines open up new routes, they offer incentives to new customers in the form of temporarily reduced rates. These tend to be heavily advertised in local newspapers—so stay alert to the possibility of coming up with a once-in-a-lifetime bargain!

● Use the toll-free or 800-numbers (listed in the telephone book) when you call the airlines.

ASKING THE RIGHT QUESTION

● Let the person on the other end of the telephone know immediately that you're bargain-hunting by asking for the lowest fare from A to B.

● Ask if there are any incentive fares.

● Find out if there are reductions for midweek flights.

● Find out about reductions for night flights—they're often offered out of main cities.

● Ask whether or not you can make a substantial savings on the flight if you fly to an area close to the Mexican border. You then cross into Mexico where public transportation is cheap.

● Even after you've arranged for a flight, continue to watch for better deals. If a bargain pops up, turn in your ticket and go with the better fare. In some cases, you'll save money even if you must pay a penalty for canceling!

SPECIAL TOUR RATES ON SCHEDULED AIRLINES

In most areas there are specialized tour companies that buy blocks of seats on regularly scheduled airlines. In some cases, these seats are sold at rates far below those offered by the airline itself.

● Get familiar with the companies in your area that specialize in low-cost airfare. They tend to advertise heavily in Sunday papers.

● Call and ask them about any upcoming offerings to Mexico.

You sometimes have to get an inside edge to know when specials will be advertised. You then call the company immediately to get a reservation on the low-cost flight!

Comparison shopping—charters

Tour and charter companies rent planes to take passengers to specific destinations. These rented planes are called charters. In a few cases the company actually owns the planes and virtually runs a sort of mini-airline.

- Charters often save you money, because seats are usually offered at a discounted rate as an incentive to use the non-scheduled plane in the first place.

- Charters often leave at weird times and are rarely on a tight schedule, but if you're trying to save a buck, they can really make sense.

- Charters must now advertise the full price of a ticket. It can't go up or down according to the number of seats sold.

- On any contract with a charter company the escrow bank and bonding company must be clearly stated.

- Charter companies must state clearly what the itinerary will be and stick to it.

- Charter companies cannot cancel a flight within ten days of the intended departure—they used to do this regularly, leaving passengers with no way of getting to where they were going.

- There are stiff cancellation penalty clauses on most charter airlines. You can take out cancellation insurance, available from charter companies and independent brokers.

- Three charter outfits:

Carefree David
955 Northeast 125th Street
North Miami, FL 33161
tel.: (305) 891-0196

International Weekends
1170 Commonwealth Avenue
Boston, MA 02134
tel.: (617) 731-9600

Wainwright Travel
803 St. John's Street
Allentown, PA 18103
tel.: (215) 432-3152

Private airlines in Mexico

A few small airlines operate on a private basis in Mexico. One of these, Aero California, is presently expanding to include charter flights to the United States in some of the western states. For information contact:

Aero California
P.O. Box 555
La Paz, Baja California Sur
Mexico 22109

Comparison shopping—clearinghouses and clubs

Clearinghouses and special airline travel clubs offer reduced tickets to countless places in the world. Basically, they pick up spaces on tours and flights that are not sold out.

- To get information on available flights and tours you pay a service fee to a clearinghouse or club. The fee is usually $35 to $45 a year.

- These clubs are geared to spur-of-the-moment travel. You may have to make up your mind to go to Mexico within only a few days of the planned trip—at a discount, of course.

- Once you pay your money, there's no time to cancel. If you "get on the boat," you go!

- Also, you have to get to the point of origin of the charter, cruise, or tour that's being offered.

- Many of these clubs have a "hot line," and you may find these lines long, detailed, and boring to listen to.

Discount travel clubs

Discount Travel International
The Ives Building 205
Narberth, PA 19072
tel.: (800) 345-8600

Moments Notice
40 East 49th Street
New York, NY 10017
tel.: (800) 253-4321

Stand-Buys, Ltd.
26711 Northwestern Highway,
    Suite 420
Southfield, MI 48037
tel.: (800) 323-6959

Worldwide Discount Travel Club
1674 Meridian Avenue, Suite 304
Miami Beach, FL 33139
tel.: (305) 534-2082

MONEY-SAVING STRATEGIES

No matter how you decide to travel, whether by tour, scheduled airline, or charter, you can usually save money by following certain strategies.

Buying tickets in advance

• Since only a certain number of seats are allotted for highly reduced fares on any given flight, you can save hundreds of dollars by buying a ticket far in advance of a planned trip. In short, the early bird does get the worm.

• Note that the airline cannot raise the price of a ticket once you've paid for it.

Keeping flexible about travel dates

• Be as flexible as possible in your travel plans so that you can take advantage of lower rates. What if you have to leave on a Thursday instead of a Friday or return on a Monday instead of a Sunday? Isn't it worth $100?

• Be sure to ask about excursion rates, with minimum and maximum lengths of stay in Mexico. It may be that, by adding or subtracting a few days from your planned trip, you can save yourself a good deal of money.

• Ask the airline whether or not a standby fare exists on the route you're planning to take. This will make sense in the not-so-popular vacation periods. Standby status is for flexible travelers, who'll do anything to save a buck.

Off-season travel

Summer is the off-season in Mexico, the time when prices drop drastically in hotels throughout the country, a time when the fishing is good and the sun is superhot.

• Check with the airline to see exactly when rates will drop for the off-season. Maybe you can take advantage of lower rates by changing your trip dates by no more than a week or two.

Using travel agents

It costs no more to buy a ticket through a travel agent than to buy one directly from the airline. The problem is that many agents do not like working with discounted fares, because they make a commission on the total dollar value of tickets sold.

• Don't be afraid to comparison shop with travel agents. Make it clear with each one that you want to know the best deal to get you from A to B.

• A few agencies (not many) now guarantee that they will come up with the lowest possible rate or refund an overpayment you've made.

• Sometimes, a good agent will come up with a tour fare that will cost you less than comparable airfare. This is getting very hard to do now, but it does happen.

Things to watch out for

• Check and recheck all airline tickets to make sure that there are no errors.

• Count the flight coupons. Make sure that you have a coupon for each flight. If you don't, you'll pay twice for the flight.

• Check to see if you've paid for the departure tax in the ticket price. If you're not sure, ask.

TRAVELING BY PRIVATE PLANE

There was a time when a private plane was the only practical way to see much of the Baja. With the road heading from Tijuana all the way to Cabo San Lucas much of what was once isolated has now opened up. Still, many areas and lovely hotels have runways geared to private planes.

Getting information

- Two of the best resources for pilots of private planes:

Patti Senterfitt
Baja Reservation Service
1575 Guy Street
San Diego, CA 92138
tel.: (619) 291-3491

Aircraft Owners and Pilots Association
421 Aviation Way
Frederick, MD 21701
tel.: (301) 428-9530

Basic tips from frequent flyers

- Pay someone to watch your plane when it would normally be unattended. Smugglers steal them.

- Much flying in Mexico is high-altitude flying—7,000 to 13,000 feet. Keep this in mind if you'll be flying frequently.

FLYING IN MEXICO

Much of the advice given on flying in this chapter applies to flights within Mexico as well. But there are a few things to keep in mind that are quite different.

Main airlines of Mexico

- The two main airlines for domestic flights in Mexico are Aeroméxico and Mexicana.

• All of their flights and fares are listed in a flight schedule pamphlet called *itinerario de vuelo*. Get one of these books immediately on arrival in Mexico, or better yet, before you go.

• You can plan itineraries with this little booklet and know ahead of time how much it's going to cost you in pesos. By comparing the prices to those of bus and trains, you can decide whether or not the extra cost will be worth the saved time and energy.

• These airlines operate frequent flights between all the major cities and towns of Mexico. The fares in Mexico are extremely reasonable, although much more expensive than bus or train travel.

• Stopovers at no extra charge are allowed on a few routes in Mexico—ask about these privileges when buying a ticket.

Private companies

• There are a number of small companies operating in Mexico. Most of them are charter outfits taking passengers to out-of-the-way ruins or to fishing camps.

• One company has been expanding rapidly in recent years and offers a number of flights from the Baja to mainland Mexico:

Aero California
P.O. Box 555
La Paz, Baja California Sur
México 22109

• Note that flights offered by these companies tend to be more expensive than flights of a comparable distance offered by either Aeroméxico or Mexicana.

Departure taxes *(derecho de uso de aeropuerto)*

• Each time you make a flight in Mexico you'll pay a departure tax. This tax is sometimes called an airport user fee.

• The fee for domestic flights changes frequently but usually is about one-fourth the fee for international flights. Ask the airline what the current fee is.

• Each time you fly from Mexico to another country you pay a stiff international departure tax. Be sure to ask what this is ahead of time so that you have pesos to cover it (note that in some airports like Cancún you can pay for this fee in dollars). Note that there may be a separate and special booth collecting these fees.

• If you buy airline tickets in Mexico, the departure tax is usually included in the price of the ticket. Ask if you're not sure. The clerk will show you where payment is marked on the bottom of the ticket.

• You should pay this fee just once.

Changing travel dates in Mexico

• Mexican airlines discourage last-minute changes in airline reservations by imposing a 25 percent charge on all cancellations and changes made within twenty-four hours of scheduled flight time.

• So make new flight arrangements more than one day in advance.

Missing a flight in Mexico

• Mexican airlines hold passengers responsible for no-shows —to the tune of 50 percent of the ticket price! If you can't make it, call and change your flight. If you're within twenty-four hours of flight time, you'll still have to pay a 25 percent fee—but that beats 50 percent.

Getting bumped in Mexico

• It's always a good idea to get to a Mexican airport early. Although you often can only check in 1 to 1½ hours before a flight, this is usually far enough ahead of time to avoid being bumped. The trick in Mexico is to get your boarding pass and seat assignment *early*.

• There is no denied boarding compensation in Mexico.

Seat assignments

• You do not always have seat assignments on flights in Mexico. The first person to the seat gets it. If you want to be in a nonsmoking section, ask ahead of time whether or not any rows have been designated for this purpose. However, Mexicans pay little attention to such regulations.

Delayed flights

• Delayed flights are so common in Mexico as to be a nonoccurrence. Experienced travelers carry a paperback to pass the time.

• Getting angry and frustrated does nothing except get you angry and frustrated.

• Many travelers accept delays as a good time to have a picnic. Carry food and drink with you at all times and don't feel self-conscious in the least about eating in public. You won't be alone.

• Write off every day of your trip that includes a flight. Getting to the airport, waiting for the plane to take off, the flight itself, the trip in from the airport—these all burn up time. Accept the fact in advance that it's a wasted day.

Carry-on luggage

• You can get a couple of good-size (not large) bags on most planes. Smaller backpacks will squeeze into overhead racks. No one really seems to care if you're on the overloaded side.

• Note that there is very little compensation for lost baggage in Mexico.

Canceled flights

• In Mexico it is common for flights to be canceled if there are not enough people to warrant a flight. Generally, you'll be switched to another flight later on. So you'll get to where you're going—you'll just have to be patient getting there.

• In short, don't take the pamphlet of scheduled flights too seriously—it's just a rough guide.

• Getting information on canceled or delayed flights over the phone can be very difficult. It's best just to go to the airport and inquire if you're having trouble getting through.

Fully booked flights

• If you want to travel on a certain day and you're told that a flight is fully booked, go to the airport.

• Get yourself put on a waiting list for the flight. The earlier you get to the airport, the more priority you have in getting on the plane.

• Mexicans admire patience, courtesy, and determination. These qualities will almost always get you on a so-called "fully booked" flight. I have done this *many* times, once in a group of three people.

• Remember that one of the ten commandments of travel in Mexico is: *You can frequently turn a "no" into a "yes."*

6

CAR TRAVEL

Over 1½ million U.S. and Canadian visitors use a car on their trip to Mexico each year. This includes travelers who drive their own cars or recreational vehicles (RVs) into the country (tips follow) and others who fly in with the idea of renting a car in Mexico (see p. 114).

TAKING YOUR OWN CAR OR RV TO MEXICO

You're really dealing with three things when you travel: money, time, and energy. Car travel is a good example of a trade-off between these three.

Advantages of car travel

Car travel is for adventurous people who are willing to pay a price for freedom. It's the best way to see Mexico if you want to strike out to unusual and colorful destinations. Sightseeing, roadside picnics, photography, sports, getting to out-of-the-way spots—all are open to motorists.

● You don't have to worry about reservations, tickets, and ticket lines.

• You don't have to travel superlight unless you prefer to.

• You're free to change or rearrange schedules at whim—without upsetting anyone.

• You don't have to put up with the poor conditions in train and bus stations (read those sections).

• You don't have to wait for delayed or canceled planes, trains, or buses.

• Most of all, you're part of the living jigsaw puzzle around you, which means you see and feel a Mexico that many tourists miss.

Disadvantages of car travel

• Car travel is expensive. Add up the preparation costs, gas, servicing, insurance, and repairs—you've got a hefty bill.

• The cost becomes more manageable as the number of passengers increases.

• The cost drops somewhat if the itinerary is limited and well planned, especially for RVers who save on lodging and dining out.

• Car travel in Mexico can be dangerous. The roads and road conditions can cause serious accidents, and Mexicans are poor drivers.

• It takes time to travel to and through Mexico by car or RV —lots of time. Distances can be overwhelming for anyone in a hurry.

• Figure an average of 150 miles per day at 30 mph as a rough guide. Naturally, distance traveled will vary each day, but the overall average will be close.

• Driving is exhausting no matter how much you like it. In Mexico it's doubly so. Long-distance drives will leave you drained.

• Two or more people driving together can share the burden, which helps considerably. But whether you're driving or not, you're still covering the same, long distances.

• If your trip is oriented to major cities, you would save lots of time and trouble by taking a plane.

• Finding a parking place in major cities can be a migraine headache. In Mexico City you'll have trouble finding a place to double park!

• Car travel can insulate you from meeting Mexicans, although in general the opposite is true.

The best cars to take to Mexico

• If it's possible, take a car that uses regular gas. Most of the new models don't, which implies that older cars that are mechanically sound are best.

• If you want to travel with a car that burns unleaded gas, be warned that you may have some engine damage to the car. Furthermore, unleaded gas is sometimes hard to find.

• Certain makes of cars are much easier to service and repair in Mexico than others. The good brands are Chevrolet, Datsun, Dodge, Ford, Mercedes, Opel, Renault, and Volkswagen. VWs are the work horses of Mexico, and most mechanics know how to work on them.

Registering your car

• Be sure to register your car with U.S. Customs before crossing the border into Mexico (see p. 373).

AUTO INSURANCE

If you drive a car or RV into Mexico, you're going to need a separate insurance policy. Your U.S. or Canadian policy will not cover you there.

Where to buy insurance

Many companies offer coverage for car or RV travel in Mexico. The best known is Sanborn's. But you can check into Atlantico and AAA coverage to compare services.

Sanborn's
P.O. Box 1210
McAllen, TX 78502
tel.: (512) 682-3402

Seguros Atlantico
200 North Festival, Suite 1702
El Paso, TX 79912
tel.: (915) 581-7918

The advantage of Sanborn's

- If you buy insurance from Sanborn's, you'll be given a free *Travelog* which will be set up according to the proposed itinerary you submit to them. It's one of the best and most complete "guides" you'll come across.

Insurance costs

- All insurance rates are controlled by the Mexican government, and they're very high. All companies offer the same rates. Some travel clubs, including Mexico West and Good Sam, are able to offer discounts:

Overland International
(Mexico West)
101 West Walnut Street
Pasadena, CA 91103
tel.: (800) 423-4403
       (800) 423-2646 (CA)

The Good Sam Club
Customer Service
P.O. Box 500
Agoura, CA 91301
tel.: (800) 423-5061

What you should know about Mexican car insurance

- All policies include a deductible amount for collision. You do not have complete coverage.

- U.S. and Canadian policies have comprehensive coverage, but Mexican policies do not. Glass breakage comes under collision, and a deductible applies.

- Personal effects and property are not covered unless they

are installed as permanent parts of a vehicle.

• Mexican policies do not cover fines, bail bonds, and legal expenses. You have to take out a different policy for these.

• Partial theft and vandalism are not covered under Mexican insurance policies. The entire car has to be stolen before insurance applies.

Trailer and boats

• If you intend to bring a trailer or a boat to Mexico, be sure to insure them with your car or RV. The regular policy will not cover them.

• Mexican insurance policies will not cover car top boats. To cover a boat it has to be pulled on a trailer.

• Be sure to register your trailer and boat with U.S. Customs (see p. 373).

Legal aid insurance

If you're worried about fines, bail bond, or paying attorney's fees, you can take out legal aid insurance. This is not required in Mexico.

• Fines for accidents rarely go above $100 in Mexico.

• Bail bond is rarely needed.

• You normally do not need to hire an attorney.

TEMPORARY IMPORTATION PERMITS FOR CAR OWNERS

If you drive a car into mainland Mexico (not the Baja), you are required to get a temporary importation permit for your car. The sole purpose of this permit is to make sure that you don't sell the car in Mexico. The car will have to leave with you.

Basics on car permits

● You are not required to have a permit for a car on the Baja, but if you intend to go by ferry from the Baja to the mainland, you'll need a permit.

● Always get the permit as you cross the border into Mexico. This is true even if you enter Mexico on the Baja with the intention of taking the ferry to the mainland. Don't wait to get the permit in port—you'll save yourself a tremendous hassle.

● The temporary importation permit is combined in one document with your tourist card, which will be stamped *con automóvil.*

● You're allowed only one temporary permit per person—not more. If you're traveling by yourself, you cannot bring an extra moped or motorcycle or car towed behind an RV. Note that some people manage to—often with a bribe (see p. 369). But don't count on it.

● Two people can bring in two vehicles, three people can bring in three, etc. Each one will be responsible for one vehicle. Each tourist card will be stamped appropriately.

● You have to be out of Mexico before your temporary importation permit expires. It can be extended with your tourist card to a maximum stay of 180 days.

● In theory, the period of validity of the tourist card and the importation permit should match since they're incorporated into one document. In fact, some tourists have reported that times have been different. In short, they had a tourist card valid for 90 days and a temporary importation permit valid for fewer days. **Make sure that your tourist card and temporary importation permit are valid for the same number of days!**

What you need to get a temporary importation permit

The border officials will give you a temporary importation permit if you have the following: a valid driver's license, valid license plates, a registration card, and proof of ownership.

- If the car is not yours, or if there's a lien on it, or if it's a company car, you must have a notarized affidavit authorizing its use in Mexico from the official owner or lien holder.

- If you cannot produce the letter, the car can be confiscated. This prevents stolen cars from coming into Mexico.

Who can drive the car?

If you have the importation permit, you and your spouse can drive the car. If you're in the car, another person can take over the driving. But if someone else wants to drive the car while you're not in it, this must be indicated on the permit. Register this person at the nearest *Registro Federal de Vehículos.* If someone drives your car without being registered, the car can be confiscated!

Expensive accessories

Expensive car accessories may be noted on tourist cards and must leave the country with you. If they don't (even if they're stolen), they'll be assumed to have been sold—you'll have to pay duty on them.

Large trailer permits

It is extremely difficult for vehicles with trailers to negotiate the narrow streets in Mexican towns.

- Any trailer more than 8-feet wide or more than 40-feet long requires a special permit to travel in Mexico. Contact the nearest Mexican Consulate for current regulations and fees (see p. 11).

- My suggestion: don't travel with large vehicles in Mexico. It just isn't worth it!

Citizen Band (CB) permits

Anyone who wants to use a CB in Mexico must apply for a permit from the nearest Mexican Consulate which will send you up-to-date regulations and fees (see p. 11).

CAR AND RV PREPARATION

Here are a few tips that you might not think about in getting your car or RV ready for a Mexico trip.

- Cactus spines can easily puncture radial tires. Tires go through constant abuse on Mexican roads. Consider putting inner tubes in *all* tires whether they're radials or not.

- Install an accessible, in-line fuel filter and have someone show you how to replace it. Impurities and water in Mexican gas can cause constant problems.

- Put a bug screen over the radiator and clean it off frequently.

- Take off all the lug nuts to make sure that you can get them off if you have a flat. Apply a little grease where necessary.

- Change the thermostat for the higher temperatures you'll encounter in Mexico.

- Reduce tire pressure for long hauls.

Special note on propane

On January 21, 1985, the Mexican government made the sale of propane for vehicles illegal. Later it was illegal only within 75 miles of the U.S. border. Who knows what's going to happen in the future? So take the following precautions:

- Get your propane tank filled completely before entering Mexico.

- Have your fuel line adapted so that it can be attached to a portable propane tank for cooking or heating water. You can do this yourself or hire someone to do it for you. This way you'll never have to worry about the propane problem (it has never been illegal for foreigners to buy propane in small, portable tanks).

Special note on dual wheels

Dual wheels are great for everything but off-road travel. If you're going to the Baja or other areas with the intention of getting off the beaten path, get a vehicle without dual wheels. The reason is that the ruts in the road have been carved out by cars and trucks without dual wheels, and you'll want to get into these grooves.

Tools and spare parts for safety

Mexico can antique a car overnight. Since spare parts and tools are extremely expensive in Mexico, consider taking them with you. Here's a checklist of suggested items for car and RV travelers.

- Note that expensive accessories, spare parts, and tools may be noted on your tourist card (see p. 99). You must take them back out of the country. If you sell or lose them in Mexico, you'll have to pay a duty on them.

adaptor
air filters
air gauge
baling wire
battery cables
bicycle
bolts and nuts
brake fluid
breaker points
car permit
CB
CB permit
chains
chairs (folding)
chamois cloth
condensers
distributor points
driver's license
duct tape
electric tape
extension cord
fan belts

fire extinguisher
fittings
flares
food
fuel filters
fuel pump
funnel
fuses
gaskets
gaskets (for water hose)
gasoline cans
generator brushes
grease
hammer (heavy rubber)
hoses and radiator clamps
hose (water)
hydraulic jacks
ice chest
ignition coil

inner tubes
keys in metal container
Liquid Wrench
lug wrench
motorbike
motor oil
paper products (towels)
plastic bags
power steering fluid
radiator coolant
radiator sealant
reflectors
shovel
siphon hose
spare tires on rims
spark plugs
tire inflator (aerosol)
tire pump
tools
towels (old diapers)

tow rope	valve cores	whisk broom
trailer	water can with	window cleaner
trailer permit	sprinkler head	wooden blocks
tube repair kit	water cans (5-gallon)	
universal joints	WD 40	

GAS

- In Mexico, gas is sold by the liter (a little more than a quart). So 40 liters is roughly 10 gallons.

- Since gas station hours and days of business are unpredictable, play it safe and try not to get below a half tank. In short, top off whenever you have the chance!

- In some instances, gas stations run out of fuel—another reason to top off frequently.

- In off-the-beaten-path areas you may have to buy gas stored in drums. This gas should be filtered through a chamois cloth —bring one if you'll be traveling in more remote areas.

- There's only one brand of gas: Pemex *(Petróleos Mexicanos).* Prices are fixed by the government and are presently comparable to those north of the border.

- The price of gas sold from drums is usually double that of gas sold in gas stations. You may prefer to carry extra gas into remote areas to avoid this rip-off.

- You must pay for gas in pesos. Credit cards are not accepted anywhere.

- Pemex Extra, lead-free *(sin plomo),* is 94-octane and sold at the silver pumps. Some stations run out (more or less permanently) of unleaded gas. For this reason it's best to drive a car which uses regular gas.

- Most rental cars do use regular gas—ask if you're not sure.

- Pemex Nova, leaded regular *(con plomo),* is 81-octane and sold at blue pumps. It is sometimes kiddingly called *"no va"* or "no go" in Spanish. You may want to mix higher (non-leaded) and lower (leaded) octane gases for extra power.

• Diesel is available at red pumps and is extremely inexpensive as support for the trucking industry.

• In tropical areas water sometimes gets into the gas. Add cheap drinking alcohol *(alcohol)* as an additive to help burn it off.

Extra tips on gas station protocol

• Make sure the pump is set at zero before the attendant starts to fill your tank.

• Ask for a specific amount of gas in pesos rather than for a fill up. This way you'll avoid gas splashing over the car onto the pavement.

• Or ask for a specific number of liters *(litros)*. If you don't, the attendant will try to squeeze every last peso out of you.

• If you ask an attendant to clean a windshield, check the oil, or inflate a tire, you're expected to tip for the service. Anytime you request a service make sure that it's actually done.

• Most drivers prefer to check the oil themselves. You may want to carry a few cans of oil with you.

• Carry small bills to pay for gas and any extra service. Attendants often claim not to have change for large bills.

• Always count your change. If it is incorrect, say, *"Me falto 30 pesos"* or whatever amount is missing.

• In remote areas, ask where the next gas can be found. "Where is the next gas station?" *"¿Dónde está la próxima gasolinera?"*

Cutting gas costs in an RV

• Plan your trip carefully with mileage in mind. Good maps and expert advice help.

• The upfront cost of a tune-up may seem steep, but it will save 8 to 20 percent on fuel consumption.

● Travel as light as you possibly can. Figure that you lose 1 percent in gas mileage per 100 pounds of excess baggage— just a rough estimate, but a good guide.

● Buy the best radials you can afford. You're trading initial cost against an added percentage in extra mileage and safety. You also get years of life from radials and much better handling.

● Don't fill your tank to the brim. Excess gas washes out and evaporates. It overflows on inclines. Check your gas cap to make sure it fits tightly. Buy locking gas caps.

● Use common sense: check tires for proper pressure, avoid roof racks (they create drag), avoid peak traffic periods (you use up gas waiting), travel early and late in the day (avoids the use of an air-conditioner), and keep windows closed (prevents drag).

DRIVING IN MEXICO

Driving in Mexico is not at all like driving in the United States or Canada. This section explains the many major differences.

Speed limits

● Maximum speed limits are posted in kilometers per hour (kph). Mexicans routinely ignore these limits. The odds of your being pulled over for a violation of a speed limit are mimimal.

● To convert speed limits or mileage signs given in kilometers to miles, divide the figure by 10 and multiply by 6. For example: 80 kph ÷ 10 = 8; 8 × 6 = 48 mph.

● On superhighways slower traffic must stay to the right. If someone approaches you from behind, you must move over to make way. Often cars coming from the rear will blink their lights as a warning signal for you to move over. If you do not move over, you can cause a serious accident.

General driving conditions

• The only fast roads in Mexico are the scattered superhighways. Other roads can be tied up with trucks (belching diesel smoke); broken-down, stopped, stalled, or stranded buses; and even herds of bleary-eyed cattle crossing the highway. Don't expect to drive quickly!

• Coastal and mountain roads must follow the natural contours of the hills, meaning hundreds of curves per mile. Passing is virtually impossible on many of these highways, although Mexicans do it routinely—blind! You'll end up moving as slowly as the slowest link in the chain, which means at the tail end of a truck hauling a full load of timber up a mountainside.

• To avoid some of the traffic start trips early in the day, just after sunrise, if possible. End all trips early—definitely before dark.

• Night driving is extremely hazardous. Under no circumstances should anyone drive at night.

• In the United States and Canada you may average 55 mph on many roads. In Mexico you might be lucky to average 30. Distances in Mexico are staggering—try to be realistic about driving times. Do not rely on charts given out by automobile clubs, the ones giving approximate driving times between cities. They're just wishful thinking calculated by some bureaucrat with dust on his bifocals!

• City driving can be tough for foreigners. The most intimidating city of all is Mexico City. Street names change without warning from one block to the next, the traffic circles (glorietas) swing you in all directions, and the traffic jams are appalling in rush hours. Come armed with a good map, lots of patience, and a sense of humor—they'll all be necessary to get you to your hotel. Once there, park the car and leave it parked until you move on!

Safety hazards

• Driving at night is a nightmare. Don't do it! Animals are

attracted to the warmth of the road and can total a car. Often vehicles break down and are impossible to see in the dark. Never drive at night.

• Markings are extremely poor in most of Mexico. You may suddenly find yourself driving across two lanes of traffic without even realizing what happened—don't assume anything. You will not believe Mexican highway engineering—or the lack of it.

• Be extremely wary at intersections. Buses think nothing of rolling through a stop sign at 80 mph. In short, don't trust signs.

• Desert areas become torrid from 11 A.M. to 4 P.M. Try to avoid midday driving through such places.

• Always carry food and water. Each person should have one gallon of water allotted per day of travel. In remote areas you should have a stockpile of food for two weeks. This is basic safety for off-road travel in the Baja. But even in populated areas, you should carry something to drink and eat with you.

• The road surface varies from washboard to smooth tar. Shoulders do not exist. Rarely are there center stripes. Expect the worst—it will often come true.

• Watch out for animals. They're often feeding by the side of the road. It is not unusual for a herd of goats or cattle to meander across a road. Burros and horses invariably find the grass greener on the edge of the pavement. Vultures light on carrion and can shatter a windshield in one quick beat of a wing. Sanborn's insurance company sums it up, "Burros don't wear taillights."

• Fog makes driving treacherous in high mountain areas. The Baja has fog in late spring and early summer along the coast.

• *Topes,* speed bumps, can wreak havoc on a car. These 3-inch high cement, asphalt, or steel bumps are not always marked, but you'll usually find them entering and leaving towns, even isolated ones with little traffic.

• Rocks, fallen or placed as markers on the road, can be hard to notice and especially hazardous. Rock slides are very common after heavy rains in mountain areas.

● Watch for one-lane bridges *(puente angosto)* and one-lane sections of highway *(solo carril)*. The driver who flashes his lights first has right of way—in theory. In fact, muscle and machismo determines all in these situations.

● *Vados,* dips in the road which act as creek beds, can be dangerous at high speeds. During the wet season the water sweeps across the pavement in these areas. Watch for them or you'll be defying the law of gravity.

● Don't drive on sand, whether you're on the beach or out in the desert. You'll eventually get stuck. Who's going to get you out before the tide comes in?

The rainy season

● If you're traveling in the rainy season (the summer months), be extremely cautious of flash floods. Never ford low areas in the rain. Water can rise suddenly sweeping your car downstream.

● Watch downpours. These cause mud slides and washouts. Anyone who has traveled extensively in Mexico realizes how serious these can be. In some areas entire concrete bridges collapse and are swept away like driftwood during a downpour.

● Make sure that wherever you go you have an escape route. If a bridge collapses, or a mountain slides over a road or gives way in a downpour, or if a river sweeps over the pavement—you can get stuck, literally for months, if there's no alternate route out!

● When in doubt, ask local bus drivers about road conditions. Bear in mind that only a catastrophe would seem significant to most of these men. Better ask in a hotel instead.

Hitchhikers

• Do not pick up hitchhikers in Mexico. Your car can be confiscated if a hitchhiker is carrying drugs. You will be guilty by association. At the very best it will be an agonizing hassle.

• Don't stop to pick up people by a stranded car. This is a favorite ploy for ripping off motorists. Let the Green Angels take care of stranded motorists (see p. 112).

Stopping on the road

• Construction and road work will often bring you to a halt. If a worker waves you back, if really means come ahead—something that can confuse the average U.S. or Canadian driver.

• The lack of shoulders makes it difficult to turn around or stop for pit stops and picnics. Try to get well off the road if you do stop—you may have to drive several miles to find a safe place.

• Stopping for photos is especially difficult and dangerous because there's no way to get off the road. Be very careful in this situation.

• If you get sick or have to go to the bathroom in the mountains, don't head into the brush on the edge of the hill. This brush is often just the top of tall trees. Each year people die in remote, mountainous areas as they fall to their deaths in just this situation.

PARKING IN THE STREET

• In most towns and cities you can park in the street during the day without any real problem. Just be sure to lock the car.

PARKING

Parking is one of the more disagreeable aspects of traveling by car. And the rules of the game are a little different in Mexico.

• Just be sure that you're not parking in a no parking zone or in front of someone's driveway.

• In a few areas you'll find parking meters. Plug in the appropriate amount for the time you'll be parking.

• Never park near a market *(mercado)*. Trucks will often double park in this area and lock you in for several hours or longer.

• In some areas kids or khaki-uniformed guards will watch over your car. Tip them a few pesos ahead of time to make sure your car doesn't have an "accident" while you're away.

• Occasionally, these guards will help you get into a tight parking place. Woodpecker tapping on the window means it's okay to back up, a loud rap means it's time to stop.

PARKING IN GARAGES OR ATTENDED PARKING LOTS

• In Mexico City you'll want to park your car in a garage. Many hotels offer garage parking to their guests, some hotels offer this at no charge. You might take this into consideration when choosing a hotel in a major city—it can save you many dollars a day.

• Cars left in the street at night tend to be vandalized even in smaller towns. If your hotel doesn't have a parking area, ask for a nearby garage. In some cities it's actually illegal to leave a car on the street overnight, so ask if you're planning to.

• Some garage attendants insist that you leave the keys with the car. In this situation you should never leave any luggage or valuables in the car.

PARKING TICKETS

• Mexican cops will remove the license plates of cars parked illegally. If this happens to you, hang around the car until the cop returns. You're in a fine/bribe situation.
• Some wily travelers put their license plate in the rear window or weld it to the car to avoid just such a situation.

Superhighways *(cuotas)*

- Most of the superhighways *(autopistas)* are commonly referred to as toll roads *(cuotas)* since you have to pay to use them.

- If you're in a hurry, they're worth the price. But secondary roads can get you to wherever you're going at no charge at all.

- Tolls vary by the day you're traveling. Prices are highest on weekends and holidays, so if you want to save money, keep this in mind.

- As in most countries, tolls are related to the size of the vehicle you're driving. And you'll have to pay extra if you're pulling a trailer or hauling a boat.

- Toll roads are indicated on most maps. You'll usually see that secondary roads skirt them and offer a good alternative to the budget traveler.

Road signs

Road signs in Mexico are relatively easy to understand. You can pick up a chart from any insurance company if you're so inclined. Travel clubs, automobile clubs, tourist offices, car rental agencies—all offer these charts free of charge.

- Here's a quick guide to the Spanish words on some of the more common signs.

Aduana	Customs
Alto	Stop
Atención	Caution
Aparcamiento	Parking lot
Autopista	Superhighway
Bifurcación	Fork, junction
Camino en reparación	Road repairs
Ceda el paso	Give right of way
Conserva su derecha	Keep right
Cuidado	Caution
Curva peligrosa	Dangerous curve
Despacio	Slow

Desvación	Detour
Escuela	School
Estacionamiento	Parking
Grava suelta	Loose gravel
Hombres trabajando	Men working
Maneja despacio—neblina	Drive slow—fog
No hay paso	Road closed
Obras	Road works
Paso prohibido	No entry
Pavimento	Paved road
Peatones	Pedestrians
Peligro	Danger
Playa	Beach
Puente angosto	Narrow bridge
Prohibido adelantamiento	No passing
Sentido único	One way
Solo carril	One-lane road

Idiosyncrasies of Mexican drivers

• Avoid contests and confrontations with Mexican drivers. You may find yourself in a macho confrontation (see p. 308). Tourists never win these.

• Railroads have stop signs. Mexicans never stop at these unless a train is coming. You shouldn't either, unless you want to be tail-ended by a Mexican who assumes you're smart enough to ignore the sign.

• Give priority to cars coming from the right. This is the easiest way to sort out traffic in any situation.

• No matter how fast you're going, someone will want to go faster, so always look into your rearview mirror before you start to pass.

• If you're following a truck, a left-turn signal means it's okay for you to pass, a right-turn signal means that there's a car coming, so don't pass. Or the signals mean the truck is turning left or right. No signal means you're on your own, the driver's asleep, or his signals are broken.

• If an oncoming car blinks lights at you, that means trouble ahead. If you're coming to a narrow bridge, it means, Stop, or I'll be the trouble ahead.

Breakdowns

• Mexico has one of the finest emergency road services in the world. Green utility trucks, nicknamed **"Green Angels,"** cruise over 37,000 miles of highway twice each day from early morning to evening looking for stranded motorists. The Green Angels hotline in Mexico City is (905) 250-0123.

• The Green Angels will help get the car running again, providing all service free of charge. You pay only for parts, gas, and lubricants.

• In Mexico City you'll find **"Silver Angels"** offering comparable service. You can call them at 588-5100.

• When you have a breakdown, raise the hood of your car as a signal that you're in trouble.

• If you don't want to wait for a Green Angel or if you're in an area where such a service is unlikely, ask a passing motorist to send help to you.

• Waving down a passing car is not always easy because of the suspicion of robbery and rip-offs. However, there is less suspicion of tourists.

• Under no circumstances should you leave a car unattended on the side of the road. Consider paying someone to watch the car if you want to find a mechanic.

Repairs

• Mexican mechanics can repair just about anything with just about nothing.

• They'll often work on your car immediately realizing that you're a tourist in a tough situation.

• If you're traveling with adequate spare parts, this will often speed up the repair process.

• Mechanics will often improvise and use used parts to get your vehicle on the road again. If you insist on new parts, you may have to pay for these in advance. Ask for a receipt *(recibo)*.

• Always get an estimate *(presupuesto)* in writing before allowing someone to work on your car.

• Stay with the car the whole time work is being done. You'll get the work done faster, the best mechanic in the shop will do it (often the owner), and you'll know what work has been done.

• Be sure to test drive the car. The person who repaired it will often come along. If you're not satisfied, let the mechanic know that something's still wrong. This process of repair can often be quite casual.

Military checkpoints

Mexico has set up military checkpoints throughout the country to check for contraband, guns, and drugs. These checkpoints are concentrated along the coast.

• Soldiers wave most tourists through these checkpoints, although they'll check most buses very carefully. So if you're driving, it would be rare for your car to be searched.

• These checkpoints come up unexpectedly. You're required to stop. Sometimes, you'll have to wait in a long line of cars before you can continue on. This can get a little tiring if it's your third check in one day—just another of a dozen reasons why driving is much slower in Mexico than you might expect by looking at a map.

Police rip-offs

If you think that the police have ripped you off, *write* a formal complaint to the following office.

Dirección de Supervision
Departamento de Quejas
Secretarío de Turismo
Presidente Mazaryk 172
Colonia Polanco
México 5, D.F.

• If you think you're being ripped off in Mexico City, call 250-8555. Ask for extension 223. Or Call 250-0123. Don't be afraid to call this office if you're right in the midst of a rip-off.

CAR RENTAL IN MEXICO

Renting a car in Mexico has the greatest appeal to travelers on vacations of less than a month. However, the freedom offered by a rental car has its price. And you may find that you really don't need a rental car at all.

People who need rental cars

• You need a rental car if you want to get off-the-beaten path to explore or to photograph unusual places and people.

• Anyone planning to visit many places in a short time without depending on public transportation needs a rental car. If you want to visit San Miguel de Allende, Guanajuato, Pátzcuaro, Morelia, Acapulco, and Taxco in one week—well, you need a car. Good luck.

• If driving is the way you *prefer* to travel, if it's emotionally satisfying, and if you exhilarate in the freedom it offers—then the high price doesn't seem too high to pay.

Travelers who don't need rental cars

• Rental cars are almost useless in most resorts. Don't be conned into renting a car there. Places like Mazatlán and Cancún have public transportation that can get you just about anywhere for just about nothing.

• You can always supplement inexpensive public transportation with more expensive taxis—more expensive, yes, but still cheap compared to the high cost of car rental.

• You do not need nor will you want a car in major cities. The hassles of weaving your way through rush-hour traffic or arguing over parking space will just not be worth it, especially in

Mexico City. You will not believe how inexpensive and good public transportation is in these larger towns and cities.

• If you want to visit sights outside major towns, take advantage of local tours. Don't like tours? Then hire a cab at a set fare to take you there! You'll find that the cost is still less than car rental. And you've got a driver and guide to boot.

• The main point: Very rarely do you *need* a car in Mexico. Many times it's actually a burden and a pointless luxury.

Car rental availability

• Major companies do not have cars available in every city and town of Mexico. However, smaller companies based in Mexico often fill the gap. If a travel agent tells you that cars are not available in town X, it isn't necessarily true.

• If you have trouble coming up with a car in a smaller town, go directly to the local tourist office and ask for rental information. You may be told about a car company you've never heard of, since it's locally based.

• How many names do you recognize in the following *partial* list of car rental firms operating in Mexico? Airways, AMSA, Arroyo, Avis, Best, Budget, Cave, Combi, Cosmopolitan, Dollar, Econorent, Fast, Fiesta, Ford, Fraiza, Hertz, Holiday, International, Max, Napeca, National, Odin, Panara, Quick, Rapsa, Volkswagen, Xelha, and Yucatán.

Car rental costs

Car rental is much more expensive in Mexico than in the United States and Canada, so much more expensive that you may figure the price isn't worth it. The overall cost includes the basic charge, supplemental costs for air-conditioning or automatic transmission, insurance premiums, mileage charges, gas refill charge, and a 15 percent tax—more about each of these later.

SHOPPING AROUND FOR THE BEST BASIC CHARGE

• Since car rental prices are government-controlled, you'll find the base price of a Volkswagen is the same from any company in the same location.

• The secret: Prices vary by location. You might pay half as much for a car in Mexico City as you would in Acapulco. So you might start a trip from the Mexico City airport with no intention of visiting the city at all in order to save a few hundred dollars.

• Using the toll-free (800) numbers in your telephone book, call major car rental firms such as Avis, Budget, Hertz, and National. Ask these companies to send you their free worldwide directories listing current car rental rates. Then study these to see which cities offer the best rates.

RESERVING A CAR IN ADVANCE

• During peak travel periods of Christmas, New Year's, Carnival, and Easter, reserve a car as far in advance as possible. Use the toll-free (800) numbers in your telephone book.

• Sometimes, companies will give you a price break for a guaranteed reservation made far enough in advance. Note that there's a cancellation penalty (usually $25) for this special offer. Ask the company for full information on potential savings, restrictions, and penalties.

• When you make a car reservation, always get the name of the person you're talking to. Ask for a confirmation number so that you have proof that the reservation has been made.

• Make sure that you have the exact address where you are to pick up the car. Ask the person to send you a map if one is available. This can save you lots of time hunting for the car rental office.

THINGS THAT UP THE BASIC RATE

• All car rental rates are related to the model and size of the car you rent. Rent the smallest car that will accommodate your party. The many advantages of small cars are covered in this section.

• Most cars in Mexico have stick shifts. You'll pay a surcharge if you want a car with automatic transmission. However, do not assume that you'll get an automatic car simply because you reserved one. It just doesn't work that way in Mexico.

• Because you may end up with a stick shift, you should learn how to operate one in advance. A competent driving instructor (preferably not a relative) can teach you how to use a stick shift in six hours or less—from the basics to starting on a 45 degree incline.

• During the sticky, summer heat of southern Mexico you'll want air-conditioning—but it's an option for which you pay a surcharge. During much of the year it's really not necessary.

THE MILEAGE CHARGE

• Many rental agreements add an additional charge for miles driven. The extra charge is actually per kilometer, roughly $\frac{6}{10}$ of a mile. You can double the kilometer charge for a rough estimate of the per mile cost—and it's steep.

AVOIDING THE MILEAGE CHARGE

• If you rent a car for more than three days (in most areas), you can get a car at a set price per day or week without paying an additional charge for mileage. This is an **unlimited mileage agreement.** Ask about these.

• Some companies claim to be offering an unlimited mileage agreement when they are really not. For example, they offer a week's rental for a set price, but then you have to pay an additional charge after the first 1000 kilometers (or 600 miles). Be sure that you're not caught in this trap. Ask several times whether there's a mileage limit at all.

• If you ask questions once in car rental agencies, you'll often be told later that you "misunderstood" because of the language barrier. The language barrier has a way of crumbling under a barrage of questions, all really the same question asked in a lot of different ways. Use the technique of *repeated* questions to get a straight answer.

INSURANCE PREMIUMS

● As in the United States and Canada, insurance charges jack up the total bill of a car considerably. Yet you really need Mexican insurance if you want to avoid tremendous hassles in case of an accident. See p. 366.

● **Note:** All Mexican car rental insurance has a deductible for which you're responsible. This applies to partial theft, glass breakage, and collision. So your insurance is really only partial insurance—a rip-off by anyone's standards.

THE GAS REFILL CHARGE

● In Mexico rental cars are filled with varying amounts of gas. Rarely will you get into a car with a full tank.

● The amount of gas to the nearest quarter of a tank should be noted on your car rental agreement.

● You return the car with an equivalent amount of gas or pay a gas refill charge—always incredibly inflated (a worldwide practice).

● Note that you pay a 15 percent tax on the refill charge. So stop at a gas station before returning the car if you want to save yourself a few bucks.

DROP-OFF CHARGES

● In most instances you cannot rent a car in one town and drop it off in another without paying a charge for this service. The charge is usually related to the distance between the two cities.

● Always ask about drop-off charges in advance and make sure to get the charge in *writing* before renting the car.

THE 15 PERCENT IVA TAX

● On *all* of your rental car expenses you'll pay a 15 percent government tax. Keep this in mind.

Who can rent a car

● To rent a car in Mexico you need: proof that you're twenty-five-years old or older, a valid driver's license, identification (passport is best), and a major credit card (or a large chunk of cash).

What kind of car should you rent

• Try to get by with the smallest car possible, especially if you'll be driving to isolated towns. Streets in Mexican villages can be narrow, torturous, and steep. Small cars can go almost anywhere. They guzzle less gas, are roomy enough if you're traveling light, can weasel into tiny parking spots, and cost less for ferries and toll roads.

• The most important point: Make sure that the car you rent is the newest model available. If you're doing extensive driving, the condition and age of the car is crucial! Make this very clear when you're renting the car.

Crucial questions

Before you leave the car rental office, make sure that certain questions have been answered.

• What is the excess charge if the car is turned in later than expected? How much per hour? How much per day?

• If time and mileage come out to be less than the amount of your unlimited mileage agreement, will you be allowed to pay that smaller amount?

• Are all the necessary documents in the car? Check to be sure there are registration papers.

• Is there a map in the car?

Get directions out of town

• Ask for directions to the road leading you to your first destination. This one step can save you an hour or more of frustration. Have the clerk show you the route on a map, if possible.

Checking out the car

• When you rent a car in Mexico, pretend that you're actually buying it. The extra time you take will pay off.

Checklist

• Are there any dents or scratches on the car? If there are, have them *noted* on the rental agreement. That way you won't have to pay for them later.

• Does the car have hub caps? Many rental cars in Mexico do not have hub caps because they get ripped off regularly. Just make sure that the absent hub caps are noted.

• Check the antenna to make sure it's there, and not bent or broken.

• Have someone show you where the spare tire is. Make sure it's there, in good shape, and fully inflated (a good reason to carry a tire gauge).

• Ask to see the jack. These are often stolen. In the Volkswagen they're located under the back seat—a good reason to leave your car locked at all times. Make sure that you understand how the jack works. Have the attendant show you if you're not.

• Try the horn, wipers, and lights. If two out of three work, you're ahead of the game. Don't settle for a car with any of these not working properly unless it's for a short, day trip.

• Give the car a quick check to make sure all fluids are up to the full mark. Don't assume they will be.

• Stick a small coin into the treads of the tire to judge the depth of the tread. Tires take tremendous abuse in Mexico and should be in excellent shape before you start your trip.

CRUISE SHIP TRAVEL

Going to Mexico by cruise ship is an old-style, romantic way to travel.

CRUISE FACTS

Most lines sail out of Los Angeles, Miami, San Francisco, and Tampa.

Common ports of call are Acapulco, Cabo San Lucas, Cozumel, Manzanillo, Mazatlán, Puerto Vallarta, and Zihuatanejo.

Booking a cabin

Travel agents specializing in cruises are your best resource. Booking a cruise is really booking a tour—the very heart of travel agency business.

The cost

- The cost of a cruise varies dramatically by line, length of the cruise, and choice of cabin.

- If you want to travel alone (single cabin), the cost will be exorbitant.

• The higher up you get, the higher the cost. Cabins on upper decks are far from engines and noise. They also offer the best views.

• Bigger rooms (or suites) cost more because space is precious. A bath instead of a shower adds to the cost for the same reason.

• Portholes, because they offer a view, add to the cost. This is an outside, versus an inside cabin.

Extra costs

• On some cruise ships tips are not included in the fare. Ask to be sure.

• Any land tours or excursions to the Mexican mainland cost extra on almost all cruise ships. These can be quite expensive, especially if they include a guide and transportation.

• Wine, beer, cocktails—all cost extra. On some lines you'll get complimentary wine with a meal.

Length of the cruise

• Most cruises last one or two weeks, providing adequate time for rest.

• A few cruises offer three and four day voyages (the first and last days are often write-offs).

Motion sickness

Some people get sick at the sight of sea water. See p. 75 for advice.

Special cruise tips

• You'll need a multiple-entry tourist card (see p. 11).

• The lowest-priced cabins on most cruises go first.

• Cruises are not geared to getting to know places. Mexico will be a backdrop, not the main performance.

• Cruises frequently offer shore excursions during mealtimes —very annoying, but a fact. Ask about the exact schedule when booking a cruise!

• Space is critical, so rooms on luxury liners are tight, and baths miniscule even for a midget.

• Bring a bottle of your favorite booze on board. This makes you less dependent on overpriced and often undersized (or watered-down) drinks.

• There are so many free snacks and edible extras on board that someone may whimsically remark that you board as a passenger, disembark as cargo.

Tipping on board

• Ask about the company policy on tipping before you buy a ticket. Tips may be included in the ticket price. If they are, the ticket is really costing you considerably less than a comparable ticket on a line where tips are not included.

• If tips are not included, tip room stewards, waiters, and other service staff for special services. The more service you ask for, the more you should expect to tip. Tips are best given immediately for such services as bringing late-night snacks.

• One very effective way of tipping: Hand the room steward or waiter an amount adding up to half the tip you expect to give him altogether. Tell him exactly what you expect. And tell him that you will give him the other half of the tip at the end of the trip (the day before you disembark). This is upfront bargaining for good service. And does it work!

8

TRAIN TRAVEL

Only a few people travel to Mexico by train, but many tourists use trains for part of their trip while traveling in Mexico.

Basic vocabulary for the train station

arrival	*llegada*
baggage	*equipaje*
change here	*cambiar de tren*
conductor	*revisor*
connection	*correspondencia*
departure	*salida*
fare	*precio, importe*
first class	*primera clase*
first class reserved	*primera especial*
no smoking	*no fumadores*
pillow	*cojín*
platform	*andén, parada*
railway	*ferrocarril*
second class	*segunda clase*
smoking car	*fumador*
stop	*parada, apeadero*
ticket	*billete, boleto*
ticket window	*taquilla de billetes*

timetable	*horario de trenes*
train	*tren*
waiting room	*sala de espera*

TRAIN TRAVEL TO MEXICO

Because of the time involved and the relatively high cost, most people prefer to fly to Mexico or to save money on a bus. If you take a train, remember that you'll have to get off at the border, no matter what time it is.

TRAIN TRAVEL IN MEXICO

Few people know very much about train travel in Mexico. Many Mexican government tourist offices more or less discourage it. Travel agents in the United States and Canada ignore it because there are no commissions and no practical way of making reservations. But vagabonds have already discovered that it's a cheap, reasonably comfortable, and low-risk mode of transportation.

Advantages of train travel

• Trains are the cheapest way to travel in Mexico, less even than buses (as much as 50 percent less).

• Train travel is relatively safe, and reasonably convenient, because it takes you from city center to city center with no transfers to pay and no weather delays (except in the high mountains).

• Train travel is far less tiring than car and bus travel. You really can relax on a train.

• Trains are much less confining than buses, and you can move around and stretch.

• You can also go to the bathroom (not always the case on buses).

- You're allowed stopovers on trains with first-class tickets, which is not the case on buses.

Disadvantages of train travel

- Trains cannot get you everywhere in Mexico. You may have to rent a car, fly, or take a bus to get to remote areas.

- Many trains are quite old, jiggle badly, and make quite a clacking racket.

- Some of the train stations in smaller towns are appalling— smelly, dirty, and even scary at night.

- For popular routes in the peak travel periods you may have to make reservations far in advance.

- Schedules change frequently and are hard to find out. You often have to go to the station to get accurate information.

- Trains are notoriously late. Mexicans joke about this constantly. Trains are often slow getting to where they are going because of frequent stopovers in small places.

- Many trains have virtually no temperature control, meaning that in winter in the high mountains you freeze and in the heat of summer you swelter.

- Trains can be very crowded, but in no way are they as crowded as most buses.

Information

If you plan to travel by train to or in Mexico, contact the following organization for information:

Mexican National Railways
1500 Broadway, Room 810
New York, NY 10036
tel.: (212) 382-2262

Mexico City Rail Information
tel.: (915) 547-8971

A HIGHLY TOUTED TRAIN RIDE

The Copper Canyon *(Barranca del Cobre)* train ride is the most publicized single train ride in Mexico. It goes from Los Mochis to Chihuahua, and vice versa.

- The train trip takes you high into the mountains to a deep and spectacular gorge, said to be larger than the Grand Canyon.

- The name of the train line is *Ferrocarril Chihuahua al Pacífico.* And the trip is 406 miles long and takes just under thirteen hours—more or less.

- Always go from the south (Los Mochis) to the north (Chihuahua) on this trip. If you don't, you will arrive at the most spectacular part of the ride in the dark!

- The best time to make the trip is in April, May, October, and November.

- The heated cars are not so heated in the winter, and both mud slides and avalanches may close down the train or catch you for several days in a shivering situation. Summer can be a season of violent storms.

- The railroad runs on central time while Los Mochis is on mountain time—make sure you're at the station on the train's, not local, time.

- The train can carry cars and RVs, but it might be easier just to make a round-trip. The fare is quite reasonable.

- The cars are sometimes advertised as vista domes. They are not. The train uses older French, Italian, and Japanese cars.

BUYING TRAIN TICKETS

- Ask a Mexican to pronounce the name of your destination,

so that the person in the ticket booth will understand you. There is a language barrier in some train stations.

● Since popular trains may sell out, buy tickets as far in advance as possible, if this is allowed.

● In some cases, you'll have to go to the train station and wait for the ticket window to open. Tickets may only be sold an hour or so before the train actually arrives. You simply show up and hope there's space.

● Bring small bills to pay for tickets. You will not make a friend if you ask the ticket person to break a large bill.

What tickets to buy

● Don't skimp unless "local color" turns you on. Train tickets are so inexpensive that traveling in the best price category available is always advised.

● First class is not always the best class available. Ask for *primera especial,* which roughly translates to super first class. It is also called *primera numerada* and *turismo* on occasion.

● Baggage is watched over somewhat in the better classes. In second, or third, it's disregarded.

● Kids under five ride the rails for free, kids five to twelve pay half fare, and all the older kids pay full boat.

● If you get on a train without a ticket, you pay an extra 25 percent.

SPECIAL TIPS FOR TRAIN TRAVELERS

Your personal safety and well-being count as much as money. Here are some suggestions regarding both.

Provisions for train travel

● If you want to eat safely on many Mexican trains, bring your own food and drink. Bring a bottle of water, or a few cans of coke, or some juice per person.

In train stations

• Train schedules use the military (twenty-four hour) system of time; so that 12:00 means noon, and 24:00 means midnight. The system is designed to keep you from confusing 5:00 A.M. (5:00) with 5:00 P.M. (17:00).

• The bathrooms in some small-town train stations are so foul that you'll prefer a hike into the woods. If you can stand the smell, be sure to bring toilet paper—there definitely won't be any.

• Some small-town train stations smell of urine, are covered with webs and strange hanging bugs, and can only be described as pits.

• Lights can and do go out at night in train stations. Always carry a flashlight with you and have it at hand!

• When the lights blink off, you can watch over your bags by flicking on the high beam. Keep your bags not just within eye sight, but right by your side!

• Travel light. Traveling by train with lots of luggage can only be compared to making frequent and unsuccessful attempts at suicide.

Getting on trains

• Although trains make frequent stopovers in small towns, these can be brief. Don't dawdle! Get on the train and then find your seat.

Aboard trains

• If you have an assigned seat, find and sit in it—unless it's already taken by someone with the same assigned seat. Be flexible, you'll probably find another available.

• Seats can swing around on many trains, but signs advise you not to do this. If you do, the conductor will undo it. Save yourself the trouble.

Sleeping on trains

● Many trains have sleeping facilities for people willing to pay double or triple the cost of a first-class ticket. If you want to use this service, make a reservation when buying your ticket.

● The sleeper ticket is called a *primera dormitorio* and there is a surcharge according to how fancy you want your bedroom. You can sleep in a dormitory car *(dormitorios)* in either an upper *(cama alta)* or lower *(cama baja)* berth. The upper is usually cheaper.

● If you want your own room and are willing to pay for it, ask for a *camarín* (private room), *camarín doble* (private room for two), *alcoba* (suite for two), *compartimiento* (suite for two), or *cabinette* (special suite for two). Note that these are not available on many trains.

Getting off trains

● Never get off a train until you've reached your final destination. You may be told that a train will be in a station for a specific time. Don't count on it. You never can be *sure* in Mexico.

9

BUS TRAVEL

Traveling by bus appeals to many people on a budget. In Mexico there are 700 bus lines going just about anywhere, which means most travelers will, at some time, end up on a bus.

BASIC CONSIDERATIONS

Deciding whether or not bus travel makes sense for you means comparing the trade-offs. Here are a few considerations to take into account.

The advantages of bus travel

- You can get just about anywhere in Mexico by bus, even to the most remote village or hamlet.

- Sometimes, bus travel is the *only* way to get to an area (unless you rent a car).

- Bus travel is incredibly cheap, only a little more expensive than train travel. It's truly a bargain.

- You meet fascinating people on buses, the kind of people who are veteran travelers, wily, and willing to put up with some discomfort to save a buck.

• Some people really like buses, no matter what the problems are. They can sleep and relax on them. If you're that kind of person, then buses leave you with lots of energy.

Disadvantages of bus travel

• Many bus stations are disaster zones with toilets so foul and waiting rooms so crowded that you feel you're in a refugee camp.

• There are some luxurious buses, but most first-class buses are second-rate. On many, Mexicans with flimsily covered machetes are jammed into the aisles for standing room only. You barely have enough room to squirm in your seat.

• Buses do not stop frequently enough to allow for bathroom breaks. Since many buses do not have bathrooms, this can be very uncomfortable.

• If you're finicky about sleep and rest, buses can be very tiring.

• The safety records of some bus companies are appalling. Anyone traveling by bus for more than a week or two will begin to hear tales that will curl your toes—I traveled with one couple who had two accidents, both serious, in just a few weeks. Bus travel is not as safe as some travel agents and travel writers would have you believe.

• Buses do not follow exact schedules. Many of them stop to pick up passengers along the route. If you're on a tight schedule, buses aren't for you.

• Buses do not always arrive in towns at a convenient time. It can be difficult and potentially dangerous to arrive somewhere in the middle of the night—this is especially true for women traveling alone (not advised).

• If you're allergic to smoke, if you can't stand stereos blasting for hours on end (many drivers have systems that would be the pride of Watts), if quick fluctuations in temperature turn you off (it's often sweltering in some buses, nearly frigid in others), then buses probably aren't for you.

Information on bus schedules

• Getting accurate information on bus routes and bus schedules is almost impossible. The only reliable way to do this is to go to the bus terminal. Times change so frequently that no one can keep track of them. Since you have to buy tickets in person, this is really the easiest way to take care of the problem.

• During the peak travel seasons of Christmas, New Year's, Carnival, and Easter, buses can be packed. You should buy your tickets as far in advance as possible. Mexicans also travel on three-day weekends. Since buses are a cheap way to get around, space can be hard to come by.

Getting tickets for inter-city buses in Mexico City

• The inter-city bus situation in Mexico City is complex because there are many bus lines and a number of terminals. You can get to these terminals by using the subway *(metro),* but you have to know which terminal handles lines heading in the right direction.

• You can get this information from most hotels, the local tourist office, and a number of free publications distributed locally. Don't be afraid to ask.

An agency handling bus tickets

• If you don't have the time or energy to pick up bus tickets in advance, you can pay an agency to do it for you for a fee. The following agency will buy tickets and deliver them to your hotel. The advantage of this agency is that it can compare fares and schedules to your advantage. Since each bus line has its own fare and varying routes, this can be quite difficult for foreigners.

Central de Autobuses
SA de CV
Plaza del Angel
Calle Londres 161 Space 48
Mexico City
tel.: 533-2047/533-2097

Important facts about bus tickets

● You cannot get bus tickets by phoning a bus terminal. You have to buy tickets in person.

● Tickets are not open-dated. If you miss the bus, you lose the money and have to buy another ticket.

● Tickets are for specific seats. The number will be stamped somewhere on the ticket, often on the back.

● There are no stopover privileges with bus tickets. You go from point A to point B, and that's it.

● There's no reduction for round-trip fares.

● You cannot refund or exchange tickets in most cases, but they're very easy to sell to people waiting in line.

Selecting a seat

● Unless you speak good Spanish, it's often hard to select a specific seat. But you can certainly try.

● Seats in the back near the bathroom can be smelly.

● A window seat *(ventanilla)* or aisle seat *(pasillo)* are easy to specify according to your preference.

● On night rides try to get a seat on the right side *(derecha)* of the bus to avoid glare from oncoming cars and trucks. You'll sleep better on the right side.

Bathrooms and buses

● Not all buses have bathrooms. Even when they do, the bathroom can be hard to get to with people standing in the aisle or it can be so foul you wish you never reached it.

● Don't drink liquids before going on a long bus trip. Shy away from coffee, colas, and tea which contain caffeine. Beer is equally bad.

● Go to the bathroom immediately before getting on the bus if you have a tendency toward a weak bladder.

● The bus will take a pee break every three to five hours.

• Bring your own toilet paper. Buses with bathrooms may run out. And bathrooms at stopover points often have none.

• If you can't wait for a stop, ask the driver to pull over. Your pee will be in public. The most private spot is directly behind the bus. You'll probably return to a series of ribald comments and a little laughter—but you can handle that.

Temperature control

• Some buses are air-conditioned. This can be a welcome treat in hot, sticky weather. If it gets too cool, you'll have to slip on a sweater or jacket. Always carry one with you.

• Some buses claim to be air-conditioned, but when you get on them, the air-conditioning turns out to be a series of open windows.

• In the evening it can get quite cool even in the tropics. Another reason to carry a sweater or jacket.

Taking care of hunger pains

• Never travel on a bus without a food pack filled to the brim with such things as fresh fruit, bread and crackers, some cheese, a chocolate bar, and something to drink. Add whatever you like, but have plenty of it.

• Many of the food stops are at restaurants that really can be quite scary from a sanitary point of view. If you have food with you, the greasy tacos won't tempt you for a second!

• Don't be self-conscious about eating in front of other travelers. Mexicans do it all the time. It's the way things are done in Mexico. So join in!

Stopovers

• Bus drivers stop every four or five hours to take a break. This gives passengers a chance to go to the bathroom or have a bite to eat.

• Buses are usually locked during these breaks. You're allowed to stay on the bus, but if you get off, you have to wait until the driver opens the door to get back on.

• These breaks tend to be quite short, fifteen or twenty minutes. Don't let the bus take off without you.

• If you're traveling with a group, have a contingency plan in case someone gets lost. If you notice that someone is missing on the bus, say, "¡Falta uno!"

Baggage on bus lines

• Traveling by bus with lots of baggage is a real hassle. Try to get by with one small bag that you can carry on the bus and stuff into an overhead rack. This way you can keep an eye on it at all times.

• If you've got a large bag or several smaller ones, you may have to put it in the luggage compartment where it can get lost or stolen. If you do put it in this compartment, watch it get loaded. You'll get a receipt for baggage in first class. But when you're traveling second class, no one bothers with such formalities.

• In some stations you'll find porters or free baggage carts (carretillas), but don't count on either—another good reason to travel light.

• Some stations have a baggage room (guarda equipaje) where you can leave your bags for little or no charge. Either you or someone else should be looking after your bags at all times!

• If your bus is in an accident, baggage will often be held. That's right—held. This can tie you up for hours or days. If you're traveling with carry-on bags, these bags will not be held.

HELPFUL PHRASES

How much is a ticket to . . .?	¿Cuánto cuesta un boleto a . . .?
What is the number of the bus?	¿Qué es el número del autobús?
What time does the bus leave?	¿A qué hora sale el autobús?
Where does this bus go?	¿Dónde va este autobús?
How many hours is it to . . . ?	¿Cuántas horas a . . . ?
I lost my baggage.	¿Se me perdió me equipaje.

Basic bus vocabulary

arrivals	*llegadas*
baggage (claim area)	*equipajes*
bus	*autobús, camión*
bus with a toilet	*pullman*
bus station	*terminal, estación de autobuses*
bus stop	*parada*
city bus	*servicio urbano*
deluxe	*super deluxe*
departures	*salidas*
destination	*destino*
driver	*chofer*
east	*este, oriente*
fare	*precio*
first class	*primera clase, deluxe*
hour	*hora*
gates	*llegadas*
get in	*sube*
intercity	*foraneo*
nonstop	*directo, sin escala*
north	*norte*
passenger	*pasajero*
reservation	*reservación*
reserved seat	*asiento reservado*
route	*ruta*
seat	*asiento*
second class	*segunda clase*
south	*sur*
stop (bus stop)	*parada*
stop (stop the bus!)	*¡bajan!*
ticket	*boleto, billete, ficha*
ticket window	*caja, taquilla*
to	*a*
toilets	*sanitaríos*
waiting room	*sala de espera*
west	*oeste, poniente*

10

ALTERNATIVE TRANSPORTATION

For some people the cost of travel is the major consideration. This chapter deals with cheap alternatives.

CAR-DELIVERY SERVICE

• You can get close to Mexico by offering your driving skill to a car-delivery service. These are often listed in Sunday papers.

• You'll have to be insured and bonded at the company's cost, and this will depend on your driving record.

• Most of these companies pay for the gas, but they leave all other expenses up to you. Only a few will pay a fee to the driver.

• Arizona, California, and Texas are frequent destinations of car delivery services, and the need for drivers is usually greatest in the fall and winter when people head to warmer climes but don't want to drive.

• Call the local office and get your name listed with the agency. By being flexible in your travel plans, you'll often come up with a delivery assignment.

HITCHHIKING

Hitchhiking is not recommended in Mexico. Not only is it difficult to get a ride, but it's also potentially dangerous. Just refusing a ride can cause a problem, since this can offend a Mexican's sense of manlihood. Since public transportation is so cheap, why bother with hitchhiking?

- Getting *to* Mexico by hitchhiking does make sense. If you disregard the advice on Mexico, here are a few tips.

Getting rides

- Go to campgrounds and RV parks and ask whether anyone will soon be traveling in your direction. This is getting a ride without hitting the road.

- Wherever you see trucks, you may be able to pick up a ride (*un ride* or *aventon*). Women are not legally allowed on trucks, so bear this in mind if a driver wants to drop you and your lady off before a checkpoint or town.

- You may be able to pick up a ride at any Pemex station. Occasionally, it helps out if you'll offer to pay for part of the gas.

Protecting your belongings

- Always carry all documents, money, and valuables on your person. Other important odds and ends should be in a little day bag which you take with you at all times—even to the bathroom.

General tips

- It's more comfortable and more productive getting rides in the early morning.

- Keep your gear light. People don't like to pick up lots of baggage with hikers.

● Stay clean—this will help you get a ride, especially if you're asking tourists for help.

● Keep knives out of sight. No one wants to pick up someone carrying a filet, hunting knife, or machete. And the police will confiscate them.

● Go through large towns using the public transportation system. Buses, trams, and the subway in Mexico City are all incredibly cheap.

MOTORCYCLING

Carrying a cycle or moped for excursions and off-road travel makes sense, but not as your only means of travel. You don't see very many bikes in Mexico and for good reason. Stick to public transportation.

COURIER SERVICE

More than 900 companies in the United States and Canada use couriers to deliver important documents to destinations worldwide. Many of them will pay for part of or all of a courier's transportation costs. Check locally with larger companies and courier services.

11

MONEY MATTERS

Protecting and getting the most for your money is on every traveler's mind.

MONEY BASICS

Following are some straightforward tips on carrying money, exchanging it, and getting the most for it in Mexico.

How to bring money into Mexico

● It's always a good idea to carry thirty $1 bills. Small bills can be used in a number of ways for everything from paying a departure tax to a cab ride. Although they are not legal tender in Mexico, you'd never know it by the way they're snapped up.

● Carry as much U.S. cash as you can afford to lose. You'll find that U.S. bills are worth more on the street than you'll get in a bank. More about the black market on p. 150.

● Bring all the rest of your money in the form of traveler's checks, which is the easiest and safest way to carry a large sum of money.

● Bring a major credit card! You'll find that it will be useful in countless ways.

Special advice to Canadians

● Canadian currency and Canadian traveler's checks can be more difficult to cash in Mexico than U.S. currency. Many Canadians convert their money into U.S. currency for travel in Mexico.

● You will lose on the exchange. If you think Canadian currency will rise against the dollar, then you'll lose even more.

● However, the convenience may be worth it.

Traveler's checks

Each year, more than a million travelers lose cash due to theft and negligence. For this reason, rely on traveler's checks as a way of carrying money throughout Mexico.

● Traveler's checks are available from American Express, Bank of America, Barclay's Bank, Citibank, Thomas Cook, and many other institutions.

● However, there is suspicion about traveler's checks in many areas of Mexico. This is as true in a bank as in a small shop or hotel. Traveler's checks from American Express and Bank of America remain the easiest checks to cash throughout the country—and even they can be hard to cash at times.

● It is possible to purchase traveler's checks in *pesos* in the United States and Canada. This would be a smart move if the dollar drops in value against the peso in the weeks following your purchase. You may avoid the long lines in banks with this strategy—but hotels and restaurants might still be reluctant to accept checks whether they're in pesos or not. You would still end up in a bank to cash them.

FEE-FREE TRAVELER'S CHECKS

Normally, you pay a 1 percent service fee when buying traveler's checks. However, if you'll look around, you'll find traveler's checks that you can buy without paying this fee.

• Many travel clubs and banks now offer traveler's checks free of any fee to members or preferred customers. It would be unusual not to find several such offers in any area at one time.

WHEN YOU BUY TRAVELER'S CHECKS

• Make sure to count them, since they're usually sold in packets containing a specific amount in specific denominations. Very rarely will a check be missing, but it does happen.

• Sign them as instructed. If you lose an unsigned check, it's gone forever. Different companies have you sign their checks in different places, but this rarely causes a problem.

• Each traveler should carry individual checks. This divides the responsibility and allows each person freedom in using them.

• Always write down the number of all the checks on a separate sheet of paper. Leave a photocopy of these numbers with someone at home—just in case you lose the checks and the original list of numbers on the trip.

• Get checks in varying denominations. Carry most of your money in $100 checks, but have an assortment of $20 checks as well. In some areas it's harder to cash the larger checks. And in some instances you may not want to convert much money into pesos.

• Get checks from different companies—a few from American Express and a few from Bank of America. The reason for this is simple: Some banks will only cash one or the other. I know it sounds absurd, but that's the way it is—trust me.

• Keep a written record of all the checks you've used. The simplest way to do this is to write all the numbers down in a safe place and to strike the number of each check cashed. This will be essential information if you lose the checks!

• Don't carry this record in the same place as your checks. If your checks get ripped off or lost, you'll lose the record as well.

CASHING TRAVELER'S CHECKS

Usually the easiest and sometimes the only place to cash a traveler's check is in a bank. Some banks refuse to cash certain brands of checks, which means you have to find another bank or a money changer who is less suspicious.

• If you're carrying a passport, you can sometimes overcome the suspicion of a clerk.

• Many times you'll be asked to get your check okayed by the bank manager. With that approval, you can then cash the check.

WET CHECKS

Mexico is a land of endless beaches, and each year a few traveler's checks end up in the drink. Although they can't swim, they do run—puddles of ink. So be wary of getting your checks wet, because it is not easy getting mutilated or faded checks cashed. In some cases it's impossible. The easiest way to deal with a mutilated or soggy traveler's check is to declare it lost and tear it up.

Personal checks

Although in some countries you can easily cash and use personal checks, such is not the case in Mexico. Leave your personal checks at home, unless you plan to pay for duty with them on your return home (see p. 372).

Credit cards

These are as good as gold in much of Mexico. There is very little suspicion of credit cards, which surprisingly raise fewer eyebrows then traveler's checks!

• The best credit cards in Mexico are American Express, Carte Blanche, Diners Club, MasterCard, and Visa.

ADVANTAGES OF CREDIT CARDS

• Credit cards are safer to carry than cash, because if they're lost or stolen, you have limited liability and no liability at all if you report the loss before they're used.

• Thieves are less interested in credit cards than cash. Very few reports of credit card theft are reported each year in Mexico.

• With a credit card there's very little hassle renting a car or signing in at a hotel. You don't need to carry large amounts of cash at any time to pay for these big expense items. Your signed receipt is all that's needed—even if you choose to pay with cash later (the receipt is then destroyed).

• When you use credit cards, you have excellent records of your expenses. This is good for trip planning and for the IRS at tax time.

• Credit card companies allow you to use their money on a float—you may not have to pay the bill for a month or two, (or three or four knowing Mexico). This ends up being an interest-free loan.

• Companies automatically convert all charges in pesos to dollars at the rate of exchange prevailing at the time the charges are submitted. This means you can avoid much of the currency exchange hassle by using the card frequently.

• Credit cards are easy to carry and honored in many shops, restaurants, car rental agencies, and hotels in Mexico. You can get a pamphlet outlining the establishments honoring the card by requesting one from the company.

• *Special note:* There should be no surcharge placed on any bill in Mexico for the use of a credit card. If someone tries to add one, refuse to pay it.

USING CREDIT CARDS TO GET CASH

Many credit cards allow you to get cash in a pinch. The regulations and fees for such a service change frequently. You might want to check with your credit card company for current information.

• If you think you'll be using this service, get a list of the places where it's available. Make sure that it's very specific.

PROTECTING CREDIT CARDS

Protect your cards like cash, and count them from time to time to make sure they're all there. Thieves are smart enough to steal just one, hoping that you won't notice.

When the money runs out

● You can phone home (collect) and ask someone to send you an international money order or wire you funds.

● The U.S. and Canadian Consulates can help in emergencies. But you'll have to repay money lent to you before you will be allowed to travel abroad again.

● If you haven't kept enough money to pay duty on your return to the United States or Canada, customs will take a personal check with two forms of identification.

Exchanging currency *(cambio de moneda)*

One of the realities of travel in Mexico is the necessity of exchanging dollars for pesos. You'll need your tourist card and passport for each exchange.

● Since the peso has been floating since 1976, exchange rates fluctuate daily. "What is the exchange rate?" in Spanish is: *"¿Cuál es el cambio?"*

● Exchange rates are sometimes posted at banks, travel offices, hotels, and restaurants. Getting the best exchange rate possible is a little like roulette. Most people exchange money according to need at the time, rather than the prevailing rate.

● Always exchange the most money you can afford to lose. This process of exchanging money is a hassle, and you'll want to do it as infrequently as possible.

WHERE TO EXCHANGE CURRENCY

You can exchange currency wherever anyone is willing to give you pesos for dollars—and that can be in the street. The main thing that counts is for you to get the best rate of exchange possible with the least amount of hassle.

● You should learn to recognize all Mexican bills and coins so that you're sure you're getting the full value for your money.

For this reason your first exchange should be in a reputable bank or at a money-changer's office.

Tips on Mexican money

Coins *(monedas)* come in a wide variety of sizes and shapes. The main unit is a peso, which is divided into 100 centavos. The 20 centavo *(veinte)* and the 50 centavo *(cinquenta)* coins are used to make local telephone calls and are worth only a fraction of a U.S. penny.

• The peso *(un peso)* comes in two sizes. The newer peso coins are the smaller of the two. The U.S. government would like to see the new pesos abolished since they can be substituted for more expensive U.S. coins in vending machines.

• The five-peso *(cinco-peso)* coin has lettering on the rim. The ten-peso *(diez-peso)* coin is eight-sided and easy to distinguish from the other coins. The twenty-peso *(veinte-peso)* coin is quite heavy. The fifty-peso *(cinquenta)* coin confuses people since it comes in two sizes—watch out for the smaller one. The one-hundred-peso *(ciento-peso)* coin stands out by its gold color.

• Study these coins for a few minutes until you're familiar with their odd shapes and sizes. Note that some of the smaller coins are worth much more than some of the larger ones—which is true of many currencies in other countries, including the United States and Canada.

• The bills or banknotes *(billetes)* come in the following denominations: 50, 100, 500, 1,000, 5,000 and 10,000. These bills come in a rainbow of colors to make them stand out from each other.

Getting the best deal on currency exchange

• The secret of exchanging money is to know the current rate of exchange. If someone offers you a more favorable rate than the official one, you've got yourself a deal.

• Generally, you get your best rate of exchange from a reputable bank. However, rates of exchange vary from one bank to the next. If saving money is more important than saving time, check several banks before you make a currency exchange. The right choice can mean a 2 to 5 percent profit.

• In most countries, you get a poor rate of exchange at airports. My experience in Mexico was the opposite, especially in Mexico City (there are several banks operating on a twenty-four-hour schedule). Just be wary of exchanging money in areas where tourists are most vulnerable.

• You usually get a poor rate of exchange in hotels. Deluxe chains including Hilton and Sheraton have tried to reverse this in Mexico. Consider checking them out before going to a bank. But note that *most* hotels consistently rip off their customers when it comes to currency exchange.

• Shops often give a poor rate of exchange. However, a few shops always give a better rate of exchange than banks as a way of encouraging shoppers to return (a kind of built-in discount). By knowing the current rate of exchange before you go shopping, you'll know whether you're being offered a good deal or a rip-off.

Money changers *(casas de cambio)*

• In most instances you'll find the same rates at money changers as at reputable banks. The big advantage: an instant transaction with none of the hassles of a bank (the good and the bad on banks follows).

The good news about Mexican banks

• The good news about Mexican banks is that they usually offer a fair rate of exchange for your money and can be found in most towns of any consequence.

The bad news about Mexican banks

• What's the number one pet peeve of travelers in Mexico? Diarrhea—pretty good guess, but not quite right. Try banks. You'll only have to go to a Mexican bank once to know how agonizingly slow the process of currency exchange can be.

● If it were slow and fair, no one would complain—that's just part of life, right? The problem is that the bank tellers are rude, insensitive, and often incompetent. Not to mention constantly allowing "special customers" to butt into the line ahead of others who have been patiently waiting for an hour (or more) to get served.

● So if you can find a place to exchange currency at a fair rate of exchange outside of a bank, jump at the opportunity—the complaints about Mexican banks are becoming legendary.

SURVIVAL VOCABULARY IN THE BANK

bank	*banco*
bank draft	*cheque del banco*
bill (banknote)	*billete*
cash (to pay *cash*)	*efectivo*
cash (to *cash*)	*cambiar*
change, exchange	*cambio*
check	*cheque*
coins	*monedas*
commission	*comisión*
credit card	*tarjeta de crédito*
dollar	*dólar*
exchange hours	*horas de cambio*
Mexican currency	*moneda nacional*
money	*dinero*
money order	*giro*
personal check	*cheque personal*
signature	*firma*
teller's window	*caja*
traveler's check	*cheque de viajero*

More bad news about Mexican banks

● Banks can run out of pesos—no joke!

● Banks often refuse to exchange traveler's checks after 12:30 P.M. Since they open at 9:30 A.M., you've got roughly three hours to make your exchange.

- Some banks won't take traveler's checks at all, as was previously mentioned.

The Black Market

You can often get a better rate of exchange for dollars (usually cash, not traveler's checks) on the black market than in a bank.

- As long as you know Mexican currency, what do you have to lose? Most travelers are delighted to sell currency at a higher rate. And they save themselves the aggravation of going to a Mexican bank!

What to watch out for in exchanging money

- Don't exchange money where you're not getting a fair rate of exchange. As was mentioned previously, this happens frequently in hotels which tend to rip off customers.

- Watch out for a service fee. Some banks charge this as a way of increasing their profit. Before you exchange money, ask if there is a commission or service fee for the transaction —"¿Cobran una comisión?" ("Do you charge a commission?").

- Watch out for a flat fee per traveler's check cashed. This can kill you. Sometimes, a fee of this nature is posted. Look for another bank! "¿Dónde hay otro banco?" ("Where's another bank?").

- Never take marked, mutilated, or torn bills. These will be rejected over and over again when you go to use them. Let the bank have the headache.

- Banks will try to stick you with as many large bank notes as possible. Large bank notes are fine if you're going directly from the bank to pay off a large bill, but they're next to useless in many shops, restaurants, and smaller hotels where change can be a major problem. Try to get banknotes in 1,000 peso denominations.

Money manners

- Don't make fun of Mexican currency. A Mexican may take it personally, even if you don't intend it that way.

- Never ask how much an item is worth in *real* money. Pesos are as real as U.S. or Canadian dollars.

- Never toss money casually to a taxi driver or to anyone in Mexico. This is considered demeaning and very rude, even though it's done frequently in the United States.

Money confusion

- Mexico, Canada, and the United States share the $ sign for their national currencies. When you see the $ sign in Mexico, it means pesos, not dollars.

- Sometimes, an item for sale or an item on a menu will have M.N. *(moneda nacional)* written behind it. This means that the cost is in the national currency or pesos.

- If a store or restaurant wants to price an item in U.S. dollars, they'll do it by adding US CY (U.S. currency) or Dlls (dollars) after the price.

Final money tip

- Never carry Mexican coins back to the United States or Canada. Many banks will refuse to exchange them for U.S. or Canadian currency. Either use them up for a treat or newspaper or convert them to paper bills. Naturally, if you intend to return to Mexico, some loose change can't hurt!

TAXES

To judge how expensive anything is going to be in Mexico you have to know about the local taxes.

Legal pickpocketing—the IVA *(Impuesto Valor Agregado)*

Mexico's Aggregate Value Tax (IVA) varies from 6 percent in the Baja to 15 percent in the rest of Mexico—it amounts to legal pickpocketing. It even soars to 20 percent on luxury items.

- The only way you can avoid it is by eating in inexpensive

restaurants and staying in inexpensive hotels and by shopping in the open market—these all cater to Mexicans who have no intention of paying any tax at all.

● Since most tourists don't eat, stay, and shop exclusively in such places, they get socked with a tax that can really add up over a period of time.

● This tax should never be confused with a service charge! You're still expected to leave a tip in appropriate situations, for example, in restaurants.

TIPPING

Many Mexicans depend almost entirely on tips for their living. Since wages are extremely low, tips take on an added importance to the average worker.

● Tips tend to be much higher in major resorts and in major cities. Tip in these areas more or less as you would in the United States or Canada.

● Tips can be much smaller in rural areas where any tip at all will be appreciated. Still, it is in these areas that need is greatest, and you might bear that in mind when tipping.

● Always carry lots of small change and small bills with you in Mexico. These will be essential for tips.

● Although tour packages generally include all gratuities for services included in the tour contract, ask about the policy on tipping before signing a contract.

Tipping on day tours

Both the driver and tour guide will appreciate a tip for their services. A dollar a day is a fair tip, more if either person offered exceptional service.

Tipping in the airport

Porters may tell you what their charge is for a bag. If they leave it up to you, tip less than in the United States, but don't underdo it.

Tipping on cruises

• Some cruise ships include the tip in the price of the voyage. Ask ahead of time to make sure.

• If tips are not included, give the waiter and steward $2 a day each.

• Some travelers prefer to give half the tip up front as an inducement for good service. They give the second half at the end of the trip.

• Always tip the day before getting off the ship to make sure that the confusion of disembarkation doesn't make tipping impossible.

Tipping in hotels

• Tip the bellboy the equivalent of the current price of a beer for his services.

• Chambermaids should be tipped for stays of longer than a few days—give at least $1 a day.

• If anyone in the hotel performs a special service for you, tip accordingly.

• In good hotels you should expect to tip the concierge for any unusual service, such as getting tickets to a sold-out performance or getting reservations at a restaurant that is nearly impossible to get into.

Tipping in restaurants

• In a few, a very few, places the tip is added onto the bill as a service charge (don't confuse this with the IVA tax of 15 percent). If a service charge has been added, that's your tip— don't add any additional tip to it.

• Most guides tell you to tip 10 to 15 percent in all restaurants. This is not what the Mexicans do. In a low-cost restaurant tip just a little. If the bill runs over $5, tip about 6 percent. If the bill tops $10, then you should tip 10 to 15 percent depending upon the service.

● Small-town restaurants don't exact the same tips as big-town restaurants might. Tip according to the area!

Miscellaneous tipping

● Give tiny tips to ushers, car watchers and gas station attendants. They don't expect much, but they do expect a little.

● You should tip washroom attendants if you use their services. Give them as little as you can get away with.

● You should tip theater (and movie) ushers who guide you to your seat—again, a very small amount will do.

When not to tip

● Don't tip taxi drivers unless they perform some special service for you (they rarely do).

● Don't tip barbers and hairdressers.

Handling beggars

Poverty is real in Mexico, and begging is common, so common that it becomes an everyday annoyance. It's an annoyance because there's very little anyone can do to alleviate the problem. So it becomes a matter of personal choice, who you give to and who you don't.

● Many travelers prefer to give food to beggars rather than money. Rarely will anyone turn you down. The hunger in Mexico is real, not the scam that you'll find in other places.

PROTECTING PROPERTY

Suspicion and wariness require energy and are not very pleasant sensations, but they do prevent trouble, which can be even more unpleasant. Mexico is a poor country, and you'd have to be naive or careless not to take protective measures.

PROTECTING YOUR BELONGINGS IN MEXICO

- Mexicans have a saying about lovers kissing in public: "Don't count your money before the poor." This same saying can be taken literally as a warning to U.S. and Canadian travelers. Never count or flash money in public. Mexicans consider this cruel, stupid, and dangerous. You're asking for trouble if you do.

- Leave all expensive jewelry at home. It's out of place in Mexico. You can pick up all sorts of gold and silver imitations for a song—that's what the Mexicans do! Follow their lead.

- Never carry all of your valuables in one place. Split up your documents and money. If you put your passport, tickets, money, traveler's checks, and credit cards in one place— they're all gone in one shot. *This is basic street sense,* and absolutely essential in developing countries.

• Keep anything valuable out of sight and in inconspicuous containers. If you have to leave something valuable in a car (not a good idea), put it in the trunk. Stow your cameras in an inexpensive carrying bag—one that looks like it could just as easily be carrying groceries.

• Never take public transportation, especially buses or trams, after cashing a large amount of money at the bank. Get the money back to your hotel safe and take just what you need for the day.

• *Just what you need for the day (or for the next few hours)* is the key phrase in Mexico. You don't need to carry a passport, three credit cards, all your traveler's checks, most of your money, and your airline tickets—leave them in the hotel safe. Take just enough to get you by for the day—one credit card will often do the trick.

• Dress casually. Ninety-nine percent of the time you do not have to dress up in Mexico. Mexicans judge travelers by their shoes and sunglasses—so keep that in mind.

How to carry valuables when you must— pickpocket proofing

There are times when everything you own is either on your body or in your bags. Violent crime is not common in Mexico, but rip-offs of bags and pickpocketing are (over 17,000 cases reported yearly). Here are some tips:

• A small, durable traveler's pouch which can be attached to a belt and worn under your pants or skirt is the *best* place to carry valuable documents and money. These can be improvised by anyone with a basic knowledge of sewing and should have a good zipper enclosure. These hidden pouches are sold in the market, as well. Get one!

• Second best but good is the inside pocket of a coat or jacket, which has been modified with a zipper. You can alter these pockets so that they're twice as deep, and twice as hard to pick. The zipper is crucial. No zipper? Use a safety pin as a deterrent to nimble fingers.

● Never carry your wallet in a rear pocket! A pickpocket can rip it off in a second. A side pants pocket is only a little better. If that's all you've got, buy a nappy-surfaced wallet or put a rubber band around it—this can give pickpockets a fit.

● If you're carrying a purse, put it in front of you with your arms crossed over it. Your wallet should be at the bottom. If your purse is to your side or behind you, a thief will slash it open with a razor blade and be gone in seconds.

Situations pickpockets like

● Pickpocketing is most common in crowded areas such as markets, buses in rush hour, the metro in Mexico City, and on beaches.

● Pickpockets prey on careless and drunk tourists—in that order. If you want to tie one on, carry only what you can afford to lose.

● Be wary of minor accidents: being bumped, having your foot stepped upon, being shoved. If your mind is not on your money, you will be vulnerable to pickpockets.

● Avoid commotions of all kinds. Pickpockets love to create them. Move away from any commotion as quickly and unobtrusively as possible.

● Pickpockets often pose as drunks. So if someone wraps his arms around you, watch your wallet—he's probably feeling for it.

Protecting valuables in a hotel

● In many Mexican hotel rooms you'll find security boxes. Make sure to get a key and instructions on how to use these.

● Many hotels have safe deposit boxes (cajas de seguridad) at the front desk. Take advantage of them. There's usually no charge, unless you lose the key—the charge for a replacement will be stiff.

● When getting valuables out of a safe, be attentive. This is one time when thieves will try to distract you.

- If you're in a budget hotel, don't leave valuables unattended. Carry them into the shower or bathroom if you have to.

Protecting valuables in airports, train, and bus stations

- If safety lockers *(gabinetes de seguridad)* are available, they provide a good way to store excess baggage or valuables. The Mexico City airport has 250 lockers that can store bags for up to one week.

- If you're traveling at night, always carry a flashlight for blackouts in train and bus stations. This will be the only way to discourage thieves—one almost carted off my bags in this situation!

- Stick with your bags—assume that if they're left unattended for a second, they'll be ripped off. Chances are good that they will be.

- Try to travel light. That way you can carry your bags with you onto planes, trains, and buses. The minute your bags are out of sight you have no way to keep track of them. On second-class buses you don't even get a receipt for your bags —good luck trying to prove they got ripped off, even if your Spanish is flawless!

Protecting valuables in cars

- Try not to leave anything valuable in a car. A good thief can get into a car or trunk in a few seconds.

- Sometimes, you have to leave things in a car. If you do, open the glove compartment to show a potential thief that it's empty. Put your gear in the trunk. Don't leave it too long, and absolutely never leave baggage in a car overnight.

- If you travel to Mexico in your own car or RV, consider a built-in safe somewhere underneath the car. It doesn't have to be large. Many experienced travelers use this "hidden compartment" for valuables and documents—it's unlikely that someone will find it.

Protecting valuables at the beach

● Leave as much as you can at your hotel, preferably in a safe deposit box.

● Pin your money to a beach robe or piece of clothing which no one would suspect as a hiding place. Leave nothing of great value in your purse or bag, which will be the first thing stolen. The purse becomes a dummy.

Losing things

It is very easy to lose things while traveling because you're constantly disoriented, frequently tired and fuzzy, and often moving at such a quick pace that it's hard to keep track of where you are or what you've got.

● Consider a special bag for things that are really important to you. Carry everything in that one bag (I'm not talking about money and valuables). You'll be less likely to forget the bag than an individual item—like a pair of sunglasses or a small camera or a favorite pen or a lighter.

● The quickest way to lose something is to set it down. You put a camera on the seat next to you and the next minute you're four blocks away and realize that the camera didn't come with you. What a sinking feeling and a mad dash to claim it—if it's still there!

● Try to establish a place for everything. This routine helps you know at all times where things are. This has a calming effect and really helps cut down on the loss of items through carelessness, fatigue, or simple oversight.

PERSONAL SAFETY

Mexico is much safer than newspaper reports would have you believe. Still, common sense and street sense will help you avoid situations that could be unpleasant.

WHAT THE MEXICANS ADVISE

Mexicans follow certain precautions as if they were second nature. They've learned not to put themselves in situations that could turn nasty.

• Don't drive at night. Not only could you have an accident, but you could expose yourself to the risk of robbery, rape, and murder. This is not the time of day to be traveling in Mexico.

• If you're into camping, do it in legal campsites. Or at the very least, do it with a group of people. Campers routinely disregard this advice and tell others that there's no problem camping out in Mexico—and they're right, most of the time. But they're wrong enough times to be scary. Ask the people who have had problems—not the ones who haven't.

• Don't hitchhike in Mexico! You're too exposed if you do. Besides, people are afraid to pick up hitchhikers. And public transportation is so cheap that hitchhiking is totally unnecessary.

● Don't go out on beaches at night. This is a sad comment and *not* universally true throughout Mexico, but in many areas beaches are no longer safe. Ask if you're in doubt.

● Before swimming in any area ask the locals about the safety of the water. Currents and undertows are treacherous in some areas, and the locals know it. No one should ever swim alone.

● Avoid off-road travel in areas where marijuana or poppies are cultivated, especially in Nayarit, Sinoloa, and Sonora. This includes some pretty large chunks of Mexico. Talk to the consulates in any area where you intend to do some "exploration."

● Don't sleep in your car by the side of the road at night. Even if you're traveling in an RV, this is a poor idea. Try to find a campsite with other people or at the very least park in the lot of a Pemex station.

● Travel with another person whenever possible. Women should never travel by themselves in remote areas—this is an open invitation to trouble.

● Finally, if you do get robbed, don't resist. Thieves are usually scared to death, they just want to get the money and run. Give it to them. Say absolutely nothing. If you don't move, resist, or talk, your chance of bodily injury is minimal—that's what the experts say!

PERSONAL SAFETY FOR WOMEN

The basic rule for women traveling in Mexico is not to travel alone. Single women are breaking a cultural taboo, and their behavior suggests sexual promiscuity. This is true even on the beach. Following are tips from women who have traveled extensively in Mexico:

● Travel light. Remember that the weight of your luggage will affect both your attitude and your vulnerability.

• Try to get by with a single piece of luggage, one no larger than a carry-on bag for a plane. This gives you freedom and mobility in every situation from public transportation to checking in at a hotel.

• Two women traveling together are much better off than a single woman, but they should still be wary and avoid provocative situations.

• Schedule most of your long-distance travel for the day. Try to avoid travel at night when you're more vulnerable.

• Women do not go out at night alone in Mexico—with the exception of prostitutes and foreigners who don't know better. Find an escort for evening entertainment or go with a tour.

• Be unattractive! This is totally contrary to what most women have been taught. Watch your hair—cover it up, keep it in a tight bun. Skip makeup, any kind of nail polish, and no perfume.

• Watch your dress. Avoid tight-fitting clothes which show off your figure. Don't wear high heels. And don't expose much of your body, especially your breasts and legs.

• Don't get into a cab by yourself and make sure that you're not the last person to be left off. You can almost always share a ride (see p. 191).

• In a hotel, have your key in your hand as you make your way to the room. You'll avoid fumbling through your purse outside the door.

• Almost all hotel rooms have bolt locks in addition to the regular lock. If the lock seems flimsy, jam a chair underneath the knob to make it difficult to open.

• It is not unknown for a proprietor of a hotel to take advantage of a pass key to make a pass. Bear this in mind when bolting or blocking a door.

• Do not accept gifts from Mexican men, unless you want a sexual relationship. The meaning of the gift outweighs its value and may force you into a compromising position.

• Remember that many bars are off-limits to women. Your appearance in a cantina could set something off.

• Simply ignore hissing and staring in the street—don't respond to any comments. If someone starts to hassle you, turn and say, *"¡Deja me!"* which roughly means, "Leave me alone!"

• If it's possible, always let someone know where you're going and when you intend to be back. This could be a friend or just someone at the front desk of a hotel.

DANGEROUS HIGHWAYS

Certain routes in Mexico have been the source of more problems than others. Any person driving through the following areas should be especially cautious:

Highway 15 through Sinaloa.
Highway 2 in the Caborca area of Sonora.
Highway 15 from Nogales in Arizona to Mexico City.
Highway 40 from Durango to the Pacific Coast.
Highway 185 crossing the Isthmus of Tehuantepec.
Highway 57 between San Luis Potosí and Matehuala.
Highway off 185 from Palomares northwest to Tuxtepec in Oaxaca.

Up-to-date information on personal safety

• Updates regarding travel in Mexico are available from the U.S. Department of State, Citizens' Emergency Center at (202) 632-5225.

• Updates are available in Canada from the Department of External Affairs in Ottawa at (613) 992-3705.

TIPS ON REGISTRATION

If you're planning on traveling extensively through Mexico or if you plan to spend several months in one area, register with the appropriate consulates (see p. 370) during your stay in Mexico.

• The consulates want to know where you are so that they can get messages or information to you in an emergency.

HOTEL FIRES

Few travelers realize how common hotel fires are because most of them are contained and cause very little concern. However, in the event of a fire here are a few safety precautions that might save your life.

• Note all exits on your floor. Try to form an accurate picture of where they are in relation to your room. During a fire it may be impossible to see exits through the smoke. Count doors to the exit, to know where it is.

• Open these exit doors to make sure that they haven't been locked and that the stairs leading down are clear. If they're locked, find out why at the front desk. Consider changing rooms if the explanation seems fuzzy.

• Check to see whether or not there's a fire escape from your room or from your floor.

• Get used to putting your key in the same place each night so that you'll always know where it is.

• If a small fire starts in your room, put it out if you can. Sometimes smothering a fire works better than trying to douse it with water.

• If the fire's out of control, leave the room immediately. Close the door behind you to contain the fire and pull the fire alarm (if there is one). Rush to the front desk and report it *immediately.*

• If you see a fire start in another part of the building, pull the fire alarm and call the fire department. Then immediately tell the front desk about the problem.

- If you don't know where a fire is and are reacting to an alarm, use the fire escape from your room or head immediately to a fire exit down the hall.

- If the door knob or door to your room feels hot, don't open it. The fire is too close and may sweep into your room as soon as the door opens.

- If the door is cool, head to the nearest fire exit.

- Always leave your room with your key in hand so that you can get back in if your escape is somehow blocked.

- If there's a lot of smoke, stay as close to the floor as you can. Cover your mouth and nose with a moist towel. But don't continue if the smoke seems too thick.

- In a fire *never use an elevator* as an escape route.

- If the stairwell going down is blocked by fire, consider going up to the roof. Many people have been saved from the top of buildings, and few people think of this alternative during the panic of a fire.

- If all fire exits are blocked completely, then return to your room. Phone the fire department and the front desk so that they know you're in trouble. Be sure to give them your room number. If you can't get through to the front desk, call the front desk of a hotel nearby.

- If you have a tub in your room, fill it with water. If you've only got a sink, fill that. Soak towels, sheets and even curtains in cold water. Stuff some of these into the openings around the door to keep smoke from coming in.

- Douse the door and surrounding area with as much water as you can. Soak the entire area thoroughly and as often as necessary.

- Try to cover vents (they can bring in smoke) if it's possible.

- If smoke does begin to filter into the room, stay low to the floor. Cover your face with a damp towel so that you're breathing through it.

- If the smoke becomes intolerable, open the outside window. The top of the window should be open twice as far as the bottom to draw the smoke from the top of the room.

● Never open a window if the air in your room is clear. You may inadvertently draw in smoke from the outside, and smoke is often more dangerous than fire.

EARTHQUAKES

Earthquakes are common in Mexico. In some years several hundred are detected, in other years very few. Here are tips just in case:

● Many of the larger buildings in Mexico City have been constructed to sway (but not give way) during major quakes. Do not be alarmed by this motion.

● Get away from walls and windows, preferably under a table, desk, or bed.

● Standing in a doorway is a good option in smaller buildings or structures that may collapse.

● Never use elevators during a quake and avoid stairways as well. You're better off staying put in a room!

● If you're out on the street, go to the center of the road if possible—watch out for panicky drivers. The façades of buildings tend to crack and fall away in earthquakes, so try to keep clear of them.

● If you're driving, slowly come to a stop and simply sit the quake out in your car.

PACKING

What to take, how to pack it—some of the most basic questions! Read this chapter to simplify the process of finding answers.

DRESS IN MEXICO

- Dress is extremely casual in most areas of Mexico. Rarely is a man expected to wear a coat and tie, comparable dress goes for women.

- Formal dress is only necessary for business meetings, dining out in elegant restaurants in Mexico City, and a few places in major resorts, and at jai alai games.

- The average tourist can get by with simple, casual clothes —nothing stylish at all. In fact, smart travelers keep a low profile while traveling in a country which is quite poor.

Dressing for the weather

- Mexico has one of the best all-around climates in the world —one of its major attractions, especially for winter travel.

- However, mountainous areas in winter can be chilly to extremely cold (watch out on the Copper Canyon ride!). Even

167

buses in tropical areas can be chilly at night or with the air-conditioning on in the day. Bring something warm even though 90 percent of the time you won't need it.

● Most of your clothes should be cotton or cotton-blend. Cotton breathes in hot climates, which makes it the most comfortable fabric to wear.

● Wear light-colored clothes. Mexicans use a lot of white for obvious reasons.

● Keep your clothes loose. Tight-fitting clothing is uncomfortable in hot weather. On women it is sexually provocative and can cause serious problems (see p. 161).

● Have a hat. If you forget, buy one in Mexico. Caps, visors, tennis hats, sombreros—any of these are fine to protect you from the sun. You'll need it.

● Keep your shoes comfortable. Forget style. Shoes can be very casual. Many young and old travelers wear nothing but tennis shoes for the whole trip. Visiting ruins, climbing steep stairs, walking on cobblestone streets, strolling along a beach —these are activities which require comfortable, casual shoes. No one cares in the least whether you're fashionable or not (except in discos and elegant restaurants).

Tips for women

● Keep makeup extremely simple while traveling. Foreign women living in Mexico suggest no makeup at all. You do not want to attract attention, you want to fade into the crowd to avoid robbery and sexual harrassment.

● Leave your valuable jewelry at home. You can buy inexpensive silver and gold imitation jewelry in countless stores and street stands in Mexico. Mexican women wear it everywhere, and you can't tell it from the real thing.

● Remember that strong perfumes and cosmetics can make you sun-sensitive. So can some antibiotics (see p. 78).

● Samples of beauty products are light, small, and easy to carry. Collect them for short trips.

- A denim skirt is more comfortable than jeans. It has all the advantages and more—it doesn't stain easily, doesn't show wrinkles, and it breathes. It's also very plain, an advantage in Mexico.

- Carry a flat, large purse for all your odds and ends—a folding umbrella, a camera (best kept out of sight), a snack—you name it. Keep your makeup in a makeup case and your money in a wallet or change purse. These fit nicely into the larger purse.

- One of the most versatile items to pack is a *long,* cotton beach robe. Not only can it be used on the beach as a coverup or beach blanket, but it can pass as either casual or elegant dress. It's extremely easy to keep clean, weighs very little, and packs tight with little wrinkling—absolutely fantastic!

PACKING LIGHT

- Do it like the pros—stewardesses, travel writers, experienced business people, correspondents—travel light. Try to get by with one piece of hand luggage. If you can't carry it on a plane, it's too large. If you can't carry it for a mile without setting it down, it's too heavy.

- It's natural for you to feel somewhat skeptical about traveling with only one piece of carry-on luggage. Questions will pop into your mind: "Can I really get by on only a few clothes?" "Won't I be embarrassed by wearing the same outfits over and over?" "Can I get by in more formal places with less than formal clothes?" "What do I do about climate changes?" "What happens if something gets stained?" And so on.

- If you choose your clothes wisely, you'll have no problem at all. The reaction to this style of travel is always the same: Are you ever smart! As long as you're clean and comfortably dressed, you'll exude an aura of contentment and confidence. Mexicans judge you more by this attitude than by your clothes!

How to pack light

- Leave electrical items at home. They're heavy, bulky, and can be damaged by varying voltage.

- Pack only items you need to survive—the essentials. I met one person who considered a toothbrush as the only item essential for travel!

- Make each item serve as many purposes as possible. A bathing suit or bikini can pass as underwear. A one-piece woman's swimsuit can be converted into a dress by adding a wraparound skirt of the same material. Shampoo can wash not only hair but the body as well—think versatility.

- Go for comfort first, style last. But the two need not be mutually exclusive. As mentioned, style is less important than attitude in Mexico.

- Make sure all clothes are light, easy to wash, and quick-drying. Test them before you leave. Pick up heavier items for special needs (such as a *serape* for cool weather) in Mexico.

- Spray water-repellant on any materials that are suited to such treatment. This will help keep them stain-free.

Basics of packing

Use the rolling technique to keep clothes wrinkle free and accessible in a small bag.

- Lay slacks or pants out on a flat surface (such as a bed) with the leg seams together. These will serve as a base.

- Fold such things as t-shirt, halter, sweater, turtleneck, or shorts in half lengthwise, with sleeves together. Lay these out evenly on both the top and bottom portion of the slacks.

- Roll the clothes into a loose ball, working from the pants legs up and hold them together with a large rubber band or slip the ball into a plastic bag—the latter is much easier.

- Clothes in a plastic bag slip in and out of luggage very easily. The plastic also protects them from dust, dirt, and any liquids that might spill accidentally.

• You just unroll the ball to get to whatever item you need later on.

Packing toiletries

• Put all liquids in plastic bottles. Place each bottle in a separate plastic bag, so that your luggage won't get soaked if it leaks.

• To prevent leaking: Gently squeeze the bottle as you put the top on to create suction. Seal the top with tape for full protection (just for plane flights).

• As you use up your toothpaste and other creams in tubes, roll tubes up tightly so that they will take up less space. Carry two small tubes of such products instead of one large one, if you'll be traveling extensively.

• Keep all toiletries in one place, like in a makeup case, so that you can get to them easily at any time.

PACKING LARGER SUITCASES

If you've decided not to travel light, here's a helpful tip:

• Plastic bags keep clothes from getting wrinkled. Slide each shirt, jacket, or skirt into a separate bag. Lay the clothes flat or folded once into the suitcase. The film of air retained between the plastic and clothes will keep them wrinkle free. Jackets and coats can be kept on hangers so that you can whip them out of the suitcase in their plastic wrap and hang them immediately in a closet. The plastic used in average dry-cleaning establishments is just fine.

Packing garment bags

• Hang a number of clothes on no more than two hangers. If you use too many hangers, the bag will become bulky and hard to handle.

• Light plastic hangers with rounded corners work best. They don't rust, jab you with pointed ends, and they help keep clothes in their original shape.

• You can stuff an incredible number of small items into the bottom of a garment bag. The temptation to do so can result in a heavy bag!

PROTECTING AND CARRYING VALUABLES

The best way to protect and carry valuables such as a passport, plane tickets, traveler's checks, and money is to make or buy a secret pocket which slides under your clothes against your hip. It is attached by loops directly to your belt.

TRAVELERS' CHECKLIST

A trip should start off relaxed, so pack well in advance of your departure. If you do, you will have a chance to check, and recheck what's packed and to remember things you've overlooked.

Use this checklist to help you pack. It's an exhaustive list, one which covers many different styles of travel. You should only take those things essential to the enjoyment of a trip and matching your particular brand of travel.

Anyone traveling by car or RV should note that there is an additional checklist included in the car travel section on p. 101.

Address book   Don't leave home without a small, light, thin address book to fill with names of new acquaintances and to refer to if you write home. Absolutely invaluable!

Adhesive tape   A good item for backpackers and anyone getting off the beaten path. Lots of potential uses!

Airline tickets   Keep these in a safe place. They're as valuable as cash.

Alarm clock   Don't rely on hotel wake-up services in Mexico. If you'll be traveling at off hours or are going to have important business meetings, take a tiny travel alarm.

Alcohol   *(drinking)*   Alcohol is cheap in Mexico. You might want to carry a flask of booze with you for flights or train trips. A bottle of imported wine makes a good gift in Mexico.

Alcohol *(rubbing)* Backpackers and hikers might want to carry some along.

Aloe vera gel This helps heal minor cuts and is good for sunburn.

Amebecide You can buy similar products in Mexico, but it can't hurt packing this with other medications, especially for remote areas.

Ammonia solution See the medical section for possible uses. Good for remote or off-road travel.

Antacid Everyone should carry a few tablets. If you've got chronic problems, take all you could possibly need.

Antiseptic ointment Carry a small tube for minor cuts and rashes. These can be quite dangerous in the tropics.

Antivenins *(scorpion and snake)* The average traveler will have no problem with snakes and scorpions, but if you'll be getting into remote areas, consider taking them.

Art supplies Hard to find and expensive in Mexico.

Aspirin A must. Take along one of the small plastic or metal boxes that contain at least a dozen tablets. For longer trips take a plastic bottle of pills.

Backpack No matter what your age or style of travel, these can make carrying gear much easier.

Baking soda For campers and off-road travel.

Ball *(rubber)* Good ice breaker with kids and stops sinks in a second where no plugs are available.

Band-Aids Bring a few. They're light and take up little space. Put them on blisters *immediately* to stop them from getting worse. Note that the Mexican version of Band-Aids are next to worthless. They won't stick.

Bandana Lightweight and very versatile. Used as sweat band, table cloths, food wrap—lots of uses.

Bathing suit Bathing suits can double for underwear if they're easy to wash, quick-drying, light, and comfortable. Fifteen minutes is all it takes to dry out a suit in the sun after swimming or washing. If you're skeptical, test the idea before you start a trip. Pick suits that don't bind or have tight elastic belts.

Bathrobe Not essential and easily replaced by a beach robe. Leave it at home!

Batteries Bring a few extra for portable radios and flashlights. If you forget, ask for *pilas* in Mexico.

Beach robe Essential. Make sure it's cotton and very long.

Beach towel Many hotels provide only the smallest and flimsiest towels for their guests. However, beach towels are hard to carry, heavy, and very bulky. Nice, but not geared to lightweight travel.

Belt   Needed if you'll be carrying a secret pouch. Can be replaced with scarves on dressier occasions.

Binoculars   Very useful for birds, whale-watching, bullfights, and even ballet. Think seriously about bringing a lightweight pair.

Birth certificate   This can be used as identification in Mexico instead of a passport. It must have a raised seal (imprinted) to be official.

Birth control pills   Bring extra, just in case you stay longer than you expect. In Spanish: *pastillas anticonceptivas*.

Blanket   Many times better and more versatile than a sleeping bag. Blankets *(cubiertas)* are sold everywhere in Mexico.

Blazer   Fine if you'll be in formal situations, otherwise useless. Travel with one made of tightly woven material, dark-colored, and stain and wrinkle-resistant. Spray with water repellant.

Blouse   Take two at most—one light-colored, one dark (or print). They should be light and easy to wash.

Boat   A small, simple boat will help fishing immeasurably. Don't get too fancy.

Boat permit   You have to have one for Mexico (see p. 320).

Body lotion   Have something to put on your skin after bathing and suntanning.

Boots   Bring a good pair of hiking boots if you'll be hiking or backpacking into remote areas. Break them in before you go to Mexico. Old boots are best.

Bottle   You'll need some sort of container for fresh juices and drinks. Plastic bottles get warm quickly and take on the odor of whatever's been in them. Glass bottles work best and can be found easily in Mexico.

Bottle opener   One of the most useful and easy-to-forget items. Many Swiss Army knifes have openers on them, but you're not allowed to bring these knives onto planes in carry-on luggage. So pick up an opener or versatile knife in Mexico.

Bottle stopper   Most grocery stores have stoppers or plugs for bottles. Essential.

Bra   Bring no more than two. Substitute a bikini top if possible. In *resort* areas the bra is obsolete.

Bucket   Either bring or buy one in Mexico if you'll be camping out. *Cubo* in Spanish.

Burner   An absolute must for cooking. The alcohol burners in Mexico are really cheap as is alcohol *(alcohol)*.

Burn ointment   Bring or buy something to take care of sunburn and burns (especially campers).

Calamine lotion   Great for relieving the itching of insect bites and bee stings. Necessary for campers and off-road travel.

Calculator Not a bad idea, if you take a slim, ultra-light kind. Good way to break the language barrier in bargaining.

Camera and film Great to have, but a hassle. Bring only if you're serious. You're allowed one camera with twelve rolls of film. Many people take more without any problem at all.

Camp cook set Keep it light and easy to use.

Can opener Absolutely essential, if you'll be shopping for meals in Mexico. Known as an *abrelatas*, just in case you forget to bring it.

Canteen Bring a canvas one, the kind that breathes and keeps water cool.

Cards *(playing)* Easy to forget, but a wonderful way to while away the hours—and there'll be lots of them.

Change purse You'll be carrying lots of change. You need change constantly, so a change purse makes sense.

Chapstick Essential. Get the kind that contains sunscreen.

Cigarettes (U.S.) Mexicans love them—a good way to break the ice, even if you don't smoke.

Coats Bring only one. A medium-weight jacket is most versatile.

Coffee *(instant)* Good for a quick lift in the morning.

Cold remedies Colds are common in Mexico. If you're susceptible to them, bring a medication which works for you.

Collapsible cups Lightweight, easy to use, and sanitary.

Comb Essential.

Compass A tiny pocket compass comes in handy for any kind of travel in Mexico. Carry one.

Corkscrew Many knives have these on them. Most travelers skip wine in favor of Mexican beer anyway.

Corn pads Hard to find when you need them. Carry a few with you.

Cosmetics Take as few as you can get by with. Keep them in a separate case.

Credit cards Very helpful, with many travel advantages.

Curling iron Can you get by without one? If not, make sure it's the lightweight, flat, plastic kind.

Currency Bring as much U.S. currency as you can afford to lose. You'll get a good rate for it on the black market. Bring at least thirty or forty $1 bills for many smaller transactions.

Day pack Small day packs come in handy for a million uses. Have one with you.

Dental floss Can be used to cut cheese and doubles for thread if you forget some.

Deodorant If you're flying, don't take aerosol cans.

Desenex   Bring one small tube if you're susceptible to athlete's foot or similar complaints.

Diapers   As if you could forget.

Diarrhea pills   The best require a prescription. Odds are you'll need them.

Diving gear   Anything to do with sports is expensive to rent or buy in Mexico. Bring your own. If nothing else, bring your own regulator.

Drain plug   A whimsical item, but very useful. A wet sock or a rubber ball work almost as well.

Dress   Take one which is easy to dress up or down. If the dress gets clingy, hang it in the bathroom while you take a bath or shower. The steam will help prevent static electricity.

Drugs   Take as many prescription drugs as you'll need for the entire trip, plus enough for a week or two to spare. Leave all drugs in their original containers. If the pharmacist puts drugs in a large container, ask him to divide the contents into two smaller bottles. In the case of narcotics, it's best to carry a prescription with you. And always ask for the generic name of a drug in case you have to get it in Mexico.

Ear plugs   If you're sensitive to noise (and Mexican hotels are unbelievably noisy!), then these are a great item to bring along. Get the easy-to-mold kind, like *Flents*.

Egg carton   Don't laugh! These can be hard to find in Mexico and are ideal for campers.

Electric razor   Small, light travel kits consisting of a compact safety razor and a few blades make more sense, but there are good battery-operated razors on the market. Check into them.

Emery board   Easy to forget.

Eye drops   Likewise.

Extension cord   Surprisingly useful.

Feminine hygiene products   No problem buying these in Mexico.

Filters *(for lens)*   Get a good polaroid filter for your camera. It protects the lens and cuts out much of the bright light.

Fingernail clippers   Very handy.

First-aid kit   Gear it to your style of travel.

Fishing gear   Bring your own—very expensive and hard to find in Mexico. There are no import regulations on this.

Fishing license   Get it before going to Mexico (see p. 319).

Fishnet shopping bag   Essential. Light, compact, tough.

Flannel shirts   Wonderful for any style of travel. The front pockets prove especially useful. Tough, easy to clean, versatile.

Flashlight   Get a good pocket-size model. Essential for walking, groping, and seeing in dark places, including your hotel room. Also helpful in dark bus and train stations when the lights go out.

Flask The metal kind are best in warm areas. The plastic take on the odor of whatever you put in them. Wash flasks out frequently to avoid the growth of dangerous bacteria.

Food Have some with you at all times for inevitable delays and snafus.

Frisbee Fun and good for digging holes in sand.

Glasses One spare of both sunglasses and prescription glasses.

Gloves Golf gloves come in handy for skin diving.

Grill A small one for cooking out.

Guns Only with a permit.

Gun permit Hard to get and expensive. See p. 329.

Hairbrush Wonderful.

Hair conditioner Often hard to find. Make sure it's in a plastic container, tightly sealed, and placed in a plastic bag.

Hair dryer Women for centuries got by without one. Can't you?

Hair spray Get by without it, if possible. If not, take a small plastic container with pump.

Halter Useful as a t-shirt or bra (or both).

Hammock Pick one up in Mexico if you'd like to be a swinger (many hotels have hooks for hammocks in the Yucatán).

Hankies Use disposable tissues instead. Buy as necessary. Not found in budget hotels.

Hat Bring one! Or buy a sombrero from a street vendor—it'll last about two weeks before it cracks.

Hatchet A good tool for campers. A machete works just as well and can be bought in Mexico.

Heater *(immersible)* A very clever gadget that heats up water quickly. Very useful and easy to use in Mexico.

Huaraches Buy in Mexico.

Hydrogen peroxide Good for throat infections, toothaches, and minor cuts. Consider for your first-aid kit.

Insect repellant Get the strongest kind you can find. Mosquitos manage to get into many hotel rooms. Absolute must if you're camping out.

International Certificates of Vaccination The "yellow card" which records your immunizations—handy to have.

International Student Identification Card All students should get one. See p. 46.

Iron If you have to travel with one, get the tiny portable travel irons.

Jacket It's warm in Mexico, but you'll still need a jacket at times. Bring one.

Jeans Accepted throughout Mexico and worn by many travelers, but quite sticky and hot.

Jewelry   Leave it at home—just a come-on for crooks and Romeos.

Juice squeezer   Pick up an *exprimidera* in Mexico for long-term travel and camping.

Kaopectate   A good diarrhea medication that comes in a plastic bottle for easy carrying.

Khakis   Better than jeans. Get a pair with lots of pockets or add extra pockets for odds and ends.

Knapsack   Accepted now almost everywhere.

Knife   You can no longer carry knives, even small ones onto planes. A good knife is invaluable, however. Buy one in Mexico. Note: knives are allowed in checked baggage.

Laces   Change the laces on your shoes or boots before going to Mexico. This way you won't have to take a spare set along.

Lamp   The light in many hotels is so dim that reading can be impossible. You can either carry a tiny lamp or buy a brighter bulb (many travelers do just that).

Laundry soap   Get a few travel packets.

Laxative   Just the opposite of what most travelers need in Mexico, but a few people have problems with constipation.

Light bulb   Pick up a *foco* of higher wattage to see in budget hotel rooms.

Lighter   Take one if needed.

Lip balm   Bring something to protect and care for your lips. They'll dry out in the sun.

Lomotil   A strong diarrhea medication that really works, but not recommended for casual or long-term use. Requires a doctor's prescription in the United States but is sold over the counter in Mexico for practically nothing.

Machete   Buy in Mexico for camping.

Makeup pencil and sharpener   So easy to forget.

Maps   Get good ones which match your brand of travel. You shouldn't have to pay for decent, serviceable maps (see p. 36).

Matches   Waterproof matches should be a part of every camper's gear.

Mattress *(air)*   Don't get a cheap one—it won't last. Bring a repair kit!

Mirror   One tiny pocket mirror is enough.

Moisturizer   Your skin takes a beating in Mexico. Come prepared.

Moleskin   Dr. Scholl's adhesive felt—better for blisters than Band-Aids.

Mosquito netting   Needed for camping out in much of Mexico depending upon the time of year. Called *pabellón* in Spanish.

Nail file   Easily packed.

Nail polish and remover   Can you get by without it? If not, be sure to put polish in a plastic bag. You may want to seal the bottle with candle wax for any plane flight. It's simply disastrous when polish leaks on your clothes. You can use nail polish to stop runs in hose.

Nasal spray Have trouble with your ears on flights? Use nasal spray before the plane makes its descent.

Needle and thread Bring one needle and a little thread (off the spool). Save travel packets given out in better hotels—these often have needles and an assortment of colored thread.

Nightgown Almost all experienced travelers do without a nightgown.

Notebook Think about it, makes interesting reading years later.

Nylons Not really necessary in Mexico.

Overcoat The same.

Pajamas Ditto.

Panties You can substitute a bathing suit for one pair. Since they're so light, bring several pairs—all nylon for fast drying.

Pants Cords and khakis are best, although many travelers go with jeans. Two pairs at the most.

Paper clips Bring a few.

Passport Not required in Mexico, but absolutely the safest and best form of identification. Bring one!

Pocket *(secret)* Carry your valuables in a secret pocket, the kind that slides under your pants or skirt. You can buy or make these.

Pen One of the most useful items abroad. Bring two—you'll invariably lose one.

Permission for minor Technically, minors have to have written permission to travel in Mexico. See p. 12.

Pillow Veteran travelers carry a small, down pillow for rides in public transportation. These squeeze down to next to nothing.

Plastic bags These have dozens of uses. One of the best is to protect cameras from dust.

Plastic plates Very useful, even if you don't plan to camp out.

Poncho Very versatile and easy to carry.

Postcards The simplest way to show someone what your home area looks like—very good.

Purse Big and flat. One of the most useful items to have.

Radio Tiny transistor and Walkman-type radios are prizes in Mexico. Use them for the trip, then trade or sell them at the end.

Raincoat Yes, bring one, even in the dry season, if you'll be traveling extensively. Just a cheap, lightweight one will do.

Rubber or nylon-braided clothesline Inexpensive, light, and useful. Great for hanging wet clothes in limited space.

Safety pins Bring one or two. Use them to keep pockets closed to protect your wallet—a secret pocket works better.

Saltwater soap   Pick this up in Mexico under the name *jabón de coco*. Great if you're camping out at the beach.

Sandals   Take a pair or pick up *huaraches* in Mexico.

Scarves   Just like gold to women travelers, because they're stylish, lightweight, compact, and versatile (they can be used as belts, skirts, and even shawls). Scarves replace jewelry, transforming one outfit into many.

Scissors   Small travel scissors prove useful, but are not indispensable. You can't have scissors in carry-on luggage anymore.

Seeds   You may think this item's for the birds, but packaged vegetable seeds make a great gift. Try to get packets with directions in both English and Spanish (can be tough to do).

Shampoo   Bring a small tube.

Shirt   Match shirts to your style of traveling. For casual trips flannel shirts work well.

Shoes   Take one pair of your most comfortable shoes. Don't bring shoes that need polishing. You don't want to worry constantly about how they look. Many people get by with a pair of tennis shoes. Think flat, comfortable, and casual. If you have to dress up, buy a pair of shoes in Mexico—it exports shoes to other countries.

Shorts   These are really out of place in Mexico except along the beach and in resorts.

Shower cap   If needed, get the light plastic kind found in hotel rooms. It scrunches down to nothing. On the other hand, you can wrap your head in a towel like a turban and do without a cap.

Skirt   Bring one that's easy to wash, dark-colored to hide stains, and wrinkle-resistant.

Slacks   You need no more than one pair. Have them baggy and comfortable with lots of pockets.

Sleeping bag   Bring a thin, down bag that will scrunch down to nothing.

Sleeping pills   Be sure to have them in the original container—carry a doctor's prescription, as well.

Sleeping sheet   Some hotels insist you have this. See p. 215 for youth hostel information.

Slip   No more than one, if any at all.

Slippers   Unnecessary. If you disagree, get the fabric kind that fold up into a tiny package. Or get slipper socks, the terry equivalent.

Snorkeling gear   Flippers are bulky and a pain to carry around. So just bring a mask, unless your whole vacation centers around snorkeling. Make sure the mask is a good one—try it!

Soap   Even little dives provide soap for their customers, although it's often already opened and used.

Socks   One pair to wear and one for a spare—of synthetic material. Both wool and cotton are preferred for hiking and heavy use, but they're difficult to wash and take a long time to dry. That's why synthetics are better for most travelers. To wash socks quickly: put them on your hands like surgeon's gloves and scrub them with a bar of soap.

Many hotels do not have stoppers in the sink. A sock works well as a replacement.

Sports coat   Only needed in a handful of hotels, restaurants, and at jai alai games. A dark color is best.

Sports equipment   No matter what's your game, bring the gear into Mexico. All sports equipment is extremely expensive and sometimes impossible to find. There are no restrictions on equipment brought into the country for personal use.

A tip: use gear once or twice to show that it's not for resale.

Mexicans will love you if you'll give, trade, or sell them equipment at the end of your stay!

Spot remover   If you travel with easy-to-wash clothes, you may not need this. If you're concerned, try Goddard's—one reader insists that it's the best.

Suit   Only necessary for business travelers.

Sunglasses   Match the glasses to how they'll be used, but bring a pair.

Mexicans love sunglasses and will trade the shirt of their back to get a good pair.

By the way, you're judged in Mexico by your shoes and sunglasses.

Sunscreen   The sun in Mexico can cause a lot of damage in a very short time. Start with protection, a sunscreen with lots of PABA. See p. 78 for detailed information on the sun.

Suntan lotion   Some lotions protect you from the sun, others just smell and feel good. The latter work best when applied after a shower in the evening.

Sweater   Bring a sweatshirt instead.

Sweatshirt   Much more versatile and comfortable than a sweater and just as warm. Bring one, especially if you'll be traveling extensively.

Swim suit   Standard issue for a country with 6,000 miles of coastline.

Swiss Army knife   Not allowed in carry-on luggage, but one of the most useful items imaginable. Get the kind with a bottle opener.

Tarp   A must for campers only.

Tea bags   Wonderful! They take up little space and weigh next to nothing.

Tennis shoes   How can you do without them?

Tent   Campers only.

Tie   Strictly for business and one or two places that are in the dark ages.

Toilet paper   Tuck a small wad into your purse or wallet. Refill as necessary. Many public toilets have zero toilet paper.

Toothbrush and paste   Bring a small tube and replenish as needed.

Tourist card   No tourist card, no travel in Mexico. See p. 10 for full details.

Towellettes   These come in many forms, some are even saturated in nail polish remover. Ingenious, and often useful.

Tranquilizers   Keep them in their original bottle and carry a prescription.

Trash bags   Can be used in countless ways and really a help for campers and RVers.

Traveler's checks   The only sane way to carry most of your money.

T-shirt   You'll probably live in it. You can also sleep in it. Mexicans love t-shirts, especially ones with snappy sayings and pictures from other countries. You'll find yourself trading t-shirts frequently.

Tucks   Available at drugstores. Very important for hemorrhoid sufferers.

Turtlenecks   Second-best to sweatshirts, but still good. Tend to be a little constraining and hot.

Tweezers   Ideal for splinters, cactus spines, and bushy brows.

Umbrella   Should be standard gear in the rainy season. If you're crossing the country in the dry season, you'll still probably hit a sprinkle or two. Get the small travel kind that folds down to less than fourteen inches.

Underwear   Use the new, synthetic-fiber underwear; easy to wash, quick-drying, and very colorful. Underwear can easily be replaced by bathing suits.

Velcro   More durable than buttons.

Visas   Necessary in Mexico only for long-term study and business travel (see p. 9).

Vitamins   Good idea for long-term travel.

Wash basin   For campers.

Wash cloth   For any traveler who needs one. Bring one with you, because they're rare in Mexico.

Watch   Wear an inexpensive brand that can be replaced for a few dollars. Leave your Rolex at home.

Wet Ones   Another version of towellettes and just as good.

Whistle   Basic survival gear for campers and off-road travelers.

Windbreaker   Ideal for cool evenings and boat trips—well-matched to Mexico's climate.

Woolite   Bring a few travel packets, if you're traveling with any wool items and cold water washables.

Youth Hostel card   See p. 215.

Zippers   The zipper is the best and safest way to have pockets closed in Mexico. Think zippers instead of buttons.

CROSSING THE BORDER

Crossing the border can be a few minutes delay or a potential hassle. This chapter will help you make the transition smoothly.

Basic Border Crossing Vocabulary

age	*edad*
baggage	*equipaje*
boat	*lancha*
boat permit	*permiso de barca*
border	*frontera*
car owner	*propietario de automóvil*
car permit	*permiso de automóvil*
chassis and motor number	*número de chasis y motor*
country	*país*
customs	*aduana*
cylinders	*cilindros*
divorced	*divorciado*
driver's license	*licencia de manejar*
guns	*armas*
gun permit	*cinegeticos*
hunting license	*licencia de cazar*
immigration	*migración*
inspection	*revisión*

insurance	*seguros*
license plates	*placas*
make of car	*marca*
marital status	*estado civil*
married	*casado*
minor	*menor de edad*
motorcycle	*moto*
number of doors	*número de puertas*
occupation	*ocupación*
outboard motor	*motor de fuera borda*
passengers	*pasajeros*
passport	*pasaporte*
pets	*mascotas*
profession	*profesión*
rabies vaccination	*vacunación de rabia*
registration	*registración*
single	*soltero*
state	*estado*
suitcase	*maleta*
title (to property)	*título (de propriedad)*
tourist card	*tarjeta de turista*
vaccination certificate	*certificado de vacunación*
widowed	*viudo*
year of car	*modelo*

THE BASICS

Here are a few of the main tips to keep in mind to avoid problems with officials when crossing the border into Mexico.

The tourist card

● No matter how you come into Mexico, you must have a tourist card *(tarjeta de turista)*. It can be filled out directly at the border or in the airport.

● This free card allows you to travel in Mexico and should be carried with you at all times. Always ask for the maximum allowable stay—presently, ninety days.

Immigration *(migración)*

- The immigration official will check the tourist card and match it to your form of identification.

- The best identification anywhere is a passport. You can use a birth certificate, but a passport is much better.

- If you're a minor, you need a notarized letter signed by both parents allowing you to travel in Mexico.

- If a parent is traveling with a minor child, then a notarized letter from the other parent granting permission for such travel is required. It's possible that you would not be allowed into Mexico without this letter. My experience: They didn't even ask for it.

Customs *(aduana)*

- Every tourist must pass through a customs inspection which varies from a few quick questions about your baggage to a thorough search through everything you've got.

- If you arrive in Mexico by plane, train or bus, these inspections tend to be routine.

- If you arrive by car or RV, you may be asked to pay a small gratuity to pass through customs quickly and efficiently. See bribes (p. 369).

- If you arrive by car or RV, your baggage will be sealed until you pass another inspection station farther inland. Don't tamper with the seals until you've been inspected the second time.

TIPS ON GOING THROUGH CUSTOMS

- Never volunteer information while going through customs. You'll seem suspicious if you do.

- Customs officials can ask you to tell them the exact amount of money you're bringing into the country and in what form you've got it.

- Always tell officials that your reason for travel is pleasure, unless you've got a visa for student or business travel.

• Say that all your belongings are for your personal use, unless it's obvious that you're bringing in a gift.

• Customs officials are suspicious of people carrying large amounts of tobacco and alcohol. Keep these to a minimum. You may even have to pay duty on amounts over the allowable quota.

• If you're entering Mexico with any expensive items, these may be noted on your tourist card. This means that you must leave the country with them or pay a stiff fee. These notations are meant to discourage the sale of items in Mexico.

• Certain items may require special permits to get through customs. Officials are very strict about guns, CBs, and movie cameras.

• If you have more than twelve rolls of film, take the canisters out of the cardboard boxes. This will show the official that the film is for personal use. Most of the time they'll let extra film pass.

• It is very useful to have a sharp filet knife in Mexico. A Swiss Army knife is equally useful. However, officials will sometimes confiscate these, especially if they're bright, shiny, and new. If you're carrying a tackle box, put the knives in the box so that they seem appropriate to the gear. Note that you can buy inexpensive knives in most Mexico markets.

• If you're bringing an unusual item into the country, such as a typewriter, expensive tape recorder, special film equipment, tell the official that you're a professional. This word seems magical. Still, it won't stop them from noting the items on your tourist card. But if often stops all the fuss about bringing the item into Mexico in the first place.

• Sexy magazines such as *Playboy* and *Penthouse* will be confiscated as pornographic material. Every official should have the right to read through such magazines as a censor, but you may cause a more thorough search wasting valuable time. Leave the magazines at home or buy comparable ones in Mexico.

● If you're bringing prescription drugs into Mexico, leave them in the original containers. Officials can get very sticky these days about pills outside the labeled bottles.

● You can bring in almost anything for personal use, but if it hasn't already been used, watch out—it can only lead to suspicion. Officials are constantly thinking gift and resale. But they'll generally accept reasonable quantities of anything—one TV, not two. Preferably black and white.

● Countries with strong agriculture are very worried about plant diseases—leave at home anything that grows or has been grown, including fruits that you might like as a snack. Eat them before crossing the border!

WHAT YOU CAN BRING INTO MEXICO WITHOUT DUTY

Personal clothing, shoes, and effects.
One camera with twelve rolls of film.
One movie camera of up to 8 millimeters with twelve rolls of film.
Used sports equipment for one person.
A limit of 20 packs of cigarettes, 50 cigars, and 250 grams of tobacco.
Fifty books.
One television.
One radio.
One pair of binoculars.
No more than 3 liters of wine or liquor.
Five toys.
Any medication. Prescription required for drugs.
Inexpensive gifts.
One typewriter.
One musical instrument.
One tent and set of camping equipment.
One canoe or kayak (not longer than 5.5 meters).
Twenty records or cassettes combined.
One bike (without motor).
Bedding.

Kitchen utensils.
One set of fishing equipment.
Two tennis rackets.
The luggage to carry these in.

The point: If it appears to be for personal use, you'll get in with it. Officials often stretch the "legal" limits if items don't appear to be for resale.

A few pointers on documents

• Keep your documents handy but in a safe place. Try to keep them in the same spot so that you don't lose track of where they are.

• Try to keep them as clean and nonmutilated as possible. Mexican officials can be very touchy about a shredded, stained tourist card.

Hassles

Not everyone whizzes through immigration with a token wave of the hand. If you haven't got much money, or, more importantly, look that way, you're in for a hassle. How you look will affect how you're treated.

• These are things that cause problems: long beards, long hair (the more unkempt, the worse), sloppy clothes, rings in your nose (women) or ears (men)—you've got the drift. The more conservatively you dress, the better.

Things not to say to officials

• Impatience and anger are the two things that really irritate Mexican officials—any impatient or sour comment, look, or attitude can only cause trouble.

• If you don't think your profession will look respectable on the tourist card, change it. Become a secretary or a business-person for a day. It isn't what you are, but what they think you are that counts.

• Never tell a Mexican official that you're coming to Mexico on business or to study. These require special visas. Just say you're a tourist—no one cares.

● Always be positive with officials. If you're nervous or uneasy, the official may pick up on this. If you treat them with respect, that's probably what you're going to get.

Where to cross borders—car and RV travel

Here are the points at which you've been able to cross the border at one time or another:

Algodones
Brownsville/Matamoros
Eagle Pass/Piedras Negras
El Paso/Ciudad Juárez
Laredo/Nuevo Laredo
McAllen/Reynosa
Mexicali
Nogales
Tecate
Tijuana

● These border crossing points are sometimes open, sometimes closed depending upon political winds and whims.

● Border checkpoint hours vary and change frequently. Any list would be out-of-date immediately. You'll have to call for information.

● By choosing more obscure checkpoints, you can avoid the long lines so well-publicized during crackdowns and capers (like kidnappings).

● Don't cross at night. Border officials on both sides of the border don't like to be bothered, and it's unsafe to drive at night in Mexico.

16

PUBLIC TRANSPORTATION

One of the simplest ways to keep travel costs down is to learn to use public transportation. It is incredibly inexpensive, very efficient, and quite fast.

GETTING SET TO TRY IT

The easiest way to learn about the ins and outs of public transportation in Mexico is to study the tips in this chapter and then try it. Many people are afraid to, overwhelmed by a perceived language barrier and the sheer number of people using the buses, trams, and subways. However, armed with information, you will find that this is one dragon that is not impossible to slay.

Public transit questions

Ask someone in your hotel to explain the public transportation system to you. If you ever get lost, go to the nearest hotel and ask again for information. Here are the basic questions:

What is the best way to get from A to B?
What is the least expensive way?
Do you have a map of the area?
Where do you get tickets? How much are they?
How do I get on the bus, tram, or subway?

- Don't be shy about this. People like to help other people. There's nothing wrong with being dependent. All travelers are.

Public transit tours

By using public transportation, you can often make tours at a fraction of the cost of organized tours. In fact, one of the best ways to get to know any town or city is to get on *any* bus or tram line and make a circular tour.

- In Mexico public transportation is so inexpensive that you can spend several hours roaming an area for pennies.

- In Mexico City you can get to all the major sites using public transportation (more on this later in the chapter).

- Always have lots of small change to pay the fares on buses, trams, and subways. You do not want to ask someone to break down large bills.

TAXIS IN MEXICO

Although you can use trams and buses in Mexico for a fraction of the cost of taxis, the latter do represent good travel value compared to fares in the United States and Canada.

Taxis and money

- In some areas, taxis are your only means of transportation, as from the airport into town. There simply may be no bus from the airport to the city center. Fares in this situation are usually government controlled.

- Before getting into a taxi in these areas ask the information booth or airline personnel for the exact fare into town.

- In a few areas, you may have to negotiate the price with the driver, but in most areas the driver must quote you the prevailing rate. Shop around if you have to.

Sharing a ride

- Your best strategy for keeping the cost of taxis down is to share a cab with other travelers.

• In many areas, shared rides are set up almost instantaneously *if* you ask for a *colectivo*. This is a magical word. A *colectivo* is a cab which takes more than one person into town, and the overall cost is divided by the passengers.

• The more people traveling, the less the individual cost.

• Sometimes, you'll ask for a *colectivo* and be put into a cab by yourself. The cab driver slams the door closed, and steps on the throttle. Stop the driver at this point. Repeat the word *colectivo*. The driver may shrug his shoulders and say something like, *"No hay pasajeros."* He's telling you that there are no passengers.

• Usually, this is a con. Each driver wants to take the fewest passengers possible so that the other cabs will have fares. It's a good "buddy system," but not so good for you. Insist on a shared fare, and you'll usually get one. Be patient!

• Since the buddy system is so strong, you're much better off setting up a shared fare before you get to the curb. This can often be done on the plane or in the airport at the baggage claim area. Be aggressive. Ask other travelers if they're going into town and if they'd like to share a ride with you.

• Your success ratio will be about 90 percent or higher. Very rarely should you have to take a cab by yourself into town. Couples can do this as easily as solo travelers.

• In some airports, you buy a ticket for a *colectivo* at a set price for the distance you're traveling. Going to a certain hotel? Well, such and such is the price. This is a good and fair system. Ask about *colectivos*.

• Mexicans share rides all the time. Smart foreigners will follow their lead. The cab takes each person to individual destinations, usually a Mexican's home or a foreigner's hotel. You'll often share cabs with Mexicans, a chance to rub shoulders with people who really know the country!

Taxis without meters

• It is always your responsibility to establish a price with the driver for any ride you want to take, whether shared or not.

- Prices should be firm and very clear. If you do not establish a price, you're setting yourself up for a real hassle. If there's a language barrier, use a pen and paper—nothing could be simpler.

- You need to be able to say only two things: your destination and *"Cuánto cuesta?"* The latter means "How much does it cost?" If you can't understand the answer, resort to pen and paper.

- Payment should be exactly what you agreed upon. Most drivers do not try to cheat you once you've agreed upon a price, but a few will. Don't let the driver intimidate you into paying more—a good reason to get all prices in writing. No one can claim that the problem is the language barrier in this instance.

- If you alter your agreement by having the driver stop for an errand or shopping, by having him drive to a new or added location, or by making any change at all, then the driver has every right to charge you more than the negotiated price. So each time you ask for a change, discuss the *new* price.

Tipping taxi drivers

- You are not expected to tip taxi drivers in Mexico.

- However, if a driver provides any extra service (like carrying bags for you), then tip for that service.

- If you hire a taxi driver as a guide (often beats renting a car for a day), then a tip is appropriate.

- In some areas, it may take a taxi driver several hours to get you to an off-beat location. Even though you have established a firm price for this service, a tip is appropriate for such long-distance drives.

Taxis with meters *(taximetro)*

- In most areas, taxis do not have meters. In Mexico City most do.

- If a taxi has a meter, it must be operating and used to determine fares.

• Make sure that the meter has been turned back when you get into the cab. Just point to the flag and say *bandera* to let the cab driver know that it has to be turned back.

Other tips on taxis

• Only use official taxis, especially in Mexico City. The odds of getting ripped off in unlicensed taxis are extremely high. Many of these unlicensed taxis seduce travelers with low prices and then really take them for a ride—watch it!

• Women traveling alone should always share a ride with another traveler. Being alone in a taxi puts you into a vulnerable position. Although rape in taxis is not common, it's not unheard of either.

• Taxis are not taking advantage of you when they add a surcharge to the fare at night. The added fee is usually 10 percent or so. Inquire locally about the custom for night fares.

• As in all countries, taxis can be extremely difficult to get in rainy weather or late at night. If it's raining, you may be smart to choose a restaurant close to your hotel. If you're going out for late-night entertainment, keep the weather and time in mind.

• Be wary of asking a hotel to call you a cab, especially if you're staying in a more expensive hotel. Many of these establishments are served by special cabs—ones that offer extra comfort (or no extra comfort) at an extra price. Insist on getting an ordinary cab.

• Although some travel guides tell you not to use cab drivers as sources of hotel information, I've found drivers to be helpful in Mexico. If you'll learn basic hotel vocabulary (p. 229), you can get the driver to take you to the kind of hotel that fits your style of travel and budget. Be explicit about what you want— and what price you want to pay.

• Some tours give vouchers for transportation from the airport to the hotel. These are not accepted as often as the tour company would have you believe. Taxi drivers sometimes refuse to take them (very common), so be sure to find out ahead of time how to use the vouchers and whether you'll be reimbursed if they're not accepted.

● In most areas, cab drivers try to charge more for a trip to the airport then you paid coming from the airport. You have to bargain aggressively to get a fair price. The simplest way to do this is to ignore the first cab and look for another one. The price often slides down immediately. Yes, this is a hassle, but you're in a rip-off situation, a very common one.

● Taxis, including *colectivos,* can be very difficult to find in peak holiday periods including Christmas, New Year, and Easter. Try to avoid all travel in these vacation times.

● Taxis can be a convenient way to cross the border from Mexico into the United States. The fare will be directly related to the amount of baggage you have (takes time and effort to clear customs with many bags). A good driver can make the entire crossing almost painless—tip accordingly.

LOCAL TOURS

Besides getting you to some local sights for a reasonable price, consider the other advantages of local tours:

● They can be used as an inexpensive way to get to another town without the fuss of public transportation. You just toss the return portion of the tour and stay in the other place.

● Tours offer a good way of meeting other people, who may be willing to join up with you as travel partners. If you're on your own, you may then share a room, or a car rental, or whatever, to reduce your travel costs.

● City tours sometimes pass by the local airport. Take the tour at the appropriate time and ask to be left off near the airport. This way you get both the tour and transportation to the airport for one price.

FERRIES

The main ferries that concern travelers in Mexico are the ones connecting the Baja to the mainland and those heading to Isla Mujeres and Cozumel in the Yucatán.

Ferry crossings

Ferries connect La Paz with Topolobampo and Mazatlán, Santa Rosalia with Guaymas, and Cabo San Lucas with Puerto Vallarta.

They also connect Isla Mujeres and Cozumel with the mainland.

Note that there is a hydrofoil between Cancún and Cozumel.

Useful ferry vocabulary

At what time?	*¿A qué hora?*
car ferries	*transbordadores de coches*
fare	*pasaje*
ferry office	*oficina de transbordadores*
next boat	*la próxima lancha*
passenger boat	*lancha de pasajeros*
pier	*embarcadero*
toilet	*baño*

General tips on all ferries

- Schedules change constantly, and there is no way for a guidebook to keep up with them.

- Local people are often as confused about ferry schedules as you are. You have to go to the ferry office to find out reliable times of departure and current costs. Do not assume the hotel clerk has either.

- There is usually an inexpensive way to get to ferries, because Mexicans use them regularly and don't have a lot of money to spare. If you want to cut costs, get to the ferry Mexican-style.

- If you keep your luggage to a minimum, you can easily take advantage of public transportation to and from ferries.

- However, public transportation and ferry schedules do not always match, so that you may have a long wait.

- Bring food and water with you when taking any ferry, not only because you'll get hungry on board but because you may get hungry waiting.

- The **classes:** *salon* (bus seat given out on a first-come, first-seated basis), *turista* (bunk which must be reserved three days in advance), *cabina* (cabin with bed and bath), and *especial* (suite with bed and bath).

- Ferries are very popular because they're incredibly cheap. This means tickets are sold out well in advance, especially for trips between the mainland and Baja (and vice versa).

- So the minute you arrive in a port, go to the ferry office and get your ticket. Go as early in the morning as possible (many Mexicans sleep out at these offices to be the first in line).

- Note that some ferries arrive at strange hours—like the middle of the night.

- Storms are the worst in September and October in the Sea of Cortez.

- If you're crossing with your car, you will not have access to it during the trip. If you want something, take it with you.

- Fares for vehicles are determined by their overall length.

Car ferries *(transbordadores de coches)*

Reservations for car ferries can be very difficult to get in Mexico. Here's some helpful advice which you won't find in other guides:

- You can only make reservations during the month that you'll be making the crossing. If you're traveling on March 17, call on March 1!

- Have someone who can speak Spanish make the call for

you. There is a distinct language barrier, and communicating on a telephone line filled with static can be difficult enough.

● Have the person get the name of the Mexican with whom he is speaking—this is crucial! No name, no guaranteed reservation—it will mysteriously disappear.

● The following office will handle this for you. You pay a service fee and for the call:

International Travel Service
3130 Wilshire Boulevard, Suite 502
Los Angeles, CA 90010
tel.: (213) 381-7707

● Most agents do not like to handle this business because there is no commission on ferry reservations. Even if there were a commission, it would be too small to matter.

Special warning to motorists

You do not have to have a car permit to drive in the Baja. However, to go to the mainland you must get one. It's much easier and faster to get this permit when you cross into Mexico than at a later time in the port of embarkation (see p. 97).

● If you do not have the correct papers with you showing that you're the owner of the car, your car will be confiscated!

PUBLIC TRANSPORTATION IN MEXICO CITY

Getting around Mexico City is an art, but one well worth learning. You can get just about everywhere in this huge town, if you just know a few basic tips.

About addresses

● Mexico City is divided into 220 neighborhoods called *colonias.* In each of these areas you may have a street of the same name, a Calle Juarez, for example. It's important to know neighborhoods as well as individual addresses.

● The *same* street or avenue may have three or four different names depending upon where you are in the city. Try to get a cross street for each address you're trying to find.

● In some areas, building numbers don't run consecutively, and this can really be a problem. Again, if you have a cross street, you'll at least be close to your destination and can ask for help locally.

From the airport into the city

Tips on getting into Mexico City from the airport follow and are arranged by mode of travel from least expensive to most expensive.

● If you have no or very little luggage, take the metro (least expensive) at the edge of the airport into the city. The metro from the air terminal subway station *(terminal aérea)* will get you to where you're going for less than a cent—unbelievable!

● There's a ticket booth in the airport for a SETTA bus which will take you to your hotel. There are different buses to different zones. The person in the booth will tell you which bus to take. This is very inexpensive.

● SETTA taxis are more expensive than the bus, but still very reasonable. Go to the *boletos de taxi* booth and buy your tickets there. These taxis are *colectivos,* and you will be paying for a shared ride according to the distance (zone) traveled.

● More expensive than the SETTA taxis are licensed taxis. Negotiate your price. Do not take unlicensed taxis no matter what fare they offer!

● You can rent a car, but don't. You do not need a car to get around Mexico City. You do not want a car in Mexico City because there's no place to park, the traffic jams are fierce, and the cost of parking is outrageous. You could go everywhere by taxi and still pay less than car rental, which is exorbitant on a daily basis. I haven't even mentioned how dangerous it is.

The metro—least expensive

The metro is the least expensive way to get around in Mexico City. The following tips will make using the metro manageable.

THE METRO—ADVANTAGES

● The subway *(metro)* is an incredible system now covering much of Mexico City. It is inexpensive, immaculate, quick, and safe—well-lit and heavily policed. An absolute gem.

● It is open from early morning to late at night and handles over 4 million passengers daily.

● You pay for one ticket, no matter how far you travel and no matter how many transfers you have to make to get to where you're going.

● You can get to most major tourist sights using the metro (occasionally combining it with other public transportation).

THE METRO—DISADVANTAGES

● The metro gets very crowded during rush hours.

● It can be hot and stuffy, again mainly in rush hours.

● Rush hours are from 8 A.M. to 10 A.M. in the morning, and from 5 P.M. to 7 P.M. in the evening.

● Crowds draw pickpockets, so you have to be wary.

THE METRO—RESTRICTIONS

● Technically, no backpacks or luggage is allowed in the metro. You're supposed to travel with no more than a briefcase, small bag, or shoulder bag.

● In reality, you can use the metro with a reasonable amount of luggage or a small backpack if you avoid the rush-hour traffic.

● You're not allowed to take photos in the metro.

THE METRO—THE RUSH HOUR

● During the rush hour certain cars are reserved for women and children only.

- If you're claustrophobic or can't stand crowded space, avoid the rush hours.

USING THE METRO

- To use the metro efficiently, get a color-coded subway map which outlines all routes and stops. Each line has its own color, each station or stop its own symbol.

- The map is available from information booths in the subway stations. Look for a booth labeled with a black "i" in a yellow circle. These booths are sometimes closed, especially on weekends.

- The map is also available in some hotels, in free tourist publications, and from tourist information offices (one is located in the airport).

- You can get around without the map, but it's much easier to have one, because it's best to plan your moves in advance.

HOW TO USE THE MAP

- Find out what metro stop is nearest your destination. You can get close to most hotels; the bus terminals, train station, and airport; to many of the finest and favorite tourist sights; and to most of the major shopping districts and department stores.

- In some cases, you'll have to combine the metro with bus, tram, pesero, or taxi rides, to get to where you're going.

- Each line has its own color. The direction the subway is going is usually the last station on the line. In some cases, it's the second-to-the-last station, which can be confusing the first time you use the system, because both stations may be used to designate one line. Example: Line 1 may be called *Observatoria* (end of the line) or *Tacubaya* (station next to the end). It's the same line heading in the same direction.

- To get to your destination you'll often have to make a connection from one line to another. Connections are made through gates marked *correspondencia*. Some of these involve quite long walks, so take a route with the fewest connections, even if it seems longer on the map!

- Maps showing all stops are located in every car. You can use these for reference. Each station also has its own symbol for quick reference and for those who can't read.

- With a map you can quickly tell whether you're heading in the right direction. By having your route planned from the start, you'll make fewer mistakes.

BASIC METRO VOCABULARY

andenes	platforms
boleto	ticket
dirección	direction
entrada	entrance
no pase	do not enter
salida	exit
taquilla (caja)	ticket booth
viaje	trip

BUYING METRO TICKETS

- Ticket offices in each station sell tickets at all hours that the subway is operating.

- Pay for the tickets with small change—do not use large bills.

- Tickets are extremely inexpensive, and there is a reduction if you buy five *(cinco)* tickets at a time.

GOING THROUGH THE GATE

- Follow the Mexicans through the gates. Simply insert the ticket into the slot and give it a light push. The machine will suck it in, and you can then push through the turnstyle.

GETTING ON THE SUBWAY

- Don't be timid, shove and push the way the Mexicans do. The strange sound you hear signals closing doors—and they slam shut!

GETTING OFF THE SUBWAY

- The area around the doors is usually packed. But try to get close to the door as your station approaches.

- Normally, you'll get out the right side of the car.

- In a few stations, you get out the left side. If you look at the route map in the subway car, you'll see these words in red under such stations: *"en estas estaciones la salida es a la izquierda"* ("in these stations the exit is to the left").

- If people are blocking your way, give a shove. Say, *"Con permiso,"* and the Mexicans will move for you.

GETTING TO THE TRAIN

- Signs will lead you to the correct platform.

- Follow the flow of traffic in peak hours. Mexicans use any available space, not paying attention to right or left in aisles or stairs.

- Use escalators whenever you can. If you don't, you may get exhausted from the high altitude. You may also want to walk at a slow pace for the first few days for the same reason.

SPECIAL TIPS

- The front cars usually have fewer people.

- The middle of the cars away from the doors offer more breathing room.

- Coming out of the subway to the street is often where you get disoriented. A small compass can help you a great deal (even though it sounds funny) and so can a good map.

Buses in Mexico City

- You can get just about anywhere in Mexico City and the surrounding area by bus.

- Buses cost more than the subway, are often very crowded, move at the snail's pace of traffic, and are favorites of pick-pockets—but they do get you to where you're going.

- Bus destinations are written on placards or white washed on the front window.

- As you get on the bus, state your destination. The bus driver will say *"si"* or *"no,"* and you'll know immediately whether you're getting on the right bus or not.

• Have plenty of small change to pay for the fare. No driver wants to change big bills.

• You get in the front and exit from the back. There's a button by the rear door which you push when you want to get off. Shout *"¡Baja!"* ("Stop!") if you're stuck in the crowd. The bus driver will wait for you to push your way to the door. Don't be timid.

Jitney cabs *(peseros)*

• Jitney cabs, cars, or combis, are *colectivos* which zip along designated routes with up to eleven passengers (sometimes more if people sit on each others laps).

• These are usually painted lime green or white with green stripes, you can't miss them.

• You have to wave them down to get in. If they're full, they won't stop. Some drivers hold their hands up to indicate open space.

• Some jitneys have automatic doors, and the driver will give you a dirty look if you try to shut them. Others don't have automatic doors, and the driver will give you a dirty look if you don't try to shut them.

• The secret to jitney cab travel is to know how to pronounce correctly the name of your destination. If the driver gives you a quizzical look, you flunked, go back to school. If the driver shakes his head or wags his finger, get in a different jitney (he may indicate which one), and if the driver nods and waves you in, you're heading home.

• The amount you pay is related to the distance you go. You don't have to pay when you get on. Drivers trust you. But when you get off, you pay. State the place where you got on so that the driver knows how much to charge. Fares are very reasonable.

Regular taxi

• The regular taxi is more expensive than the metro, buses, and jitney cabs, but fares are still quite reasonable.

- In Mexico City the fares on the meter do not represent pesos but a number which corresponds to a fare quoted on a price schedule *(lista)*. The units on the meter relate to distance and time as is true for taxis worldwide.

- This system can be confusing to foreign travelers. You have every right to ask to see the fare schedule to make sure that the quoted fare really does match the number of units registered on the meter.

- If you have any problem with a cab, write down the cab number and license plate. Have someone who speaks Spanish convey the complaint to the following number (588-6526). Lost items? Call 571-3600, ext. 14 or 15.

Sitio taxi

- Cab stands are listed in the yellow pages under *Sitio*. These cabs have their own little territory.

- They always charge more than regular cabs, even if they're hailed in the street. *Sitio* is written on the sides of these.

- You can call them to your hotel, but you'll pay for the service.

- Always establish a price immediately for any trip. You may end up relying on regular taxis after a bad experience with a *sitio*.

Turismo taxi

- Turismo cabs sit outside hotels like salmon-colored, sleeping sharks.

- The drivers usually stand next to the revolving door with a solicitous grin and a constant *"taxi, señor"* on their lips.

- The meters in these cabs are usually covered with a black hood. Don't let the wake be yours! These cabs charge exorbitant rates. Skip them and hail a regular cab in the street—it just takes seconds.

Getting from Mexico City to the airport

• If you have little or no baggage, you can backtrack to the airport using the metro. Go to the *terminal aérea* metro stop, not the *aeropuerto* metro stop (the latter doesn't get you all the way to the terminal).

• If you prefer to take a cab, ask your hotel to get a *colectivo* for you. Make sure you get the price clearly understood from the hotel employee. When the cab arrives, make sure that the price quoted by the hotel matches the driver's expectations.

• Note that these *colectivo* cabs don't always show up as scheduled, so give yourself plenty of time as leeway. You may end up hailing a regular cab in the street.

17

WHERE TO STAY

You'll want to match the wide variety of accommodations in Mexico to your budget and preferred style of travel. Whether you choose a deluxe hotel or a campsite on a secluded beach, here are some helpful suggestions.

GETTING WHAT YOU WANT FROM A RESORT

If you are one of the many people traveling to Mexico strictly for rest and relaxation in a resort, then this section is for you.

About the best-known resort areas

Matching the overall area to your personality is the first step in getting what you want from a Mexican trip. The following brief descriptions will help you narrow the field to one or two places:

ACAPULCO: Really a city curving around a broad bay with beautiful beach areas—noisy, crowded, and lively with prices for all pocket books. Known for its shopping and lively night life. Location and choice of hotel is crucial.

CABO SAN LUCAS/SAN JOSÉ DE CABO: Remote hideaways on the southern tip of the Baja. Geared to luxury travelers and jet setters seeking sun, fishing, and isolation in a desert-like setting. Easy access from California.

CANCÚN: A bit like Miami Beach with a Mexican accent (not quite so crowded). Very commercial—lots of topflight, luxury hotels on a series of small, pure-white beaches. Appeals to couples or families looking for safety, sun, and varied activities. Lots of shops, restaurants, and aggressive types trying to sell just about everything.

COZUMEL: The place to go for diving and snorkeling—the preoccupation of most visitors, who demand little else. Remote and peaceful.

ISLA MUJERES: Laid-back little island off Cancún. Appeals to backpackers and budget types content with sand, sun, seafood, and snorkeling.

IXTAPA: Luxury living in enclave by the sea. Very fine commercial hotels with all the trimmings, including facilities for tennis and golf. A bit of a country-club atmosphere, cut off from the Mexico of Mexicans.

LORETO: Moderate resort geared mainly to avid fishermen and Californians seeking refuge from hectic Los Angeles. Nice, but nothing fancy.

MANZANILLO: An "in" place with lots of charm. Geared to heavy spending and hard playing. Offers good sail fishing. Some of the finest accommodations in Mexico for someone willing to pay the price.

MAZATLÁN: Really a city cum resort area. The best hotels and beaches stretch to the north. Not as warm and sticky as resorts farther south. Varied restaurants, shopping, and night life. Good sail and marlin fishing (large fleet). Appeals to travelers on a moderate budget.

PUERTO ANGEL: What popular resorts were decades ago. Similar to Puerto Escondido in its attractions.

PUERTO ESCONDIDO: Laid back, low key—for the budget and backpacking set. People who come here form a free-floating family, often staying for weeks or months. Good seafood at reasonable prices. Good, if highly unorganized, fishing. Surfing as well.

PUERTO VALLARTA: A mini-mining town with cobble-stoned streets converted to a sophisticated and very popular resort. Best hotels are on the north and south of the city. Hotels in town are noisy and cheap. Broad beach, shopping, and frenetic night life. Fully discovered.

SAN BLAS: Lazy "jungle hideaway" with so-so to moderate hotels. Popular with explorer and hippie types willing to put up with nasty nauseums (bite like hell). The bugs have kept the area from developing despite its intrinsic beauty.

ZIHUATANEJO: The Mexican counterpart to Ixtapa and only a short drive away. Assorted beach and hillside hotels look onto charming bay filled with a handful of moored yachts. Small and manageable, but now well-known with constantly rising prices (no longer a bargain).

Choosing a hotel within a resort area

Can a resort hotel give you what you want? Does it cost what you're willing to pay? Fundamental questions when choosing a resort hotel!

WHAT ARE YOU WILLING TO PAY?

Although price and quality do *not* always go hand in hand, they are assuredly related more often than not.

If your demands are high, then expect to pay for them accordingly. However, even in expensive resort areas like Cancún and Acapulco, you can come up with functional, budget hotels which will keep the rain off your head for $10 or $15 a double.

WHAT DO YOU WANT?

The time to get what you want is *before,* not after, you get to the resort. Some hotels specialize in tennis or golf, others are geared to lazy life on secluded beaches, and still others offer pools with swim-up bars and hibiscus flowers floating in pineapples filled with potent drinks—so pick your place with what you want in mind.

RESORT CHECKLIST

☐   What's the weather like? Is it humid? Is it windy?

☐   Where is the hotel in relation to the town? Is it a good location? Can you get a map showing the exact location of the hotel?

☐   Is there free transportation to and from the airport to the hotel? Is there a parking lot? Does the hotel have cars?

☐   What kind of people go to the hotel? Does it take tours? Is it family-oriented? Do many singles go there?

☐   Is it a large or small hotel? Would you call it intimate? Or is it a large, commercial complex?

☐   Is the hotel on or near the beach? Does the beach come right up to the hotel?

☐   What's the beach like? How wide is it? What's the sand like? Are there beach chairs?

☐   Is the water good for swimming? Is it clear enough for snorkeling? Can you swim in the area? Is there an undertow or any problem swimming in the area (very real concern)?

☐   Are there any rooms with access directly to the beach?

☐   What kind of rooms are available? Any special rooms? Any special suites? Any villas?

☐   Is there a road between the hotel and beach (very noisy and disagreeable)? How close are other hotels to this hotel? How far from a main road is the hotel?

☐   Does the hotel have a pool? If so, is it used or just a token pool? Does it have water in it (no joke—some don't!). Is it kept up? Does it have a life guard (very few do)? Are there chaises longues for the guests? Is it in a good, open location or blocked off from the sun much of the day?

☐   Does the hotel have tennis courts? How many? Do you have to pay extra to use them? What surface do they have? Are they maintained? Is there a pro? What about equipment for sale? Are courts lit for night play? How far in advance do you have to make reservations? Do guests have priority?

☐   Is there a golf course? How far in advance do reservations have to be made? What are the greens fees? Are there carts and do they work? What's the best time of year to play? Is there a pro? Any equipment for rent or sale? What's the cost? Who has priority?

☐   Will your room face the ocean? Or will your room have an ocean view (a euphemism for seeing the water out of the corner of your eye while leaning over the balcony).

☐   Are hotel plans available showing where your room is located?

☐   The room has a balcony. Great! What size is it? Can it be used? Does it have a table and chairs? Can breakfast be served there?

RESORT CHECKLIST

☐   If you're using a travel agent, has he been to the hotel? Has he stayed there?

☐   What's the food like? Do you have to eat in the resort (you don't want to be forced to)? What's included in the full-board price? What's not? Do you have a choice in what dishes you can order with full room and board?

☐   What size are the rooms? What kind of beds do they have? Is there a bath or a shower? Is there hot water (silly question—no one ever knows). Are beach towels provided?

☐   What kind of water sports are there? Are masks and fins available? What about boats? Windsurfing? Water skiing? Parasailing? Fishing? How much do they cost? Is the equipment in good shape?

BEING REALISTIC

The resort hotel checklist is meant only to point out that glossy brochures are just that—paper with some words written on them. Photographers can do marvelous things with next to nothing. The questions you ask can help you get what you want.

Yet, you have to be realistic when traveling to Mexico, which means being willing to bend. Hot water, for example, comes and goes, even in deluxe hotels—you have to go with the flow. And that may mean taking baths or showers at odd times.

Requesting what you want is smart because it increases your odds of getting it. But don't count on it. Even such a basic thing as reservations can be bungled or disregarded in Mexican hotels.

FISHING HOTELS IN THE BAJA

There are certain people who go to Mexico to fish—and that's it. Fishing hotels in the Baja are unique. They're friendly, club-like, and very original. In some hotels you won't find telephones and TVs, because no one wants them. Such hotels attract a special breed of traveler—sophisticated and fun. Many of these hotels can be reached by private plane or charter flights.

- Some of the better fishing hotels in southern Baja include Cabo Baja, Cabo San Lucas, Finisterra, Hacienda, Los Barriles, Mar de Cortez, Palmas de Cortez, Palmilla, Punta Colorada (fabulous roosterfish fishing), Punta Pescadero, Rancho Buena Vista (World Festival of Fishing), and the Twin Dolphin.

- Reservations should be made as far in advance as possible in these hotels during the peak seasons.

- The following club specializes in travel to the Baja and has current fishing reports available to members:

Mexico West Travel Club
2424 Newport Boulevard, Suite 91
Costa Mesa, CA 92627
tel.: (714) 662-7616

CLUB MED

Club Meds have become a household word. These vacation resorts combine elegance and casual living with good food and good times. Although they once appealed mainly to singles on the swing, many are now opening up to families as well. Costs tend to be on the high side, but are a good value. There are three regular Club Meds in Mexico: Cancún, Ixtapa, and Playa Blanca.

Club Med
Box 29822
Phoenix, AZ 85038
tel.: (800) 528-3100
       (602) 352-3102

Club Med
40 West 57th Street
New York, NY 10019
tel.: (212) 977-2100

Club Meds at archaeological sites

Club Med opened up small complexes at the major archaeological sites throughout the country. No membership is required to stay overnight. Single rooms are available and stays of less than a week are allowed. There are no buffets as in regular Club Meds, but you'll find a pool and tennis in each. Libraries with information on the sites are maintained for those interested.

Club Meds are located at the following archaeological sites:

Cholula   Teotihuacán
Chichén Itza   Uxmal
Coba

VILLAS AND APARTMENTS

If you'd like to rent a villa or apartment for a stay in Mexico, check into the following organizations:

Creative Leisure   Travel Resources
951 Transport Way   3314 Virginia Street
Petaluma, CA 94952   Coconut Grove, FL 33133
tel.: (800) 426-6367   tel.: (800) 327-5039

At Home Abroad, Inc.   Villa Leisure
405 East 56th Street, #6H   P.O. Box 1096
New York, NY 10022   Fairfield, CT 06430
tel.: (212) 421-9165   tel.: (203) 222-9611

HOME EXCHANGE

If you'd prefer to exchange your home with a Mexican, here are two organizations with information on this process:

Vacation Exchange Club, Inc.   International Home Exchange
12006 111th Avenue   250 Bel Marin Keys
Youngtown, AZ 85363   Ignacio, CA 94947
tel.: (602) 972-2186   tel.: (415) 382-0300

INTIMATE AND ROMANTIC INNS

Many people want to stay in smaller, more intimate places that either have charm or class. Following are some of these special places, which offer something unique. Note that prices vary widely from moderate to deluxe in this special classification.

Acapulco

Villa Vera
Hotel Boca Chica

Alamos

Casa de los Tesoros

Cabo San Lucas

Twin Dolphin

Cuernavaca

Cuernavaca Racquet Club
Las Mañanitas

Guadalajara

Guadalajara Racquet Club

Guanajuato

Hacienda de Lobos
Parador de San Javier

Mazatlán

Balboa Club (requires introduction)

Mexico City

Hotel de Cortez
Maria Isabel

Morelia

Villa Montaña
Virrey de Mendoza

Oaxaca

Convento

Puerto Vallarta

Garza Blanca
Posada Río Cuale

Querétaro

Jurica

San Miguel de Allende

Casa de Sierra Nevada
Posada de San Francisco

Taxco

Hacienda del Solar
Hostería Don Carlos
Monte Taxco

Zihuatanejo

Villa del Sol

BUDGET CHOICES

The budget traveler has many options for low-cost rooms: inexpensive hotels, boardinghouses *(pensiones* or *casas de huéspedes),* furnished homes *(casas con muebles),* apartments, private homes *(casas particulares),* youth hostels, bungalows *(cabañas),* bathhouses, restaurants (believe it or not), and even whorehouses—all of which add up to anything from great to grubby.

- The key words are *bueno y económico*—good and cheap!

- There's only one way to come up with these places. Ask! Many remain totally undiscovered by U.S. and Canadian travelers and even companies producing budget guides.

YOUTH HOSTELS

The youth hostel movement is just beginning in Mexico, but you may still want to take advantage of the limited accommodations.

The American Youth Hostels (AYH) association issues youth hostel cards, which you must have if you're planning to stay in Mexican hostels. Costs vary according to your age. You can get information from any local branch or the central office:

American Youth Hostels
1332 I Street, N.W., Suite 800
Washington, DC 20005.
tel.: (202) 783-6161

Canadian Hostelling Association
18 Byward Market
Ottawa, Ontario K1N 7A1
tel.: (613) 230-1200

Asociación Mexicana de Albergues
de la Juventud
Av. Francisco I. Madero 6
Ciudad de México 1, D.F.
tel.: (915) 521-9191

Basics of hostels

- The age limit for a stay in a Mexican youth hostel is twenty-seven. However, parents are allowed in with children. And older hostelers with valid cards are accepted if space is available.

● Bring a sleeping sack (like a sheet), which you can make yourself or pick up from:

The Metropolitan New York Council
75 Spring Street
New York, NY 10012
tel.: (212) 431-7100

● Save money by eating in the communal dining rooms. The meals are always filling, and occasionally good.

Ground rules for hostels

● You help with the cleaning.

● Neither smoking nor radios are permitted in the sleeping area.

● There's a fifteen consecutive day limit on stays (unless there's room available).

● Lights out by 10:00 P.M., and you get up by 7:00 A.M. (Not necessarily adhered to).

● Hostels can close from late morning to late afternoon—so get there early to register for the coming night!

● If you want to reserve a room in advance, write to the hostel requesting a reservation. Enclose one night's fee and enough international reply coupons to cover an air-mail reply.

CAMPING

Camping is geared to a loose, free-flowing style of travel that is not compatible with limited time. If you've got the time, however, you'll find that campgrounds are well organized, often offering facilities that include showers and stores. You'll find many of them in Mexico, even near major cities.

Official warnings

● Mexicans will tell you not to camp by yourself or in a small group in remote areas.

- You should be wary camping in beach areas, unless you're with a large group.

- In short, you're much better off in recognized campgrounds which offer protection in numbers.

- Note that many campers and even some writers of camping guides tell you that these warnings are not true. Yet, the police reports I've seen would indicate that they are.

Other warnings—not quite so official

- Listen to discreet warnings about travel in certain areas. Someone's trying to tell you that you're going to stumble into a marijuana or poppy patch.

- Shy away from borders. They tend to be heavily patrolled and less than friendly places. In short, don't camp out near Guatemala.

Solo camping

- Officials say no one should camp out at anytime alone in Mexico.

- Some ardent supporters of camping out would say that the rule only applies to women. Nevertheless, everyone agrees that a woman camping alone in Mexico is inviting serious trouble. Don't do it.

International camping carnet

- Get an International Camping Carnet, the campers' passport, which entitles you to small reductions in campground fees.

For this card, contact:

National Campers and Hikers Association
7172 Transit Road
Buffalo, NY 14221
tel.: (716) 634-5433

Camping information

You can get guides and camping information from the following sources:

AAA (American Automobile Association)
8111 Gatehouse Road
Falls Church, VA 22047
tel.: (703) 222-6000

KOA, Inc. (Two campgrounds in Mexico)
P.O. Box 30558
Billings, MT 59114
tel.: (406) 248-7444

Sanborn's Mexican Insurance Service
P.O. Box 1210
McAllen, TX 78502
tel.: (512) 682-3402

Camping-gear checklist

Here are a few items which you will find essential for camping in Mexico.

Air mattress Get the best one available and bring a patching kit.

Alcohol burner This will be your stove. Alcohol is cheap in Mexico and easy to find. So are the burners.

Canteen The best canvas canteens breathe and cool the water even in the hottest weather.

Flashlight Absolutely essential. Bring a few extra batteries.

Grill This should be tiny, just large enough to cook something on. Carry it in a plastic or canvas bag.

Insect repellant The little stick kind is the most convenient. Get a really strong one.

Knife Don't get anything too fancy or shiny. It will be confiscated by the police. A decent Swiss Army knife with a bottle opener is best.

Lantern Not essential, but really nice.

Matches One container of waterproof matches.

Mosquito netting The single most important item to carry.

Plastic containers Enough for a variety of solid and liquid foods.

Pots For cooking.

Sleeping bag Can be replaced with a blanket or hammock.

Tent   Featherlight.

Toilet paper   Needed everywhere in Mexico.

Tools   To match your brand of camping. Pick up a machete in Mexico.

Water containers   Need a gallon of water per day per person.

Tips on camping equipment

● Know your gear before you go to Mexico, which means trying it out at home. Nothing's worse than a so-called water-proof tent which leaks or a mosquito net that's worn through.

● Bring the minimum gear for your brand of camping—for some that can be quite elaborate.

● Note that white gas can be difficult to locate in Mexico, which is why the alcohol burner makes sense.

The value of a good hammock

One of the most enjoyable ways to cut costs and enjoy the warmer areas of southern Mexico is to camp out with a hammock. Some hotels offer discounts to travelers who hook up their hammocks instead of using regular beds.

● Buy the S-shaped hooks made especially for hanging hammocks. They'll save you lots of time and are the easiest to use.

● Never hang your hammock so low that you'll scrape the ground. This will ruin the hammock quickly.

● Don't use the hammock as a place to sit or swing on. You should lie down in it, or you'll stretch the hammock in the wrong direction making it uncomfortable for sleeping.

● Mosquitos are a problem in many areas where hammocks are most enjoyable. Put a blanket down in the bottom of the hammock to protect your backside at night. Use mosquito netting over the hammock to protect you from night attacks.

● Store your hammock in a bag or container to protect it from rodents or insects.

Where to camp

You can camp almost anywhere in Mexico for free, since there are no laws prohibiting it. Note that beaches are public and cannot be privately owned (although access can be). Here are some free campsites:

NO-COST CAMPSITES

beaches (hassles with sand and salt mist)
bridges (just off to the side)
cemeteries (just outside)
churchyards
dams (look for the sign indicating *presas*)
gas stations
hot springs
microwave stations (look for *microondas* signs)
national parks
parking lots
plazas
quarries
schoolyards
side roads
soccer fields
spas
town halls

Other popular places to camp may cost a token amount. Here are a few low-cost campsite suggestions:

campgrounds
cheap hotels
thatched huts *(palapas)*
trailer parks

Where not to camp

There are certain campsites where you're asking for trouble. Following are some spots you'll want to avoid:

archaeological sites (officials discourage this)
hills (noisy with lots of trucks)
markets (busy at the break of dawn)

riverbeds (flash floods)
trails (dangerous)
villages (noisy with lots of kids)
swimming holes (noisy with even more kids)
windy areas (tough on you and tents)

Basic camping suggestions

• Always ask for permission to camp. It will rarely be denied. *"¿Por favor, podemos pasar la noche aquí?"*

• If you don't find anyone to ask, go ahead and camp. If someone shows up and asks you what you're doing, just say, *"Pasando la noche. Está bien?"*

• Leave the campsite spotless despite the incredible litter you'll see throughout Mexico.

Special precautions

• Never camp or sleep under a coconut palm *(coco)*. The coconuts drop with an alarming thud—one that can cause a great deal of damage to cars, tents, and unprotected heads.

• Don't eat any strange fruits. The manzanillo tree has both a poisonous sap and poisonous fruit.

• Always have a place that you can get to when the mosquitos hit at night.

• Read about scorpions on p. 76.

• If privacy is important to you, then have a place that you can block off as your own. Mexicans are fascinated with foreigners and will watch you for hours.

Getting your body clean

• One of the biggest problems in traveling on a shoestring is keeping clean.

• If you are by the sea, use coconut soap *(jabón de coco)* to wash with. This does the same thing as more expensive salt water soaps.

• Stop in at some of the RV and trailer parks and pay for a shower.

• In some areas as on Islas Mujeres you'll find showers in some of the beachside restaurants.

• Cheap hotels offer yet another alternative to get clean. Some will allow you to pay for a bath only.

• Public baths *(baños públicos)* offer inexpensive showers *(regadores).*

• With over 10,000 hot springs in the country you may come up with an ideal bathing spot for free. Watch for quick changes in temperature!

• And you can bathe for free in any number of streams, rivers, and lakes.

Tips on bathing in public

• Don't strip completely when bathing. Nudity can be a serious offense (see p. 333 for exceptions).

• Men and women should not bathe together, certainly not in public even if they are partially clad.

• The key word is discretion.

Getting your clothes clean

• No one expects a vagabond to be completely clean. You may want to carry one set of clothes for special occasions and live in a second set. Most Mexicans are not offended by dirt.

• Many women will gladly wash your clothes for a token amount. Settle on a flat rate for the bundle and provide them with a bar of soap *(barra)* or with powdered soap *(jabón en polvo).*

• Be specific on when you want your clothes back—if you aren't, you may not see them for days.

• You'll find laundromats in Mexico, but they're rarely do-it-yourself operations. You'll pay a flat fee for a load.

RV LIVING

RVs have become very popular with people traveling to Mexico, especially older people who would like to spend the winter in a warm, relatively inexpensive area. There are now many trailer parks throughout the country. Much of the advice given in the camping section applies to RVers. Here are a few speical tips:

Tips just for RVers

• You may no longer be able to buy propane for use in vehicles in Mexico. You can still buy the small containers, however. So fill up on propane before you come into Mexico, and convert your gas pipes to a hookup to portable tanks.

• RVs are big, and there are no shoulders on most Mexican roads. Never stop in the road, because you could cause a serious accident. RVs can make it through most towns and cities, but plan your route carefully and take the advice of others who have been there before—I saw one RV stuck in a narrow street with no way to get out (they probably had to dismantle it).

• Trailer parks by the sea fill up fast. The sooner you can get to your appointed place in late fall or early winter, the better off you'll be.

• Some trailer parks double as bordellos, which are not illegal in Mexico. If you're traveling with a family, keep this in mind.

• An awning is invaluable in Mexico because of the bright sun. Have one installed if you haven't got one already.

• There are very few dump stations in Mexico, so don't spend a lot of time looking for them.

• In emergencies you can leave your RV in Mexico. Check locally for exact details if you have to leave the country without it.

• Mosquitos can get fierce in some areas. If your screens are old or filled with tiny holes, the bugs will get in. Replace them.

● Here's a club devoted solely to RVers and which has cara-vans to Mexico each year:

The Good Sam Club
International Headquarters
P.O. Box 500
Agoura, CA 91301
tel.: (800) 423-5061
    (800) 382-3455 (CA)

● Odds and ends that are easy to forget: a water hose with extra gaskets (these break with frequent use or get indented so that water leaks out), roof sealer (should be applied yearly), velcro (great for tying curtains back), paper towel rack (you'll be using a lot of paper products), fly swatter, small rugs, exten-sion cord (plenty long), laundry bags (good for many uses), plastic garbage bags, soft soap, fire extinguisher, spare bulbs, nuts, screws, spare rotor, hydraulic lift (two of these are ideal for emergencies), and a superb tool kit.

ROOM RESERVATIONS

Reservations are not necessarily essential for enjoyable travel, but they certainly can help, especially for brief and highly organized trips. A poorly made reservation may be worse than none at all, however. Here are some tips on doing it right.

When reserving a room makes sense

● Have a reservation for the first night in Mexico. Since you'll be exhausted when you arrive, you don't want to look for a room.

● Make reservations if you want rooms of great charm or value, especially during the peak seasons.

● Always have room reservations if you're traveling in the period of Christmas (Navidad) to New Year's, or at Easter time (Semana Santa).

● Mexicans also jam hotels on three-day holiday weekends,

particularly around Mexico City. Just keep that in mind for the towns in that region.

● During the summer, major tourist towns in mountain areas fill up on weekends, because they offer much cooler weather.

● If you're on a short trip with little time to waste, have reservations for every night in Mexico. You can't afford the hassle or the time involved in looking for rooms on your own.

● Have rooms reserved for resort vacations if you want to stay in fancy and famous hotels—these fill up months in advance during the winter, with February being the prime time for winter sun.

● If you'll be going to a town during a festival, make reservations. You won't find a room in Mazatlán during Carnival, for example.

Disadvantages of reservations

● You may have to pay a fee for room reservations and also foot the cost of cables and telephone calls.

● You're usually renting sight unseen. Unless you have great confidence in your "source," you may end up disappointed.

● You'll end up paying for higher-priced rooms or paying the highest price a room will rent for. Reservations take away your bargaining power and make it very difficult for you to shift from one room to another.

● Reservations tie you down. If you're on a short trip, this will make no difference, but when a trip stretches to three weeks or longer, a reservation schedule can begin to feel like an ill-fitting shoe on a 10-mile hike.

● Reservations in Mexico are sometimes not honored, or are blatantly disregarded.

● If you cancel a reservation, you may not be able to get your deposit back. More about this later.

Avoiding getting bumped by hotels

Many hotels routinely overbook by 10 to 15 percent. Even with written confirmations, you could be one of those bumped.

• Make reservations as far in advance as possible. For hotels in resort areas during the peak season this could mean booking a room six months or longer ahead of time.

• Get your reservations confirmed in writing. If you know that you'll be arriving at a hotel after 6:00 P.M., make sure that the hotel knows this. And have this late arrival time noted on your room confirmation slip.

• Pay a substantial deposit on the room. With money in the bank, hotels are less likely to bump you. Deposits are commonly required by better hotels.

• If you make reservations through a travel agent, choose one with clout—so that you will have someone to lean on if things go awry.

• If you get delayed unexpectedly (very common), notify the hotel. Few hotels will rent out a room if you have contacted them. Get the name of the person you talk to.

Canceling a room

The refund policy of Mexican hotels varies with each hotel. In some instances, you may lose your entire deposit for canceling a room too late.

• Before making a reservation requiring a deposit, ask for a copy of the cancellation policy—preferably in writing.

• Getting money back can be a problem. See p. 371 for a way to get this resolved quickly.

Travel agents' reservations

• Most agents charge nothing at all for making room reservations, unless doing so involves a special service, such as telephoning or cabling (their commission is paid by the hotel).

• Ask the agent whether you'll be charged for cables or telephone calls—or for anything else, for that matter!

• If the agent insists that there is no charge at all, ask whether a surcharge could be added to your hotel bill on the other end.

• If the agent says that no such commission need be paid, ask for a letter typed on the agency stationery stating this in straightforward terms. If a hotel then tries to stick you with a surcharge, produce the letter and refuse to pay.

Making your own reservations

• Larger hotel chains with many establishments in Mexico have toll-free (800) numbers listed in the phone book or available from information (call 1-800-555-1212). All you have to do is to dial the number and make a reservation. Be specific about repeating dates and ask them to send you some sort of confirmation in writing. Also ask for a reservation or confirmation number.

• You can write directly to hotels listed in guide books. If you use business stationery, request information on business discounts (up to 30 percent).

• Send your letter by air mail. Include international reply coupons (available in main post offices) to cover the cost of the hotel's air mail reply. Tell the hotel to reply by air mail!

• Most hotels will reply with a request for a deposit to show good faith. An international money order will do the trick. Sometimes just a check is good enough, but Mexicans are very suspicious of them.

• Another method that's expensive but effective: call the foreign hotel during local business hours (remember the time-zone difference). Ask for the front desk, where you'll probably find someone who can speak English. Talk very slowly and very clearly. Repeat the dates of your intended stay several times. Ask for a written confirmation. And be sure to get the name of the person with whom you're talking.

Credit card reservations

• Note that with some credit cards you can get a confirmed room reservation in major hotels. These guaranteed rooms have a penalty for cancellation. Call major credit card companies and hotel chains for current information on making these special reservations.

• Always get a confirmation number when making a room reservation with a major credit card. You can produce this number as proof that the reservation was made if someone cannot seem to locate it.

Hotel representatives in the United States

The following companies handle hotels in Mexico. You or your travel agent can make a reservation by dialing the toll-free (800) number of these hotel representatives.

Alexander Associates 1-(800) 221-6509
American International 1-(800) 223-5695
Best Western 1-(800) 528-1234
Club Med 1-(800) 528-3100
Fiesta Americana 1-(800) 223-2332
Holiday Inn 1-(800) 238-8000
Harry Jarvinen 1-(800) 421-0767
Hotel Service International 1-(800) 231-9860
Hyatt International 1-(800) 228-9000
John Tetley 1-(800) 421-0000
Loew's Reservations 1-(800) 223-0888 or 1-(800) 522-5455
   (NY).
Princess Hotels 1-(800) 223-1818
Quality Inn 1-(800) 228-5151
Ramada Inns 1-(800) 228-2828
Robert Warner 1-(800) 223-6625
Sheraton 1-(800) 325-3535
Travmex (612) 941-5305
Utell International 1-(800) 223-9869 or 1-(800) 223-9868
Westin Hotels 1-(800) 228-3000

Reservations in Isla Mujeres

For reservations on the tiny island of Isla Mujeres off Cancún, contact Arlene Coates from May to December at her Wisconsin address. Ask for Laura. From December to May send a telegram to her in Isla Mujeres. She charges a flat fee of $10 per person for reservations, which are essential at Christmas, during Carnival, and for spring break.

Arlene Coates
1322 Forster Drive
Madison, WI 53704
tel.: (800) 872-5464 (ask for Laura)
    (608) 244-4341

Arlene Coates
Lista de Correos
Isla Mujeres
Quintana Roo
México

Basic hotel vocabulary

air-conditioned	*aire acondicionado*
apartment house	*apartamentos*
back	*al fondo*
baggage	*equipaje*
bar	*bar*
bath	*baño*
bathroom	*baño*
bed	*cama*
double bed	*cama matrimonial*
extra bed	*cama extra*
bedroom	*recámera*
bellboy	*botones*
bill	*cuenta*
blanket	*cobija, cubierta*
boardinghouse	*pensión, casa de huéspedes*
by the week	*por la semana*
by the month	*por el més*
car	*coche*
cheap	*económico*
cheaper	*más barato*
child	*niño*
to close	*cerrar*
clothes	*ropa*

cot	*catre*
credit card	*tarjeta de crédito*
dining room	*comedor*
electricity	*electricidad*
elevator	*elevador*
fan	*ventilador, abanico*
floor	*piso*
for rent	*se renta, se alquila*
for sale	*se vende*
for . . . days	*por . . . días*
front	*al frente*
furnished	*amueblada*
garage	*cochera, garage*
hammock	*hamaca*
hangars	*ganchos*
hotel	*hotel*
house	*casa*
how much	*cuánto*
How much is . . . ?	*¿Cuánto cuesta . . . ?*
ice	*hielo*
I like it	*me gusta*
I don't like it	* no me gusta*
inn	*posada*
key	*llave*
kitchen	*cocina*
landlord, owner	*dueño, dueña*
maid	*criada, camarera*
manager	*gerente, dueño*
May I see it?	*¿Puedo verlo?*
minimum	*mínimo*
motel	*motel*
night watchman	*velador*
noise	*ruido*
office	*oficina*
open (to open)	*abrir*
parking lot	*estacionamento*
pillow	*almohada*
porter	*mozo de servicios*
quiet	*tranquilo*

refrigerator	*refrigerador*
room	*cuarto*
single room	*cuarto sencillo*
double room	*cuarto doble*
for two people	*para dos personas*
for three people	*para tres personas*
with bath	*con baño*
with meals	*con comidas*
without meals	*sin comidas*
safe (adjective)	*seguro*
safe (for valuables)	*caja de seguridad*
sheet	*sabana*
shower	*regador, regadera*
soap	*jabón*
stairway	*escalera*
stopped, plugged	*tapado, tapada*
stove	*estufa*
swimming pool	*alberca, piscina*
tax	*impuesto*
toilet	*taza*
toilet paper	*papel sanitario*
towel	*toalla*
view	*vista*
water	*agua*
cold water	*agua fría*
hot water	*agua caliente*
with	*con*
without	*sin*

HOTEL STRATEGIES

Getting the room you want with the amenities you want at the price you want—no mean trick. That's what this section is all about.

Hotel reservations

Making a hotel reservation which will be honored is also no mean trick in Mexico. Here are a few tips.

IF YOU HAVE A RESERVATION BUT GET BUMPED

With a reservation you've already decided where you're going to stay, but the hotel may have a different idea.

- If you have a written confirmation, insist that the hotel come up with a room.

- Patience often pays off. Park yourself in the lobby. Don't get angry. Let them know that you're assuming they can handle the problem.

- If they can't find a room for you, ask them to get a room in a comparable hotel at a comparable price. Ask them to pay the cab fare to get you there.

GETTING BUMPED WITHOUT A WRITTEN CONFIRMATION

Unless you have a written confirmation, you can expect no sympathy. A telephone conversation with someone's name is very helpful, but not necessarily enough. That's why you should insist on written confirmations.

- Again, don't get angry. Remain calm, patient, and friendly. Ask for help. Mexicans admire courtesy and patience and will often help you out in this situation. You're thinking that it's all their fault. And they're just trying to get through the day. They'll get to it, just don't expect it to be done immediately. Take out the paperback and start to read.

Finding your own room—without a reservation

The big advantage of traveling without reservations is the overall freedom it gives you. Many people *prefer* to travel in this fashion. Another advantage is that you get to see the room (and the hotel) before you rent. That advantage pales in extremely crowded cities during the peak season, but the fact is that you often do better on your own than when others book rooms for you. It's quite easy and can save you a bundle if you know a few basic principles and techniques.

THE GRAPEVINE

- Sometimes, simple is best. The most effective way to find

a room in Mexico is to ask. If you're traveling by plane, ask someone in the information booth in the airport. If you're in a taxi, ask the driver. If you're traveling by bus or train, corner foreigners you're riding with—they have the same concern you do.

● This informal grapevine is often more accurate and up-to-date than any travel guide! Travel in Mexico has a way of drawing people together. The sharing helps the entire group overcome mutual problems.

● Once you find a hotel that matches your personality and budget, ask the hotel personnel to make recommendations in other cities. They often know spots that have never even been written about in the United States or Canada.

USING A TRAVEL GUIDE TO FIND LODGING

● Each travel guide is aimed at a specific market, usually according to budget. If you're on a tight budget, use a student guide. Not so tight? Try any of the more popular guides with varied listings.

● These guides are all out of date before they're printed. Many have given up listing prices—for good reason! But they all list a batch of hotels which fall into certain price categories. Although prices may have risen, the listed hotels will fall into the "budget" or "moderate" or "luxury" categories—that, in itself, is the value of the guide.

● The tip: Go to *any* of these hotels which most accurately matches your idea of what you want. The hotel may or may not have a room available, but that really doesn't matter. What you need is help. And almost all hotels will suggest other hotels nearby, and many hotel owners will call those hotels for you. This strategy works 99.9 percent of the time.

FINDING HOTELS BY AREA

● If you're interested in a specific area of a town, if you want to be near or on the beach, if you want to be near the market or shopping, or whatever—check out the area nearest whatever interests you.

• Hotels that fall into similar price categories often cluster together. If you're looking for budget hotels, you'll usually find a bunch of them in one location. In the old part of Acapulco you'll find half a dozen cheap hotels all in the same general location on the side of a steep hill.

• The secret of this strategy is to be traveling light. Or, if you're with another person, have him watch over the bags while you go out in search of the "perfect hotel." A short walk can be a good way to get to know an area, and you'll be surprised with the unusual finds you come up with.

WRITE YOUR GEMS DOWN

• When trying to come up with hotels, it always helps to share your finds with others. They in turn help you out, so keep a log of all the places that offered good value and would interest others.

TOURIST OFFICES

• If you come into a city during a peak travel period, during a holiday or fiesta, you may need help locating a room. Ask for the nearest tourist office *(turismo).*

• Tourist offices close at weird times and often take a break for a siesta. But they can help you locate a room where none are to be found. You may end up in a private home, but that in itself could be a great experience.

CALLING AHEAD FOR RESERVATIONS

• Major hotels will make reservations for you if you want to stay in another link of the chain.

• If you're in a budget hotel and know that you'll be arriving late at your next destination, consider having someone in the hotel phone ahead for a reservation. Their Spanish could be the key to getting you a room. You're out the cost of the call or calls, but you're assured of a place when you arrive.

BEATING THE "NO VACANCY" SIGN

It can be frustrating at times, this process of finding a room on your own. It's particularly frustrating when you find "No Vacancy"

("*Occupato*") at every turn—a dirty word when you're looking for a room. When things look very bleak, try some of the following techniques to help you come up with a room.

- Find out when the check-out time is. Often people change their minds at the last minute and leave. In Mexico things are casual, and in many places the staff really has no idea how many vacancies there will be—timing is key. So if someone tells you a place is booked solid, come back at check-out time.

- Many times you'll be told that there is no room in a larger hotel simply because the clerk doesn't want to be bothered with the fuss of looking. Don't assume anything. Tell the clerk that you'll wait awhile to see whether anything opens up. Now he's got to look at you staring at him for the next half hour or so—this often produces a room.

- When you walk up to a clerk and the first thing you hear is, "How long do you intend to stay?" you've got to answer, "A week," or there may suddenly be no vacancies. Short stays cost hotels more in overhead. If the clerk tells you that they've only got a room for one night, take it. Once you're in a place, you're rarely booted out. And, if one night's enough, fine.

- The secret in Mexico is patience, the aura of calm determination and tranquility.

Judging hotels

- Never judge a hotel by its exterior or lobby. Some very bleak exteriors hide sumptuous interiors. And some charming lobbies with flower-filled gardens cannot make up for bug-infested and dirty rooms. Ask to see the room.

- Never judge a hotel by its official rating, just jargon that's misleading. A first-class hotel can have an empty swimming pool and surly staff while a budget inn with no stars may provide friendly service and rooms with fireplaces—you just never know. Ask to see the room.

CHECKING OUT A ROOM

- Make sure the room is clean. Don't worry about the glasses, half the time they haven't been washed. Just see whether or not you can live with the colony of bugs or the dust on the tables.

● Does the room smell fresh and clean? Well, maybe that's pushing it. Does it smell okay?

● Does the price posted in the room match the one quoted to you—it's supposed to.

● Are the faucets dripping? Is the toilet churning? Turn on the hot water to see if there is any.

● Check the bathroom. Are you willing to stand in the shower or bathe in the tub? Does it seem clean enough?

● Check the bedding. If it's cool outside, ask whether or not there are extra blankets.

Bargaining on room rates

Once you find a room you like, you'll want to come up with the best price possible. Although it may go against your grain, bargaining in various ways is acceptable. Naturally, it's only effective in an area with many open rooms, and for that reason it's done more successfully in the off-season.

● During the off-season the hotel may volunteer a drastic price reduction. You barely even hint at it, and it's yours.

● In the peak season, you have to be more subtle. Tell the clerk that the room is great, but that it's too expensive for you. This will often bring the price down.

● Or be blunt: Tell the clerk that you like the room and will pay such and such an amount—a lower, but still fair, price. This works frequently, but you have to have the right temperament to try it.

● Ask if there's a room that is just as nice but costs less. What you're checking on is the variability of pricing in the hotel.

Room-rate discounts

• Rates shown in rooms are the maximum allowed by law. In the off-season there should be a discount.

• Always ask about discounts for prolonged stays (usually three days or longer). If none exist, the hotel will tell you so. You can then either accept the standard rate or shop around.

• Ask if the hotel offers weekend discounts. This tactic works best in large cities.

• Some hotels will give discounts for people in different professions. Ask to see if such an opportunity exists.

• Occasionally, a hotel will offer a business discount if you make a reservation on a company's stationery—it's worth a try.

Hotel costs and services

Check-in is the time to get everything straight on costs and services. Avoid any potential conflicts by asking questions right away.

• You'll find that all rooms have a base price. Ask to have this written down.

• In most hotels (but not all) you'll pay an IVA tax. The tax is 6 percent in the Baja and 15 percent in the rest of Mexico. However, in hotels catering mainly to Mexicans on a budget you may have no tax at all. Ask if any tax will be added to the base price.

• Occasionally, a hotel will tack on a service charge which ups the bill considerably. You'll want to know about this charge in advance, because it can add a hefty percentage to the bill. Again, ask.

• Note that single rooms are almost the same price as doubles (just a little less, actually), so you can't get much of a benefit by traveling alone.

• Ask if there are any additional charges for telephones and television. Many hotels do make a small charge per day for these two items. Find out what it is in advance.

● Air-conditioning can add a substantial price increase to a room. If you're willing to settle for a ceiling fan, the cost drops dramatically.

● If you don't have a bath in your room, ask if there is an additional charge to take a bath. Find out if towels cost extra as well.

Room and board

The term *American Plan* (full room and board) means that you're staying in a hotel and eating all three meals there. *Modified American Plan* (half room and board) indicates that you're skipping either lunch or dinner at the hotel. In Mexico it usually means lunch is left out. Most hotels offer good rates for both full and half room and board.

● Some hotels will force you into an American Plan before they will rent you a room. In the peak season you may have to submit to this racket if you want to get into a particular hotel.

● Ideally, you want to be able to choose to eat in any hotel, no matter what plans are available. This gives you the option of eating out or deciding that the hotel food warrants a full or half room and board plan.

● If you do stay on a room-and-board basis, find out if there is an extra charge for anything, such as wine, dessert, or coffee.

● Most hotels offering half or full room and board post specific meal times. If you miss the meal, you still pay for it.

● And most hotels offer a choice of two or more entrées with each meal, so that you have the feeling of some control—not much, really.

Payment

● Fancy hotels will ask you to produce a major credit card at the time of check-in. They will imprint the information on a charge slip as collateral. When you check out, you can either fill in the total or pay in cash and have the credit card slip destroyed.

• Budget hotels will ask for a cash *(efectivo)* payment upfront for the first night's rental.

• You do not want to use a traveler's check to pay a hotel bill in most instances, because very few hotels give a fair rate of exchange. Always carry enough money in pesos to pay your hotel bills.

• When you pay the bill, ask for a receipt *(recibo)*. If you pay with a credit card, check the total before signing. Be sure to keep all receipts until the charges have come in.

IDIOSYNCRACIES OF MEXICAN HOTELS

Half the pleasure of travel comes from discovering the difference between them and us. However, some differences come as a shock. Here are some bridges for cultural gaps in hotels.

The front desk

• Always have room prices written down for you when checking in. This avoids any discussion of a language barrier.

• Don't assume that your name is easy to spell or read. Write it down for the clerk.

• If you have any valuables, ask the front desk about safe-deposit boxes. Normally, there is no charge for these. Better hotels have them, many budget hotels don't. But you won't know for sure until you've asked.

• If you don't have a map, ask for one at the front desk. They usually have tourist-oriented information.

• If you use the front desk for wake-up services, wait until as late in the evening as possible to request the service. This way you have a good chance of talking to the person who will wake you up in the morning.

Porters

- Porters expect a reasonable tip for carrying baggage, even if it's feather-light.

Concierge

- Luxury hotels have a concierge, a kind of jack-of-all-trades who can arrange or get just about anything done. Use the concierge for any kind of unusual request and tip according to its difficulty. You will be amazed at what they can accomplish —they are truly street smart.

Travel agencies

- Moderate and upper bracket hotels often have travel agencies in the lobby or nearby. These can set up city tours or excursions to nearby tourist sights. They can arrange for tickets to performances of any kind, usually at an inflated price.

Baggage room *(garda equipaje)*

- If you're checking out before you have to leave a town, use the baggage room for storage. Your bags are generally secure in these protected areas.

- Many hotels offer such a service free of charge.

- Always get a receipt for each bag stored in a baggage check room.

Time

- Hotels work on the military system of time. Checkout at 13 hours equals checkout at 1 P.M. You'll see a placard in your room explaining the checkout policy. It will read: *"Su cuarto se vence a . . ."* ("Your room must be vacated by . . .")

- If you do not check out on time, the hotel can legally ask you to pay for another night's lodging.

Telephone

- Most hotels charge a small fee per day for the use of a telephone or a small fee per local call.

- Most (but not all) hotels charge a surcharge for long-distance calls. You should ask ahead of time what the surcharge is, if any.

- Hotels add a charge to your bill for any collect calls as well. The charge can be higher if the collect call was not accepted. Again, ask what the charge will be.

Television

- Quite a few hotels add a charge for television in the room. Some charge nothing at all, it's just built into the overall price of the room. You have to ask to avoid any surprises.

Parking

- In major cities, hotels will charge a steep fee for the use of parking facilities. There are exceptions to this rule, and you can save many dollars a day if the hotel offers free parking to its guests. If you'll be driving in Mexico City, try to make a reservation in a hotel which offers free parking.

- Street parking is not advised, so no matter what the charge, it's worth getting your car into a guarded area or parking lot. Smaller hotels often have a courtyard where you can park overnight, and they rarely charge anything for this service.

Elevators

- The elevators in most hotels do not work like Swiss watches. The clunk when you push the call button means it's heard you. The whine means it's on its way. The second clunk means the maid has intercepted it on the third floor and will now head in the opposite direction.

- Once you've cornered the elevator, remember that PB *(planta baja)* means main floor.

Bathrooms and showers

- In small hotels you'll find soap in the bathrooms, but it has usually been opened and used before. If you're fussy, bring your own.

● Water barely manages to escape from the shower heads in some hotels. A few wily travelers have found that enlarging the holes by force does wonders for the flow.

● Light a match in smelly toilets. The sulfur seems to dissipate the smell.

● If there are no plugs for the sink, just use a sock.

● Sometimes, a toilet won't flush. Lift off the back and see whether the tank is full. If not, fill it up with water from the faucet and flush—usually takes care of the problem, but not as well as a good plumber would.

● *Caballeros* is the sign on a men's bathroom, *damas* signals relief to ladies.

Hot and cold water

● In small hotels with a central water heating system you may be out of luck (and hot water). As a matter of fact, the same is often true in large, fancy hotels. You'll have to learn the best times for bathing if you're fussy about hot water.

● C *(caliente)* on a faucet means hot, which confuses many people from English-speaking countries. Cold in Spanish is *fría*. After running the hot water for five minutes and getting none, assume the plumber was illiterate, or, more likely, the hotel is out of hot water.

Mattresses

● If you're the kind of person who doesn't have to jump to sink a basket, ask to see the bed in a room before renting it. You may have to settle for a double bed on which you can lie diagonally.

● You'll run into a mattress every now and then which gives you a spinal tap for no extra charge. Just toss it on the floor and sleep there.

● If you want to slide two beds together to make one, place the box springs side by side, but always place the mattresses *across* them. If you don't, someone will disappear in the night.

The shrinking sheet epidemic

• Budget hotels have fallen prey to the shrinking sheet epidemic which has swept across Mexico in waves leaving all sheets 6 inches too short for the bed—it is incurable.

Hammock hooks

• Those strange claws on the walls of hotel rooms in the Yucatán are hammock hooks, perfectly suited to hanging hammocks so that they land squarely on a bed. Move the beds if you have to, and always ask for a discount if you're a swinger —after all, they don't have to clean the sheets!

Lights

• To beat the poor light in many smaller hotels carry a flashlight.

• If you want stronger light for reading, pick up a high watt bulb. It's the only way to beat the system.

Guests

Hotels can be strict about inviting guests to your room. The landlady will look at you and your new friend heading up the stairs and say, "Excuse me. You paid for one person, not two."

• If you are expecting, or hope to find, a partner, pay for two from the start. It's rarely much more than the single price.

• It is *not* illegal for unmarried people to share a room, but in small inns it might be extremely indiscreet. Pretend to be married.

Unwanted guests

• Hotels detest pets in Mexico—best to leave yours at home.

Other unwanted guests

• You'll want to send bedbugs packing after your first experience with these invisible but voracious feeders. They leave little red spots that itch like crazy. Don't scratch them, they just get worse.

Curfew

- Not many places close up early, but a few do. Still, it seems to go against tradition, with everyone strolling about until well after midnight.

- When there's a strict curfew, someone will let you know in advance.

Mosquitos

- Mosquitos hum and bum their way into many hotel rooms despite the screens and attempts at protection. They are very annoying, and carry malaria, which makes them more than just a nuisance.

- If you're in a bug-infested area, invest in mosquito netting, insect repellant, and a long-sleeved shirt. If you're in a hammock, put a thin blanket down to protect your rump.

Air-conditioning

- Air conditioning can be a must during the hot, humid months of the rainy season. It can add a surcharge to your room.

Fans *(ventilador)*

- Fans whine, moan, and make strange gyrating sounds, but they prove effective.

- The switch on the wall controls their speed, usually a casual luffing to a kind of frenzy that seems to be pulling the fan off the ceiling as it jiggles and bumps in all directions.

- If you're tall, don't have a pillow fight on the bed or reach up to put on your sweatshirt. Many of the fans hover inches above your head.

- Fishing rods and spear guns will not stand up to the concerted attack of a ceiling fan—keep that in mind.

Fireplaces

- Fireplaces with a warm crackling glow and wonderful scent

can be found in mountainous areas. Tip for extra wood—it's worth it.

Noise

• If you're at all sensitive to noise, if you're a light sleeper, or if you prefer to listen to your own brand of music, bring ear plugs.

• Mexico is the land of the constant crowing, lowing, mating of cats, grinding of gears, unloading of cement blocks—and a dozen other noisy gerunds. You simply will not believe it!

• When checking out a hotel, pay attention to noise: Are you just above the lounge or disco? Are you right next to the reception area? Near the elevator or public toilet? Is your room overlooking the *zócalo* (main square) or right on a busy highway? You've got the picture.

Smells

• You can tell almost immediately whether or not a room has a strong smell. If it does, move.

• However, in many hotels you'll get nearly asphyxiated in the middle of the night if you're near the laundry room or if the wind shifts and the smell of diesel from the flues hits you with full force. This happens in even better hotels and suggests a quick look at the chimney line on the way to your room.

Safety

• Single women take note—there are pass keys, and some owners of smaller hotels have been known to use them. Jam a chair under the handle of the door if you have any suspicion of this (or change hotels).

• Read the section on protecting your property and yourself on p. 161.

Maids

• Unless you put small odds and ends in a drawer or in your

luggage, they may disappear. They're usually not being stolen, but are being thrown away.

Washing clothes in your room

● By hand-washing your clothes you'll save money and time (hotel laundries take forever). Besides, today's modern fabrics are practically maintenance free.

● Roll clothes in a towel to collect excess moisture and speed up drying before you hang them up. (But don't wring out drip-dry clothes).

● Be sure to bring a braided rubber clothesline from which you can hang wash to dry.

Hanging clothes to dry

● Never hang your laundry out a window to dry in major cities. In budget hotels or resorts, you can lay out clothes on chairs or over the edge of the balcony to let them dry in the sun.

● In humid areas, the only way to get clothes dry is to get them into the sun!

● Don't lay wet clothes on stained wood surfaces, since they'll bleach the wood and end up stained themselves.

● When possible, separate the back portion of any wet clothing from the front. This speeds up the drying process. This is really only possible with hangers or a rubber clothesline.

● Smooth out the material to eliminate potential wrinkles.

● Button the top two buttons of a shirt or blouse and set the collar in the correct position.

Laundromats

● Since hotel laundries take long and cost a bundle, look for a local laundromat (lavanderia automática). In some of these places you do everything yourself, in others you leave off your clothes. Here are the key words:

bag (plastic)	*bolsa*
chlorine	*cloro*
dry	*secado*
soap	*jabón*
tokens	*fichas*
wash	*lavado*

Wrinkles, lint, and stains

● To get rid of wrinkles in shirts, slacks, or dresses after they are dry, hang them in a steamy bathroom.

● Another solution: Dampen the wrinkles and run them across a hot light bulb (acts just like an iron).

● Use any kind of tape to pick up lint off clothes. Just wrap the tape lightly around your fingers and brush gently. The lint sticks to the tape.

● Soak blood stains in *cold* water and scrub vigorously to remove them.

● Sprinkle salt or soda on wine stains and talcum powder (or something similar) on grease stains to help absorb and remove them before washing.

● One of the best stain removers to carry with you is *Goddard's.*

Drinking glasses

● In better hotels you'll be given drinking glasses wrapped in plastic as proof that they've been sterilized. Unfortunately, this happens once—when you arrive. The glasses are then left in your room until you leave. The problem: The maids wash them out each day in tap water.

● In budget hotels there's far less pretense and protection— many of the glasses are filthy.

● Suggestion: Have a personal cup for traveling or carry some plastic cups which can be used and then tossed—you can buy them in most stores.

Water

- People who worry about water in Mexico are not all wet. Skip tap water in hotels and don't brush your teeth in it.

- Some of the larger deluxe hotels claim to have pure tap water. They probably do. Some of the smaller hotels make the same claim. They probably don't. Be suspicious of tap water.

- In some hotels big jugs of purified water *(agua purificada)* are found in individual rooms or in the hallway. Just tip these to get water out, unless they have a little spigot at the base.

- Some hotels provide bottles of pure water by the sink. Or they have carafes filled with what they claim is pure water. Frankly, I'd be suspicious.

- Why not carry bottles of mineral water *(agua mineral)* with you? You can find them in some stores either in small or large bottles, with or without carbonation.

Servi-bars

- The better Mexican hotels often have servi-bars in the room. You open these little boxes with your room or specially provided key. Inside, you'll find fruit juices, colas, beer, wine, mini bottles of booze, and an assortment of snacks. You pay for these, often through the nose.

Tipping

- When you stay in a hotel for three days or longer, be sure to tip the cleaning lady—do it in person to make certain she gets the tip.

DINING OUT

The food in Mexico can be excellent ranging from *cabrito* (goat) in Monterrey to *langosta* (spiny lobster) in Isla Mujeres off the coast of Cancún. Most of the time it is average, and occasionally it drops to bad. This chapter covers the ins and outs of eating in Mexico. *Buen provecho!*

FOOD AND MONEY

You'll want good value for your money in Mexico. You'll also want to be fair in your demands and tips. Here are a few pointers.

À la carte versus set-price meals

• There are two basic ways of ordering food in Mexican restaurants: à la carte or set-price menu. À la carte means that you order and pay for each item on the menu separately. A set-price menu means that you order an entire meal, from soup to nuts, for a set price.

• A set-price meal is usually a better deal than an à la carte meal. Most set-price meals include the cover charge *(cubierto)* and are usually offered at breakfast and at noon—less rarely at night. The set-price noon meal is called the *comida corrida*. It is sometimes posted out in front of a restaurant, and at other times it is added as a note to the menu. In a few places you have to ask the waiter about the set-price meal.

Cover charge *(cubierto)*

● In more formal restaurants you pay a cover charge *(cubierto)* the moment you place an order. The charge covers bread, butter, the table setting, and extras such as pâté.

● In small, informal restaurants you'll rarely see a cover charge.

● The price of a *comida corrida* (set-price menu) almost always includes the cover charge. If you're not sure, just ask.

Mariachis

● In some restaurants mariachis stroll from table to table singing favorite Mexican songs.

● If you request a song, you're expected to pay for it—call it a tip. You're also expected to tip if it's obvious that the restaurant is *not* picking up the tab for the music. You can tell if people at other tables have been tipping.

● If you do not want music at your table, just say, *"No, gracias."* This can be difficult to do, but if that's the way you feel, do it.

The bill *(la cuenta)*

● Mexicans do not automatically bring bills to tables. This would be considered rude as it would imply pressure for you to leave.

● If you want the bill, you have to ask for it: *"La cuenta, por favor."*

● Do not expect the bill to come immediately. This is a good time to catch up on some reading or carry on an extended conversation with a friend. Your anxiety about getting going is not shared by the waiter—in fact, you're anxiety would be viewed as neurotic.

Checking the bill

• As you're ordering, try to keep a rough idea of the total cost of the meal.

• Check the bill carefully for errors. If the bill seems especially high, ask to see the menu again.

• Mexicans do not like to make separate checks for customers. They much prefer overall bills for large groups of people. One person should pay the bill.

• In funky, little places catering mainly to Mexicans you won't find every dish or bottle of beer or dessert, noted on a bill. They'll just charge you an overall price for the group. I've found that this is usually done to the *customer's* advantage.

• However, this is rarely done in restaurants catering to tourists, although a round of free drinks or a free dessert is occasionally offered to friendly and large parties of foreigners as a goodwill gesture.

Tax *(impuesto)*

• All restaurants catering to tourists charge a 15 percent government tax on the total bill. This tax is not a tip, it is not a service charge, it is not going to the waiter.

• In small, informal restaurants catering mainly to Mexicans you will rarely see this charge added to the bill.

Tips *(propinas)*

• Wages for waiters are very low, and they make most of their income from tips.

• Most guides tell you to tip between 10 and 15 percent. This is not quite accurate. You only tip that much in fancy restaurants. In smaller, less formal places a more modest tip is in order.

• Furthermore, tips should be related to the area. You tip

more in resorts and in big cities than you do in rural areas.

• A few, a very few, restaurants add a tip or service charge to the bill automatically. If this is done, do not tip. You have already paid the tip! If you're not sure if the tip has been included, ask.

Cutting Costs

- One of the simplest ways to cut costs in Mexico is to eat less—a good idea for your health in a hot and high country.
- Don't order breakfast in hotels or restaurants. Improvise your own with pastries, fresh breads, tropical fruits, and "home-brewed" tea or coffee.
- Carry an immersion heater (available in many hardware stores) to bring a cup of water to boil in seconds.
- Eat your biggest meal at lunch to take advantage of the *comida corrida,* an inexpensive set-price meal that gives you everything from soup to nuts at a reasonable price.
- Try inexpensive Mexican combination platters. These usually come with oversize portions, easily enough for two.
- Or skip lunch and settle for a picnic! Mexicans do this frequently. Fresh bread, a few slices of cheese and canned ham, peanuts, a bar of chocolate—what more could you ask for?
- Eat in thoroughly Mexican places where the local dishes are a fraction of the price of the more commercial tourist spots.
- Typical Mexican restaurants don't charge the 15 percent IVA tax—yet another reason to travel as the Mexicans do.
- Stick to hearty, simple dishes like soup. And fill up on inexpensive staples like rice, refried beans, and tortillas (stacks of the latter can be purchased for pennies).
- Share a meal with a friend, if you're really strapped. Just ask for another plate. Mexicans don't mind.
- Omelettes make a tasty, large, and reasonably priced meal—lots of protein at very little cost.
- Buy snack and picnic foods in the local markets. Prices for fresh fruit and nuts are always a bargain there!
- Stick strictly to local wines, beers, and liquors. All imported brands have a huge tax added to their cost and rarely are worth the extra charge.
- Skip coffee at the end of a meal, if you can, because it's expensive and has little food value.
- Always carry food with you on buses, trains, and planes to avoid both high prices and unsanitary conditions—a *basic* rule in Mexico.

Credit cards *(tarjetas de crédito)*

• Mexicans like and trust credit cards. You'll find many restaurants willing to take them.

• Be sure to keep the receipts filed until the charges come in —that could be several months later in the case of some Mexican charges.

MEAL TIMES

In a typical Mexican household you might eat five meals a day. The average tourist settles for two or three.

When Mexicans eat

• Breakfast *(desayuno)* time is very elastic, it can stretch from early in the morning to noon. However, in some hotels and boardinghouses you'll find a very strict schedule for breakfast, usually 7:30 to 9:30 A.M.

• Mexicans like to eat lunch *(comida)* a little later than most of their northern neighbors. You'll be on time if you stop at a restaurant about 1 P.M.

• Dinner *(cena)* times vary considerably throughout the country. In fashionable restaurants you might not begin to eat until 9 P.M. In average restaurants dinner begins a couple of hours earlier. These places really have an early and a late sitting. Dinner time is later in big cities and some resort areas.

EATING AND HEALTH

One of the unpleasant aspects of Mexican travel is the amount of effort you have to make not to eat or drink things that could make you sick.

The standard advice

Most health organizations and guides give out a kind of standard health sermon which goes something like this:

- Drink only purified water.

- Don't eat lettuce or salads.

- Don't drink milk or eat any milk products unless they're made from pasteurized milk.

- Don't eat ice cream.

- Don't have ice in your drinks.

- Don't eat raw shellfish.

- Don't eat mayonnaise, custard, or any egg-based products which have not been properly refrigerated.

- Don't eat any cold snacks.

- Don't eat any cold fish.

- Don't eat fruits unless they can be peeled.

- Don't eat food sold on the street.

My reaction to the standard advice

- They're right, of course. You can get sick from all of these things. And people do every day. But no matter how many precautions you take, you can still get sick.

- Mexico is a developing country. The standards of hygiene are low. It only takes one fly on one piece of food to undo all the precautions that you've so religiously taken not to get sick.

- However, I'd like to see how these health specialists would handle eating in remote or rural areas—I guess they would pack food in and make their own meals three times a day (not a bad idea).

What you don't read in most guides

- There are some doctors who suggest that much of the diarrhea in Mexico could be prevented if people would not drink alcohol or would drink a lot less. Alcohol lowers your resistance to infection. It actually promotes the growth of harmful bacteria. So while this may throw a wet blanket on one of life's pleasures, what can I say?

● The altitude of many Mexican cities can cause problems if you overeat. One of the simplest solutions is to eat a lot less. And do what the Mexicans do—eat more at noon and less at night. Altitude affects digestion and causes gas. Finally, it doubles and triples the effect of alcohol, so that one drink can have the punch of three at sea level.

● Altitude causes another problem: dehydration. Drink lots and lots of liquids. Fresh fruit juices, purified water, soft drinks —lots of these can help you counteract the effects of high elevation.

● Frankly, I don't know how it's possible to eat in Mexican restaurants without eating many of the "dangerous" foods outlined earlier. Are you really going to send back a coke that's been poured over ice? What are you going to do with a fresh salad with ripe tomatoes sliced neatly on top? Mexico's favorite dessert, *flan,* is made out of milk, so is rice pudding, and so are countless cheeses—how do you *know* whether they've been made from pasteurized milk?

● Furthermore, just eating in a fashionable restaurant or high-class hotel does not solve the problem—you can get just as sick in these as from fly-covered food handed to you from a street vendor.

● The point: You're either going to get sick or you're not. Follow your common sense, and hope God is looking over your shoulder.

FASHIONABLE RESTAURANTS

In Mexico fashionable restaurants are found in the major cities, in world-class resorts and occasionally, but rarely, in remote areas. Mexico City has more superb restaurants than the rest of the country together. Most of these restaurants are very well-known. If you'd like to know about them, simply ask—they are not state secrets.

Reservations

Better restaurants usually require reservations, especially in Mexico City and major resorts like Acapulco. It's best to call immediately on arrival to make sure that you'll get in.

- Reservations are most difficult in the evening, so if you're willing to eat your major meal at noon as the Mexicans often do, you'll have a better chance of getting in.

- There are exceptions to this. For example, if you go to the Bazar Sábado (Saturday Market) in Mexico City's San Angel district, the inn there will be packed with tourists at lunch—causing problems with both the service and the food.

- If you have trouble making reservations, ask someone in your hotel to call for you. If you're in an expensive hotel, ask the concierge to do this. You're expected to tip him for this service.

Best times for best meals

Mexicans tend to eat their big meal at lunch which usually begins at 1 P.M. or later. Prices at lunch are often much lower than they are in the evening, especially for the set-price meal. So if you're mainly interested in an elegant meal at an excellent price, lunch is the best time in fashionable restaurants.

- If you're traveling alone, try to make a reservation for an off-peak period. Go early for lunch and early for dinner. Since dinner for Mexicans tends to be late, going early means going to dinner at 7 P.M. Most restaurants frown on diners eating alone, because they take up a table which could be used for more people. By avoiding the prime dining time, you'll have better and friendlier service, and you'll still have a chance to enjoy a finer restaurant.

- Still, it's more enjoyable to go to a fine restaurant with another person, because the livelier atmosphere at the peak dining time is part of the fun. Furthermore, if you're a single woman, you'll avoid many hassles by finding a dinner partner for the evening (see p. 161).

Dress requirements

When making a reservation at a fine restaurant, ask about dress requirements. In Mexico only a few places have stringent dress codes—mainly in Mexico City.

• Legally, you're not supposed to be turned away from a restaurant because of what you're wearing. But you'd feel uncomfortable dressed inappropriately in an elegant place.

• Appropriately would be a coat and tie at the most for men. And comparable dress for women.

• In resorts such as Acapulco you can go with the tide which often means zany and outlandish costumes for the "in" places —festive and beachy.

Drinking with meals

Fashionable restaurants charge fashionable prices for drinks. If you order any imported liquor or wine, you're going to be stunned by the bill. A bottle of imported wine could double your entire bill!

• Start off with a purely Mexican drink made from Mexican liquor. Or do what the Mexicans do—order beer with your meal. It goes extremely well with most Mexican dishes.

• If you want to drink wine, try one of the Mexican varieties. Start with a glass to see whether it suits your taste and then order a bottle.

• Very few foreigners know anything about Mexican wines, which vary from poor to fairly good. Don't hesitate to ask the waiter or wine steward for advice.

• Be sure that you know the price of any bottled wine that you order. This will avoid confrontations at bill time.

Service

Slow service is not considered bad service in Mexico. Fine restaurants allow you to enjoy a meal at a leisurely pace. Poor service is common only when the owner goes on vacation, usually once or twice a year in fancy places.

SEAFOOD RESTAURANTS

Mexicans love seafood and are willing to splurge to get it, especially when they're on vacation with their families. Here are a few tips on these special restaurants.

Getting the most and best from seafood restaurants

- The best seafood restaurants are right on the sea, often right on a beach. They don't have to be fancy to be good. You may eat in the open covered only by the fronds of a palapa.

- Ask to see whatever you intend to order. If you want lobster, ask to see the lobster. If you want shrimp, ask the waiter to bring a few out to you. Seafood is very expensive. You want to make sure that what you're ordering is fresh.

- Smaller lobster are more tender than larger ones, larger shrimp are nicer and more expensive than smaller ones, large fish tend to be more expensive than small fish.

- Fresh shellfish can be delicious but be wary of them. If they come from polluted waters, you can get serious food poisoning.

- Go to seafood restaurants at noon—the fish will be fresher than in the evening. Some places have only poor to fair facilities for keeping seafood cool and fresh.

- Cold beer goes extremely well with fresh seafood. It's what the Mexicans drink. Many times the empty bottles will be left on the table as a way of tallying your overall bill for booze.

HOTEL RESTAURANTS

Hotel restaurants are a good, conservative choice for someone traveling through Mexico.

About hotel restaurants

● Some of the best restaurants in Mexico can be found in the better hotels. The prices are high, but the food is reliable.

● In some resort areas you'll be required to eat your meals in a hotel if you want to stay there. These meals vary considerably in quality. Try to rent rooms without meal prices included. This gives you the option of eating in or trying restaurants in town.

● You do not have to stay in a hotel to eat in its restaurant. There are a few exceptions to this. But you may have to call ahead to make a reservation for a meal. If you want to eat in the restaurant of a very special inn or romantic retreat, you might have to make reservations several days in advance.

● Many small hotels offer exceptionally good prices on set-price meals both at noon and at night. This is a big advantage to budget-minded travelers who will find it hard to locate set-price meals in restaurants in the evening. Check out some of the smaller hotels!

● In rural areas and small towns you may find the best food is in the local hotel. In some cases it may be the only reliable place to eat. You'll have to check out the options and go by your gut reaction. In a few instances you may choose to buy food and make your own meal—just to be safe.

GOOD BUT CHEAP RESTAURANTS

It's tough finding good, but cheap restaurants in Mexico. They are not as easy to come up with as you might hope.

Finding budget restaurants

● If you're staying in a budget hotel, ask someone where a good, but cheap restaurant is located. They'll usually be glad to offer a suggestion or two.

• Be sure to define the amount of money you're willing to spend to avoid a wild-goose chase.

• Your idea of good is very subjective. You might want to be more specific. Who has the best chicken in town? Where can I get *fresh* fish? Who makes the best guacamole?

• Ask other travelers about their finds! This is one of the simplest and most effective ways to come up with current information—much better than most books. Remember that if you don't ask, God doesn't hear—a popular Mexican saying.

• Look around. When you're out sightseeing or shopping, check out the little places that are available. Start to get a gut feeling about the options. This intuitive sense can become finely tuned like a snake's tongue or a bug's antennae—don't take that personally!

• Eventually, you may discover that you're thinking in terms of cheap, but good dishes, rather than cheap, but good restaurants.

Cheap, but good, dishes

• Some so-so restaurants have some fairly decent dishes, and you may have to settle for this.

• Vegetable soup, no matter where you order it, tends to be hearty and good. It may even be hot. Since the vegetables are cooked, you don't have to worry much about intestinal problems. Soup usually comes with bread.

• Fresh bread in Mexico can be fantastic. In some cases it's almost as good as French bread made in France—okay, that's rare. But most of the time the bread is better than good.

• Tortillas—these are almost always fresh and warm. You can order as many refills of the basket as you want, and you'll rarely be charged extra.

• Omelettes make an excellent and inexpensive meal. They're usually made from eggs laid that morning—chickens are everywhere in Mexico. You wake to their crowing and clucking each morning.

• You guessed it—chicken. How can you go wrong? If you want a breast, ask for a *pechuga*. Flap your arm a couple of times to make sure the waitress gets the picture. If she flaps back, she either understands or wants to mate. Your chances of getting a breast have now risen to 50–50.

• Fresh fruit plates—slices of oranges, moist mangos and papayas, a wedge of watermelon, and cubes of cantaloupe—not cheap, but usually next to great.

• As are the freshly squeezed fruit juices. Don't leave Mexico without asking for a large glass of orange juice. Simply delicious.

• An excellent buy in any coastal area is the fish of the day. If you're trying to keep the bill down, stick to something simple like a small red snapper. The cost of this kind of fish is very reasonable.

• Soft drinks—okay, they're not exactly a dish. And they're more expensive than tap water, but you can't drink the tap water, so you're stuck. Soft drinks fill a void, are safe, and reasonably priced. You won't be able to live without them. Neither can the Mexicans.

• With these dishes in mind you can be on a starvation budget and still not starve.

MEXICAN IDIOSYNCRACIES

By knowing ahead about some of the customs of Mexico you can make the necessary attitude adjustment to have a relaxed and enjoyable time.

Never go to a Mexican restaurant hungry

• I kid you not. Don't be too hungry when you go to a Mexican restaurant because the service will be slow. If you expect and accept this slow pace, then everything's fine. If you go in hyperactive, you're going to leave disappointed and irritated.

Getting the waiter's attention

- It's fun watching people trying to get the waiter's attention. Some hiss, others snap fingers, a few whistle lightly, one will wave his hand—obviously, this is an art form.

Order in groups of foods

- You're used to ordering by person. I would like this, this, and this. Then on to the next person. It's much easier in Mexico to order in groups of foods: four tacos, two omelettes, eight cokes, and tortillas. This will save a lot of time and confusion.

Expect the unexpected

- Or when you least expect it, expect it. If you think you're always going to get the dish you ordered, you're living in an unreal world.

- Accept whatever you get with good grace. Either they didn't have the dish you ordered, couldn't understand the order, or sincerely felt that you'd be better off with the dish you got than the one you ordered—this happens frequently. Is it worth getting angry?

The term bistec is confusing

- Most tourists think that *bistec* means beefsteak. A *bistec de res* is a beefsteak, a *bistec de puerco* is a cut of pork, a *bistec de pescado* is a filet of fish, and a *bistec de tortuga* is the flank of a turtle—got the picture?

Soup *(sopa)*

- The soup *(sopa)* course does not just cover soups. Included on the menu are also rice dishes and many varieties of pasta. These are thought of as *sopas* in Mexico, which can be confusing.

Hot and spicy

- Mexicans adore hot and spicy food. You'll find sauces on the table that can turn an ordinary dish into cinders. Watch the sauces! Sometimes, restaurants make up their own special house sauce *(salsa casera)*.

Basic manners

● If you sit down at a table with a Mexican, wish him *"Buen provecho"* or "good appetite" before he starts to eat. This custom is common in many countries and really appreciated despite its simplicity.

Communicate your reactions

● If you really like a dish, tell the waitress how good it was. Compliments are often appreciated more than a big tip—although that's appreciated too!

PICNICS

Mexicans love picnics, which are an ideal alternative to eating in restaurants or hotels. Picnics are inexpensive and safe in areas where sanitary conditions may be primitive.

Keeping foods fresh

● Shop daily for the foods which you'll be using to make up a picnic basket. Many Mexican foods do not contain preservatives.

● Buy fruits according to their stage of ripeness. The term for ripe is *madura*. If you want to eat something right away, say to the vender *para hoy*. If you want to eat it later, say, *para más tarde*.

● Watch for soft spots and spoilage. Without preservatives fruit and vegetables can die in a day.

● Purifying fruits and vegetables in an iodine or bleach solution (see p. 55) will help reduce spoilage and make them safe to eat.

● Never wrap fresh fruits and vegetables in plastic—they'll go bad quickly. Use paper if you want to protect them. Wrap each piece individually. They're best stored in an ice cooler.

• Certain foods last a long time, are safe, readily available in Mexico, and good buys: avocadoes, bananas, cheese, chocolate, coconuts, cucumbers (sliced in sandwiches), eggs (boiled), limes, melons, nuts, oranges, peanuts, and squash (if you intend to do a little cooking).

• Note that small hotels will be delighted to boil eggs for you if you'll offer a small tip—all you have to do is ask.

• On a daily basis you can supplement these basic items with milk (in cartons), soft drinks or beer; fresh bread, tortillas, and pastries; as well as canned goods ranging from sardines to imported ham.

Cooking

• You don't have to cook to enjoy picnics in Mexico, but on longer trips it helps.

• Alcohol burners are cheap in Mexico, so is alcohol—think about picking these up.

SHOPPING FOR SUPPLIES

You can find foods in everything from small stores and supermarkets to the open-air market. Shopping is one of the great experiences in Mexico.

Supermarkets *(supermercados)*

• You'll find supermarkets in larger towns and cities. They're similar to those found in the United States or Canada with a wide assortment of goods all carefully marked. Visiting a supermarket is a good idea to get an overall sense of prices in Mexico.

• Familiar supermarket names are Aurrera, Comercial, Mexicana, Gigante, and Sumesa.

Small stores *(tiendas)*

- Small stores are often poorly stocked in out-of-the-way locations.

- The farther away you get from main cities, the higher the price of packaged goods. Stock up when you can at places with better prices.

- Do not assume that what you see on the shelves is all that the store carries. If you're looking for something specific, ask for it. It may be hidden away somewhere under a counter or in the back room.

- Many stores do not price their goods, and this can be frustrating. If you're buying an imported product, ask the price before you buy it—it might be outrageous.

- Prices vary enormously from one store to the next. You may have to shop around—even in a small town—to come up with the best price. Wherever you can find Conasupo stores, you're in luck. They often have the best price in the area. Check it out for yourself.

- Sales are posted with *Oferta, Ganga,* or *Especial*—the old and new prices will be given.

- Stores may not be able to exchange large bills, so always carry a good supply of small bills and change. This is a basic rule in Mexico!

- Mexicans carry bags with them to do their shopping, so should you. Fishnet bags are light and big enough to carry lots of items. Either bring or buy one in Mexico—it's absolutely essential.

Specialty shops

- You get bread in a bakery *(panadería),* pastries in a pastry shop *(pastelaría),* and tortillas in a tortilla shop *(tortillería).*

- The lines give the best times to shop in these away. Bring something to carry things in.

Determining price

- Weight often determines the price of items you buy. This is true with many fruits and vegetables, meats, and cheese.

- Mexicans use the metric system of measurement. A kilo is 2.2 pounds and is divided into 1000 grams *(gramos)*. Prices for vegetables and fruit are usually (but not always) quoted per kilo of weight.

- If you're hesitant about how much you get for a certain weight, start with 100 grams *(cien gramos)* of a particular item and work up or down from there.

- Liquids are sold in liters *(litros)* which equal 1.1 quarts. A half liter *(medio litro)* is roughly a pint, and a quarter liter *(cuarto litro)* comes out close to a cup.

- Several foods are sold by the piece *(por pieza)*. You pay so much per egg with a discount thrown in for a dozen (eggs are sometimes sold by weight, as well).

- The size of an item may raise its value. Big shrimp sell for more per kilo than small ones, so do shiny, ripe tomatoes and onions. You want big ones? Okay, you pay a bigger price. Naturally, fresh produce will be more expensive than old.

Shopping in open markets

- You'll love the color, excitement and life of Mexican markets—this is what travel is all about.

- If you're driving, never park near a market *(mercado)* because you may get blocked in for hours by heavy traffic and trucks.

- Markets are usually best in mid-morning. By this time everyone has come in with their produce.

- Market days *(días del mercado)* vary by area. Just ask if you're not sure. An Indian market may be called a *tianguis*.

- To find the market ask for the *mercado* or *plaza commercial*.

● Don't go to a market without a shopping bag. The average vendor sells produce, not bags.

● Carry small change! You're not dealing with wealthy people. They may have very little or no change for larger bills. Furthermore, you don't bargain and then pull out a wad of large bills.

Bargaining

● Bargaining is expected in all markets. If you don't bargain, you'll appear the fool. You're not playing the game by Mexican rules.

● Always greet a vendor with *"Buenos días"* before asking the price. *"¿Cuánto cuesta?"*

● The vendor replies with a price in pesos. If you don't understand, use sign language or a pad and pencil or a calculator—use whatever you need to communicate.

● Offer less than what you think the going rate is. You'll get a counter offer. Settle for what you think the fair price would be in Mexico. It takes awhile to learn what's fair.

● If you're not satisfied, move on. Bargaining can be very rapid. Sometimes, no more than a shake of a finger or nod of a head. And there may be twenty stalls selling the same thing. You can afford to wait.

● Bargaining can take place without either party losing face. Here's how: The vendor asks for 20 pesos for two oranges. You agree to pay that price for four oranges. You both win. This works 90 percent of the time—try it! The implication: Always ask for less than you really want or need to begin with.

What you should know about common foods

Here are a few suggestions on saving time, and tummy trouble in Mexico:

ALFALFA SEEDS

● Sprout lovers, avoid these! They're often treated with chemicals.

AVOCADO *(AGUACATE)*

- A basic ingredient of guacamole, a dish found in every Mexican restaurant. Best in late summer, but easily found in markets year-round. Safe and delicious to eat.

BANANA

- Many varieties are sold in Mexican markets. They are extremely cheap and safe to eat anywhere.

dominicos—tiny, "finger" bananas
manzano—short and chubby
platano (macho)—cooking bananas
platano morado—sweet and purple
tabascos—like ones found in grocery stores

- Note that in the Yucatán bananas may be referred to as *manzanas* or *manzanos*.

BEEF *(CARNE DE RES)*

- When you order beef from a butcher, it will often be whacked into tiny bits—the way most Mexicans would want it. If you want a whole piece, ask for *pedazo entero*.

- When buying meat, ask for an amount worth a certain number of pesos, 200 or 400 pesos worth of hamburger, for instance.

- Tenderloin is called *lomo* or *filete* and is occasionally sold at a price just a little higher than hamburger. However, Mexican butchers are beginning to catch onto the value of specific cuts of beef.

- Note that Mexican beef tends to be much tougher than meat in the United States and Canada.

BREAD *(PAN)*

• Mexican bread can be outstanding and is usually very inexpensive.

• Bakeries have varying hours in each area. You simply have to ask when fresh bread will be available. Bakeries often bake limited amounts of each item, so you have to get to the bakery at a specific time to get what you want.

• In most bakeries you'll find metal trays and large "tweezers" to pick up the bread, rolls, or pastries. You then get them priced before going to a cashier who takes your money. Just follow the lead of the Mexicans around you.

CHEESE *(QUESO)*

• In major supermarkets you can buy cheeses of any kind without health problems. However, in rural areas you should not eat cheese made from unpasteurized milk. Since it's almost impossible to know how the cheese has been made, it's best to avoid it.

• Edam cheese stays fresh in hot areas and is excellent for picnics. Any packaged cheese is easy to carry in a food or backpack.

• Cheesecloth or paper wrapped around cheese will keep it fresh for days.

CHICKEN *(POLLO)*

• Chickens are often butchered on the spot. If you don't want the heads or feet, give them away—Mexicans love them.

• Chicken dishes are found throughout Mexico in even the smallest restaurants. You'll hear the clucking outside. It's a safe and modestly priced main course anywhere.

CHILIES *(CHILES)*

• Chilies are a staple in Mexico and vary from mild to liquid dynamite.

- Don't be fooled by some of the sauces that mask the effect of chilies—you may suddenly feel like you're on fire.

- *Chiles rellenos,* a dish found in many restaurants, is a stuffed pepper cooked in egg batter and smothered in sauce. When it's made properly, it's a dish fit for a gourmet.

- Mexicans believe that if you overdose on chile, the best cure is eating salt, bread, or rice. Most foreigners reach for the water glass instead.

- Watch out for the word *chile*—it means penis in Mexican slang.

CLOVES *(CLAVOS DE ESPECIA* OR *CLAVOS MOLIDOS)*

- If you ask for clavos in Spanish, you'll get a bag of nails. Finish the phrase off correctly, and you'll get cloves.

COCONUT *(COCO)*

- Coconut milk is known as coconut water *(agua de coco)* in Mexico, and it is safe and refreshing to drink.

- If you're not packing a machete, then coconuts can be hard to open. Ask the vendor to do the whacking for you—quick and easy. The meat inside is called *carne.*

COFFEE *(CAFÉ)*

- Instant coffee is known as *Nescafé* throughout the country. If you want coffee beans, you can find and have them ground in a number of shops.

CONCH *(CARACOL)*

- Although you'll find conch on many Mexican menus, it's considered an endangered species—probably because it's so easy for divers to locate and catch.

- Conch can be cooked in a variety of ways. It's usually overcooked which makes it tough and rubbery.

CORN-ON-THE-COB *(ELOTE)*

- Boiled corn-on-the-cob is sold on most street corners by

sad-eyed little old ladies who would be delighted if you gave it a try.

● It's cheap, tough, and often served with lime juice and chili powder. Most travel guides would tell you to avoid street food, but many people eat corn with no worse effect than typical restaurant fare.

CUSTARD *(FLAN)*

● Custard is Mexico's most popular dessert. It often comes with a delicious, sugary sauce. You'll find it on most menus.

EGGS *(HUEVOS)*

● You'll find fresh eggs in every market and delicious egg dishes on every menu. This is one of the cheapest and most consistently good items in Mexico.

● In the market, don't ask someone for *huevos,* use the term *blanquillos.* In slang, "Do you have *huevos?"* means "Do you have balls?" Good for a laugh anywhere.

FISH *(PESCADO)*

● Once a fish *(pez)* has been caught, it's called *pescado.* Fish should be cooked slowly but not too long—just long enough for the flesh to congeal. In Mexico fish is frequently under- or overcooked.

● Not-so-fresh fish can cause lots of problems, which is why many travelers only eat fish early in the day and in areas where you can smell the sea at your side.

● The size of a fish often determines the price, whether you're in the market or in a restaurant. Mexico offers a delightful variety of saltwater fish, and most are very reasonably priced.

● Fish are often cooked whole with head and fins intact. The flesh underneath the eye on the jaw is considered a delicacy, although it is often no more than a fleck. Whole-fried fish is called *pescado frito.*

● Marinated chunks of fish (usually mackerel) make up the

popular dish *ceviche*. Each area has its own recipe, and you'll see it on many menus.

• Many doctors now advise travelers to avoid raw shellfish anywhere in the world. They often come from polluted waters and are a consistent source of food poisoning.

• If you decide to avoid this warning (they are delicious), make sure they're fresh. Note that it's technically illegal for foreigners to gather shellfish in Mexico, although it's done all the time.

• In the market, you have to be very careful when you buy fish fresh. Make sure the flesh is firm (poke it) and the gills are bright red (the brighter, the better).

• Fish is sold whole *(pescado entero)* or cut into filets *(filetes)*. Naturally, the price will rise for filets.

• Fish last longer if only the guts and gills are removed. Leave on the head, fins, tail, and scales.

• Shop for fish *early* in the morning or buy them directly from the fishermen (technically illegal, but very common). Fishing boats rarely have the facilities for keeping fish refrigerated.

ICE CREAM *(HELADO)*

• Ice cream is one of the most popular treats in Mexico because of the constant heat and bright sun. It is usually, but not always, safe.

• Popular flavors are: *coco* (coconut), *chocolate, nuez* (walnut), *piñon* (pine nut), *vainilla* (vanilla), *café* (coffee), and *pistache* (pistachio).

• Ice cream is occasionally called *nieve de leche* while sorbet is sold under the name *nieve de agua*. These are as safe as the water they're made from—you can never be sure.

LIME *(LIMÓN)*

• Most of the yellow fruits sold as lemons in Mexico are really limes, so whether the sour fruit is green or yellow, it's a lime or *limón*.

• Mexicans believe that lime juice kills bacteria. For this reason it's used frequently, especially on salads. The juice is squeezed over the lettuce and left on the salad for fifteen or twenty minutes before it's eaten. You'll be served slices of lime with just about everything including soft drinks and steaks.

LOBSTER (LANGOSTA)

• The lobster you'll find in Mexico doesn't have the big claws of a the Maine variety, because it's a spiny lobster—equally delicious, however!

• Try to find a restaurant which serves them fresh—not frozen. You'll find these along the coast in the appropriate season.

• Legally, you're not supposed to fish for spiny lobsters, but many tourists do. You can snag a lobster with a *gancho,* a fish hook at the end of a pole. Since you'll be looking for them in coral reefs, a leather glove (a golfing glove works great) will protect your hand. Note that lobsters begin to show themselves late in the day—but so do sharks.

• The best way to clean a lobster: Pull one of the spines off the head and insert it in the anal opening. Push it in all the way and then pull out—the guts will come with the spine which is covered with tiny barbs. You can then twist off the tail from the head or insert a knife in the joint and cut them apart.

MANGOES (MANGOS)

• Mangoes, a popular fruit in Mexico, come in countless varieties and are best when fully ripe and juicy. They're often peeled, cut into fancy shapes, and stuck on sticks as a treat on the street or in marketplaces—you can't miss kids sucking on them.

ORANGES (NARANJAS)

• Don't judge Mexican oranges by their color—they just haven't been dyed. Juice oranges *(naranjas para jugo)* are quite inexpensive as is fresh orange juice sold just about everywhere as *jugo de naranja*—really delicious.

PINEAPPLE (PIÑA)

• Ripe pineapples give off a sweet aroma and give slightly to the touch. You'll find them in many markets and small stores at very inexpensive prices.

● Have the vendor cut off the thick skin and slice the pineapple for you. Put the slices in a plastic bag and enjoy the fruit immediately. If you want to save the fruit for later, get a sharp knife in a local store.

SANDWICHES *(TORTAS)*

● Fist-size sandwiches made from small bread loaves or rolls are called *tortas* and are sold in every corner of the country. You may prefer to make your own *tortas* out of avocado, sardines, cheese, and ham—or whatever fresh ingredients are available.

SAUCES *(SALSAS)*

● Sauces are a Mexican specialty, and you'll find them on every table served in little glass containers. Most of them are quite spicy.

● *Moles* are special regional sauces made for dishes containing turkey, chicken, or beef. The ingredients, such as unsweetened chocolate, can be quite unusual.

SHRIMP *(CAMARONES)*

● If you like shrimp, you'll find some of the biggest and best in Mexico. Don't miss the *azules,* tasty prawns. Almost as big and good are the *cristales.* The *regulares* are smaller yet, but still delicious.

● You can sometimes buy shrimp directly from the boat, and you can often buy them frozen from shrimp processing plants in large quantities.

TAMALES *(TAMALES)*

● One tamal, two tamales—whether singular or plural, the real tamales will be ground-corn dough wrapped in corn husks or banana leaves and served hot—a true Mexican specialty.

TOMATOES *(JITOMATES)*

● If you want big, red tomatoes, ask for *jitomates! Tomates* are small, green tomatoes used only to make sauces.

TORTILLAS *(TORTILLAS)*

• *Tortillas* are corn pancakes made from boiled ground corn or wheat flour. They are either cooked on a hot skillet or made commercially at a *tortillería*—you'll see lines where Mexicans wait for *tortillas* hot off the press.

• *Tortillas* are served with almost every meal in Mexico, replaced occasionally by bread as a courtesy to tourists. They come in little cloth-lined baskets or small covered pots. If you run out of *tortillas,* just ask for more—usually at no charge.

• Think of a *tortilla* not only as a food, but as a utensil—watch the Mexicans for an example.

• As soon as a *tortilla* is combined with another food, it changes names. Here are a few of the most common *tortilla* dishes: *burritos* (only in northern Mexico—means little burros in the south), *chalupas, chilaquiles, enchiladas, flautas, quesadillas, sopa de tortilla, tacos,* and *tostadas.*

• There is no consistent style in tortilla dishes throughout Mexico. Each restaurant seems to create its own version of each, and that version can be completely different from the restaurant next door. Usually, these Mexican dishes are very inexpensive.

WATERMELON *(SANDÍA)*

• Watermelon comes with every order of fruit salad or fruit plate and is usually cool and delicious.

• *Note:* Some health departments claim that watermelon is unsafe to eat in Mexico because farmers inject the fruit with unsafe water to make it heavier and worth more in the marketplace. You be the judge.

Mexican drinking idiosyncracies

• Many drinks in Mexico are served at room temperature *(al tiempo).* This includes cokes and beers, which most tourists would like to be ice cold. You won't get it that cold, but you will get it mildly cool if you'll ask for it *fría.*

- If you're at all anxious about the ice in a bar or restaurant, ask for your drinks *sin hielo*—without ice. Don't worry about ice in fancier places. It's made from purified water.

- The normal toast in Mexico is a hearty *salud*. You raise your glass, look the person in the eye, and drink to his health.

- Women are not welcome in many Mexican drinking spots. They won't be allowed into a *pulquería*—nor are most male tourists welcome here. They'll rarely feel comfortable in a *cantina,* which is male-oriented (urinals are sometimes located right next to the bar).

- A drink is *una copita* or *un trago.* If you accept a drink from a Mexican, you may be in for an all-night drunk. Once you've accepted a drink, you've entered into the macho world of everyday Mexico. Declining the next drink and the next and the next will be nearly impossible and very insulting—you could actually get into a fight. My advice: Politely but firmly decline all offers of a drink unless you have three days to spare in an all-out drinking binge.

- Note that Mexicans often deliberately get drunk, especially in fiestas. This behavior is shrugged off as normal.

- Bottles once opened will be finished off. Bottles are often left on the table as a way of keeping track of the total bill. It's macho not to be able to see across the table because of the stack of bottles there.

- If you're invited to a Mexican home, let the host fill all glasses.

BEER *(CERVEZA)*

- Mexico's seventeen breweries put out Mexico's favorite drink. Beer goes perfectly with Mexican cooking. It's also safe and cheap to drink.

- Once you've tried a Mexican beer, you'll be hooked. They're truly exceptional. It seems that every traveler has a personal favorite. Here are a few terms to help you get the kind of beer you like: light *(clara),* dark *(oscura),* semi-dark *(semioscura),* and draft *(de barril).*

• Mexicans often sprinkle salt and lime on the lid of a beer can before drinking. Can beer *(cerveza de late)* costs more than bottled beer *(embotellada).*

• There is a deposit for beer bottles. Sometimes, you'll need a receipt (get it at the time of purchase) to get a refund on beer bottles. Bottles will be marked either returnable *(retornable)* or nonreturnable *(desechable).* You may have to return the bottles where you got them to get a refund.

• Some bottles of beer come with an indentation in the bottom which is used to pop off the cap of another bottle of beer. This way you don't have to use your teeth if you forget your bottle opener—really ingenious!

• Other useful beer-drinking terms: case *(carton),* six-pack *(canastilla),* can *(bote),* bottle *(botella),* liter bottle *(caguama* or *ballena)*—the latter offer excellent value for your money.

• Cases of beer are sold at the *agencia* or *deposito de cerveza* in each town.

BLENDED DRINKS *(LICUADOS)*

• Mexicans like drinks that are prepared in blenders. These drinks are made from water, milk, sugar, eggs, and fruits—countless varieties of tropical fruits.

• Blended drinks are not always pure. You have to judge the sanitary conditions for yourself. Rarely do these places wash out the blender, rarely do they clean the glasses properly—best be wary.

• Frozen *licuados* are like popsicles. They're called *paletas,* and they too are only as pure as the water they're made from.

CHOCOLATE DRINKS

• The hot chocolate *(chocolate caliente)* in Mexico is extremely thick and rich. It's usually more expensive than tea or coffee.

• If you want your chocolate cool or cold, ask for it *fría.*

COCONUT MILK *(AGUA DE COCO)*

• You'll find coconuts for sale in many markets throughout Mexico. Coconuts rarely are contaminated. The coconut milk or water can be extremely refreshing.

• If you don't have anything to open the nut with, ask the vendor to whack it open with his machete. They're used to this request. Just make a nonverbal whacking motion—he'll understand. Have something with you to catch the milk.

COFFEE *(CAFÉ)*

• Coffee is a very popular drink in Mexico. It's as popular in the mid-afternoon with a sweet roll or pastry as it is in the morning.

• Most Mexicans do not drink coffee with a regular meal. They wait until the end of the meal to have it.

• Many restaurants use instant coffee to make coffee instead of brewing it from freshly ground beans.

• If you want your coffee black, ask for *café negro.* If you want milk *(leche),* cream *(crema),* or sugar *(azúgar),* you'll often have to ask for it. Service in Mexico tends to be very casual—whatever you ask for may or may not arrive within the half hour.

• ***Café con leche*** is very popular in the morning and late afternoon. If you order it, the waitress will bring you a large glass. She'll pour coffee into it until you signal her to stop. Usually, just a little coffee will do. She then fills the rest of the glass to the brim with hot milk. You add sugar to taste.

• A special note: In some people coffee causes diarrhea. If you have diarrhea, switch to tea until it's gone. You may want to stick with tea for the rest of the trip. This is really very common.

HORCHATA

• *Horchata,* a Mexican specialty, is a strange brew, milky white and made from a number of ingredients including cantaloupe seeds. Like any *licuado,* it's only as pure as the ingredients from which it's made.

JUICES *(JUGOS)*

• Fruit juices may well be your best overall buy in Mexico. Fresh orange juice is available in most places at anytime of the day.

• Juices are so good that a small glass *(chico)* may not be enough. The word for large is *grande,* and you'll end up with a milkshake-size glass filled to the brim with freshly squeezed juice.

• When juices are mixed together, they're called *cocteles de fruta.* You can ask for a number of unusual combinations according to taste.

• The most popular juices: *jugo de naranja* (orange juice), *jugo de tomate* (tomato juice), and *jugo de toronja* (grapefruit juice).

LIQUOR

• Imported liquor and wine are sold at many times the price of domestic liquor and wine. Since Mexican brands are usually more than adequate, most travelers skip all imports because of the exorbitant cost.

• Bottled liquor is available in supermarkets, liquor stores, and in cantinas (in the latter at an inflated price.)

• Particularly good buys are Oso Negro gin (100-proof and truly excellent); Bacardi, Castillo, and Potosí rums (very dry and smooth); and Kahlua liqueur—much less expensive in Mexico than in the United States or Canada, because it's made there.

• Plain alcohol *(alcohol)* goes for a song and is sold just about everywhere. Usually 190 proof, it will knock your socks off, even if you're not wearing any. It also makes an excellent fuel additive in wet weather when water gets in your gas.

PULQUE

• *Pulque,* a popular drink among Mexican workers, is made

from the juice of the agave plant. It's only mildly alcoholic, and if it were made from pure water, might be quite healthful.

● It is often made from impure water, and tourists should skip it. Furthermore, it's sold in *pulquerías* which pass as informal Mexican clubs where tourists are not really welcome.

REGIONAL DRINKS

● If you travel extensively in Mexico, you'll begin to run into regional drinks which vary from mild to explosive. Here are a few: *Acajul, Balche, Chi Cha, Coatepec, Colonche, Crema de Lima, Curados, Damiana, Moscos, Rompope, Sangre de Pichon, Sidra, Sotol, Tesguine, Tuba, Xtabentum.* And then there's *Holanda, Holcatzin . . .*

SANGRÍA

● *Sangría,* a real winner on a hot day, is a mixed fruit and wine punch—lots of lemonade, red wine, and slices of fruit floating in a cool pitcher.

● You don't see *sangría* very often—you may have to ask for it. Do it in a place you love and trust. It's very festive, romantic, and often quite expensive.

SANGRITA

● Don't confuse *sangrita* with *sangría.* They couldn't be more different. Imagine the taste of a drink made from tomato juice, grenadine, orange juice, and chilies—then try it without wincing (much better than it sounds).

SOFT DRINKS *(REFRESCOS)*

● Coca Cola has the largest truck fleet in the world, and one visit to Mexico will tell you why. You can be in the most remote area of Mexico, and a sign for coke will dangle from a tiny hut shaded by a single cactus restraining a tired mule.

● Soft drinks, not water, quench the average Mexican's thirst. Soft drinks are safe—that's all that has to be said.

● There is no such thing as a standard price for anything in Mexico. When you buy cokes, you'll soon understand free enterprise or the saying that cokes are 80 pesos in English and 35 *en español.*

SWEET WATERS *(AGUAS FRESCAS)*

• Drinks made from fruit juices mixed with water are called *aguas frescas.* They are much less expensive than fresh fruit juice and often impure. The more popular drinks: *chia* (made from chia seeds), *flor de jamaica* (hibiscus flower), *limón* (lemonade), *naranjada* (orangeade), *tamarindo* (tamarind), and *tepache* (pineapple).

TEA *(TÉ)*

• You can order tea in many restaurants, but it's not as popular as coffee. Many times you'll have to bring your own tea bag if you insist on a certain brand (not a bad thing to carry with you).

• Tea is a great drink for travelers because it's so easy to make. A simple immersion heater (available in many hardware stores) can heat a glass or cup of water to boiling in just a few minutes. If you're carrying tea with you, you've got a cup of tea moments later.

• Tea can calm an upset stomach and is often used as a cure for simple diarrhea.

• Following are teas commonly found in Mexican restaurants: black *(negro),* camomile *(té de manzanillo),* dog *(té de perro),* mint *(té de yerba buena),* and orange-blossom *(té de azar).*

• If you want iced tea, ask for *té helado.*

TEQUILA AND MEZCAL

• Tequila is one of the most popular drinks in Mexico, either drunk straight or in Margaritas and Tequila Sunrises.

• Traditionally, Mexicans drink tequila with a lick of salt and a squeeze of lime. The salt protects the inside of your mouth by causing you to salivate. And the lime covers the aftertaste of this potent drink. Salt first, then the shot of Tequila, and finally a squeeze of lime—that's the procedure.

● The better tequilas are aged *(anejo)* and turn yellow. Here's the normal progression: *joven* (aged three months), *extra* (aged roughly a year), *hornitos* (aged longer), and *commemorativo* (aged six or seven years).

● The most famous brands of tequila are José Cuervo and Sauza. Naturally, you pay the most for older tequilas from name-brand companies.

● Bootlegged tequila is quite common. Real tequila comes from Jalisco, Nayarit, or Tamaulipas. Look for DGN on the label—that signifies true tequila.

● Mezcal is less popular than tequila but made from the same kind of plant—the agave. Some bottles contain a worm which Mexican machos eat with a flourish (rumors are that these unfortunate worms are quickly and quietly disappearing).

WATER *(AGUA)*

● Bottled water is not as easy to find as you might think. You may often have to replace it with soft drinks or bottled beer.

● If you want water in a restaurant, you'll have to ask for it. After the first request, try again.

● Mineral water is *agua mineral,* and it comes carbonated *(con gas)* or noncarbonated *(sin gas).* If you order bottled water in a restaurant, the seal should be broken at the table. Don't count on this in Mexico.

● Shy away from tap water unless you've been told it's safe. Don't even use it to brush your teeth!

● Most hotels provide purified water *(agua purificada)* for their guests. This might be a bottle of mineral water, a huge jug in the hallway or in the room itself, or just a carafe of water. I have a strong suspicion that much of this water has not really been purified in the smaller, budget hotels.

● *Ice* is just frozen water—brilliant, right? But many travelers forget that it's only as pure as the water it's made from. Good hotels and restaurants buy ice that's made from safe water. You can get packaged ice made from purified water in many stores and at some Pemex stations.

WINE *(VINO)*

● Not very many Mexicans order wine with their meal, because it tends to be overpriced, not exceptionally good, and not appropriate with most Mexican food.

● Imported wines are sold at exorbitant prices and are rarely served except in top restaurants and hotels. There's a 100 percent tax on imported wines, a good reason to avoid them.

● If you want to sample some local wines *(vinos del país),* ask your waiter or wine steward for advice. Mexico does produce some decent vintages.

● However, quality control is low. If you get a bad bottle of wine, don't hesitate to send it back.

● If you're in doubt about Mexican wines, why not try a glass first? Here are a few terms to help you make a choice: *blanco* (white), *tinto* (red), *rosado* (rose), *champaña* (champagne), *dulce* (sweet), and *seco* (dry).

● You can buy bottled wine in liquor stores and supermarkets. Forgot a corkscrew? It's called a *sacacorchos.*

● One final tip: In rural areas if you order a *vino blanco,* you'll end up with a shot of tequila. Order a *vino blanco de uva*— they'll probably just shake their heads as they send out one of their kids to fetch a bottle on his bicycle.

Basic restaurant vocabulary

breakfast	*desayuno*
check, bill	*cuenta*
cup	*taza*
delicious	*delicioso*
dinner	*cena, comida*
fork	*tenedor*
glass	*vaso*
goblet	*copa*
good	*bueno*
knife	*cuchillo*
lunch	*almuerzo, comida*
meal	*comida*

menu	menú, carta
napkin	servilleta
plate	plato, platillo
rare	poco cocido
snack	antojito, botana
specialty of the house	especialidad de la casa
spicy	picante, picoso
spoon	cuchara
supper	cena
table	mesa
tasty	sabroso, rico
tax	impuesto
tip	propina
toothpick	palillo
to the side	al lado
waiter, waitress	mesero, mesera
well-done	bien cocido

BREAD (PAN)

bizcocho	biscuit
bolillo	roll
buñuelo	bun, cruller
galleta	cookie, cracker
pan	bread
pan dulce	sweet roll
pan tostado	toast

SOUP (SOPA)

caldo	broth
caldo de pollo	chicken broth
consomé de camarón	shrimp consomme
consomé de pollo	chicken consomme
consomé de res	beef broth
gazpacho	cold vegetable soup
médula	bone marrow soup
menudo	tripe soup
sopa clara	chicken consomme
sopa de ajo	garlic soup

sopa de chicaros	pea soup
sopa de flor de calabaza	squash flower soup
sopa de lentejas	lentil soup
sopa de lima	lime soup
sopa de pescado	fish soup
sopa de verduras	vegetable soup
sopa juliana	vegetable soup
sopa tártara	chicken consomme with egg

MISCELLANEOUS

ajo	garlic
aceite	oil
azúgar	sugar
mantequilla	butter
canela	cinnamon
mayonesa	mayonnaise
mermelada	jam
miel	syrup
miel de abeja	honey
mostaza	mustard
pimienta	pepper
queso	cheese
sal	salt
salsa	sauce
vinagre	vinegar

MEAT *(CARNE)*

ahumado	smoked
alambre	shish kebab
albondigas	meatballs
ancas de rana	frogs legs
asado	roast
barbacoa	barbecue
bistec de res	beefsteak
cabrito	kid goat
caracoles	snails
carne	meat
carne fría	cold cuts

carne molida	ground meat
carne deshebrada	shredded meat
carne asada	broiled beef strips
carne de res	beef
carnero	mutton
carnitas	deep-fried pork
cerdo	pork
chicarrón	deep-fried pigskin
chorizo	sausage
chuleta	chop, cutlet
conejo	rabbit
cordero	lamb
filete	tenderloin, filet
ganso	goose
hígado	liver
jamón	ham
lengua	tongue
manitas de puerco	pig's feet
pancita	tripe
pato	duck
pavo	turkey
pechuga	chicken breast
perdiz	partridge
pichón	squab
pierna	chicken leg
pollo	chicken
puerco	pork
res	beef
riñones	kidneys
rosbif	roastbeef
salchicha	sausage
sesos	brains
ternera	veal
tocino	bacon
venado	venison

FISH (PESCADO) AND SHELLFISH (MARISCO)

abulón	abalone
almejas	clams

anchoas	anchovies
arengues	herring
atún	tuna
bacalao	codfish
cabrilla	grouper
caguama	turtle
calamar	squid
caracol	conch
camarones	shrimp
cazon	shark
corvina	sea trout
dorado	dolphin
escalopas	scallops
filete	filet
huachinango	red snapper
jaiba	crab
jurel	yellowtail
langosta	lobster
lenguado	flounder, sole
lisa	mullet
lobina	bass
merluza	hake
mero	sea bass
mojarra	perch-like
ostion	oyster
pámpano	pompano
pescado	fish (dead)
ahumado	smoked
a la gabardina	breaded
a la milanesa	breaded
a las brasas	coal roasted
a la parilla	grilled
al mojo de ajo	garlic-fried
brocheta	brochette
empanizado	breaded
frito	fried
natural	boiled
rostizado	roasted
pez	fish (alive)

pez espada	swordfish
pez gallo	roosterfish
pez blanco	whitefish
pulpo	octopus
robalo	snook
sardinas	sardines
sierra	mackerel
solo	pike
trucha	trout

VEGETABLES *(LEGUMBRES)*

aceituna	olive
aguacate	avocado
alcachofa	artichoke
apio	celery
arroz	rice
betabel	beet
calabaza	squash, pumpkin
camote	yam
cebolla	onion
champiñones	mushrooms
chayote	squash-like
chicaros	peas
col	cabbage
col fermentada	sauerkraut
coliflor	cauliflower
ejotes	string beans
elote	corn
ensalada	salad
esparragos	asparagus
espinaca	spinach
garbanzos	chickpeas
frijoles	refried beans
jicame	turnip-like
jitomate	tomato
lechuga	lettuce
nopales	cactus leaves
papas	potatoes
pepino	cucumber

pimiento verde	green pepper
rábanos	radishes
tomates	green tomatoes
zanahoria	carrot

EGGS *(HUEVOS)*

a la Mexicana	mixed with onion, tomato, herbs
cocidos	hard-boiled
con chorizo	with sausage
con frijoles	with refried beans
con jamón	with ham
con tocino	with bacon
crudos	raw
duros	hard-boiled
estrellados	fried
frescos	fresh
fritos	fried
motulenos	mixed with tortilla, ham, cheese
poches	poached
rancheros	fried, on a tortilla with sauce
revueltos	scrambled
tibios	soft-boiled
omelet de champiñones	mushroom omelet
omelet de jamón	ham omelet
omelet de queso	cheese omelet
omelet surtido	mixed omelet
tortilla de huevos	omelet

FRUITS *(FRUTAS)*

cerezas	cherries
chabacanco	apricot
ciruela	plum
ciruela pasa	prune
dátiles	dates
durazno	peach
frambuesa	raspberries
fresa	strawberry
guanabana	guanabana
guayaba	guava

higo	fig
limón	lime
mamey	mamey
mango	mango
manzana	apple
mandarina	tangerine
melón	cantaloupe
membrillo	quince
naranja	orange
papaya	papaya
pasas	raisins
pera	pear
piña	pineapple
plátano	cooking banana
sandía	watermelon
tamarindo	tamarind
toronja	grapefruit
tuna	prickly pear
uva	grape
zapote	zapote
zarzamora	blackberry

DESSERTS *(POSTRES)*

arroz con leche	rice pudding
flan	custard
helado	ice cream
nieve	sorbet
pastel	cake
pay	pie

NUTS *(NUECES)*

almendra	almond
cacahuate	peanuts
coco	coconut
nuez	walnut
nuez de la India	cashew

BEVERAGES *(BEBIDAS)*

agua	water
aguardente	brandy

café	coffee
café con leche	coffee with milk
café americano	weak coffee
café negro	black coffee
café con crema	coffee with cream
cerveza	beer
cerveza clara	light beer
cerveza obscura	dark beer
chocolate caliente	hot chocolate
chocolate fría	chocolate milk
coctel	cocktail
crema	cream
ginebra	gin
jugo	juice
leche	milk
limonada	lemonade
refresco	soft drink
ron	rum
sangría	lemonade and red wine
sangrita	spicy tomato drink
té	tea
vino	wine
vino blanco	white wine
vino de champaña	Champagne
vino tinto	red wine
vodka	vodka
whisky	whisky

COMMUNICATING

Don't let the language barrier discourage you from getting what you want out of a trip to Mexico. Naturally, you can become better acquainted with Mexicans if you can really speak Spanish, but you can still have a good time in Mexico with very little knowledge of the language. Throughout this book you'll find the key words to get what you want in a specific situation.

SPEAKING

You'll have little trouble communicating in areas where there's heavy tourist traffic. You'll usually find someone in most hotels, restaurants, shops, and travel terminals who can help you out.

However, when you get off the beaten path, you'll run into a language barrier. But you'll get by combining a few key words with sign language.

The fundamentals

Since it takes years to learn a foriegn language, most people don't even try. However, you should take the time to learn a few basic expressions and how to count, not only because it will prove helpful but also because it's the right thing to do.

No book can show you how to pronounce foreign words correctly! Have a native speaker pronounce them for you (and don't be afraid to ask). Most people are complimented that you're taking the time to try.

BASIC EXPRESSIONS

These are the everyday basic expressions that you should know before traveling in Mexico. People will really appreciate it if you use them.

hello (good day)	*buenos días (in the morning)*
(good evening)	*buenas tardes (in the afternoon and evening)*
(good night)	*buenas noches*
good-bye	*hasta luego, adiós*
please	*por favor*
thank you	*gracias*
you're welcome	*de nada*
yes	*sí*
no	*no*
I don't understand	*no entiendo; no comprendo*
I want	*quiero*
How are you?	*¿Cómo está usted?*
slowly	*despacio*
How do you say . . . in Spanish?	*¿Cómo se dice . . . en español?*
Do you have	*¿Tiene usted?*
How much is it?	*¿Cuánto cuesta?*
who	*quién*
where	*dónde*
when	*cuándo*
why	*por qué*

NUMBERS

Knowing numbers is essential for anyone interested in keeping costs down and knowing what's going on around them.

0	*cero*
1	*uno*
2	*dos*

3	*tres*
4	*cuatro*
5	*cinco*
6	*seis*
7	*siete*
8	*ocho*
9	*nueve*
10	*diez*
11	*once*
12	*doce*
13	*trece*
14	*catorce*
15	*quince*
16	*diez y seis*
17	*diez y siete*
18	*diez y ocho*
19	*diez y nueve*
20	*veinte*
30	*treinta*
40	*cuarenta*
50	*cincuenta*
60	*sesenta*
70	*setenta*
80	*ochenta*
90	*noventa*
100	*cien (ciento)*
200	*doscientos*
500	*quinientos*

DAYS OF THE WEEK

Monday	*lunes*
Tuesday	*martes*
Wednesday	*miércoles*
Thursday	*jueves*
Friday	*viernes*
Saturday	*sábado*
Sunday	*domingo*

HELPFUL ADJECTIVES

bad	*malo*
beautiful	*hermoso*
broken	*roto, quebrado*
cheap	*barato*
clean	*limpio*
closed	*cerrado*
cold	*frío*
comfortable	*cómodo*
dangerous	*peligroso*
difficult	*difícil*
dirty	*sucio*
drinkable	*potable*
early	*temprano*
easy	*fácil*
expensive	*caro*
fair	*justo*
far	*lejos*
fast	*rápido*
friendly	*amable*
good	*bueno*
happy	*contento*
heavy	*pesado*
high	*alto*
hot	*caliente*
ill	*enfermo*
large	*grande*
late	*tarde*
long	*largo*
low	*bajo*
old	*viejo*
open	*abierto*
pretty	*bonito*
short	*corto*
slow	*lento*
small	*pequeño*
ugly	*feo*

Tricks for communicating

- Don't be complicated. Say "Menu, please", not "I would like a menu, please."

- Repeat statements or questions only once—slowly and without raising your voice. No go? Smile and say, *"Gracias."*

- If your comprehension is limited, try to communicate in writing. Carry paper and pen, and get waiters and clerks to write down prices for you.

- By all means, try. Say something, even if it's in English. Silence is considered rude.

- In short, don't be intimidated by the language barrier. Don't let it stop you from venturing into remote areas that have barely been touched by modern tourism.

Some confusing words

- A library is called a *biblioteca,* while a bookstore is a *librería.*

- The Gulf of California is known as the Sea of Cortez or *Mar de Cortez* in Spanish.

- Mexicans refer to the Rio Grande as the *Río Bravo.*

- *Monte* doesn't mean mountain. It's the word for jungle or forest or brush.

- *Señorita,* which means Miss, can be used with women of all ages unless you know they're married. If they are, the correct term is *señora.*

- México can mean Mexico (the country), Mexico (the State), or Mexico City.

Asking directions

Asking directions is a real art, one which comes with experience and common sense. The skill varies with each country, and Mexico has some ringers for you to learn.

TRICKS TO ASKING DIRECTIONS

• Ask directions from men, especially in rural areas where women will often avoid contact with foreigners.

• Always greet someone before you ask any questions. This is considered basic good manners. *"Buenos días, señor,"* is all it takes.

• Keep your question ultra-simple. Don't get fancy. All you want to do is to get to where you're going.

• The simplest way to do this is to use the word *a* in Spanish. This means *to* and is pronounced "ah" as if you're showing your tonsils to a doctor. Follow *a* by the place you want to get to. For example, "ah" San Miguel de Allende, or "ah" Acapulco, or whatever destination. Now say this to a Mexican as a question, and you've found the simplest way to ask a direction.

• If you're not going in the right direction, the Mexican will shake his finger and point you in another direction. If you're going in the right direction, he'll just nod and say, *"sí."* You do not need an extensive vocabulary to communicate directions!

SENSE THE NATURE OF THE RESPONSE

• It is considered more polite in Mexico to give a wrong answer than none at all. You can sometimes tell when someone really doesn't know the right direction.

• Some people may be confused by your accent or your looks. They don't really listen to what you're saying, because they're intrigued by how different you are.

• If you don't trust an answer, ask again—but this time ask someone else. If you get a different answer, ask yet another person. You're trying to get a consensus.

THINGS NOT TO DO

• Don't take out a fancy, multicolored map and ask a peasant to show you the right direction to San Miguel de Allende. The odds are he's never seen a map before, and you'll spend the next twenty minutes showing it to him.

● Don't get angry if someone doesn't understand you. It's not their fault that you're lost. In fact, never think of yourself as being lost. You're just experiencing a part of Mexico you've never seen before.

OTHER TIPS ON DIRECTIONS

● A small compass can be very useful on any trip. If you're traveling in remote areas, this can at least get you headed in the general direction.

● Remember that some areas may have more than one name. This can be very confusing and is usually only a problem in off-road travel.

USEFUL VOCABULARY

You don't have to speak fluent Spanish to travel widely in Mexico, but it helps to know a few words relating to directions:

Where is . . . ?	*¿Dónde está . . . ?*
to the right	*a la derecha*
to the left	*a la izquierda*
straight ahead	*(sempre) derecho*
one block	*una cuadra*
on the corner	*en la esquina*
in front	*en frente*
near	*cerca*
far	*lejos*
here	*aquí*
there	*allí*

WRITING

Letters from home, and the postcards you send, can be especially important while you're traveling. No news may be good news, but news is still fun when you're far away from home.

Useful vocabulary in the post office

address (return)	*dirección (del remitente)*
airgram	*aerogramo*
airmail	*correo aéreo*
box	*caja*
certified	*certificado*
change of address card	*tarjeta de cambiar*
duty, tax	*impuesto*
envelope	*sobre*
express	*urgente*
general delivery	*lista de correos*
insurance	*seguros*
letter	*carta*
package	*paquete*
postage	*porte, franquero*
post card	*tarjeta*
poste restante	*poste restante*
post office	*correo*
printed papers	*impreso*
receipt	*recibo*
registered	*registrado*
return receipt	*acuso de recibo*
special handling	*entrega immediata*
stamp	*estampilla, timbre*
string	*cuerda*
weight	*peso*
wrapped	*envuelto*

Staying in touch

- Duplicate your itinerary to give to friends and relatives you'd like to keep in touch with. If you don't have an exact itinerary, approximate your plans as best you can.

How mail should be addressed

- Ask correspondents to write "Tourist Mail—Hold for Arrival" followed by the approximate date on all mail.

- Ask friends to *type,* not write, the address on the envelope.

Your last name should be in caps and underlined. Do *not* have them use your middle name! This only confuses Mexicans. An address typed in this way has a much greater chance of getting to you.

● Ask them to address each envelope to an individual person, not to a couple. Otherwise, the couple may have to show up to collect it.

● Never have packages mailed to you in Mexico. They will either be lost, stolen, or held in customs until you go through unbelievable red tape to collect them—not to mention the duties you'll have to pay.

About Mexican addresses

● Some cities are divided into neighborhoods to make mail delivery much easier. In Mexico City these areas are called *colonias.* Each neighborhood might have a street of the same name, so including the *colonia* in the overall address can be crucial.

● *Calle* in Spanish means "street," and it's often omitted in addresses. *Y* means "and" which is used in addresses to connect streets. *S/N (sin número)* means that a place has no number at all. *X* means "by the corner of" and is used in many addresses in Mérida.

● If you're trying to find a certain address in Mexico City, you may be confused by the numbering—it's not always consecutive. No wonder the mail doesn't always get through!

● Note that in looking up addresses the letter "ñ" will be listed in words in the phone book as if it were a separate letter of the alphabet. So *anzuelo* would be listed before *añadidura* in the dictionary.

● Note too that "ch", "ll", and "rr" are considered separate letters in the Spanish alphabet.

COMMON ABBREVIATIONS

Apto.	**Apartado postal**	P.O. Box
Av.	**Avenida**	Avenue

C.	**Calle**	Street
Calz.	**Calzada**	Boulevard
DDT	**Departamento de Tránsito**	Transit department (cops)
D.F.	**Distrito Federal**	Federal District
E.,	**Este**	East
EUM	**Estados Unidos Mexicanos**	Mexico
EE.UU or E.U.A.	**Estados Unidos de America**	U.S.A.
Hnos.	**Hermanos**	Brothers
KM	**kilómetro**	kilometer
kg.	**kilogramo**	kilogram
Kph.	**Kilómetros por hora**	Kilometers per hour
Lic.	**Licenciado**	Lawyer
MN	**Moneda Nacional**	Mexican Currency
N, Nte.	**Norte**	North
NO	**Noroeste**	Northwest
No.	**Número**	Number
NE	**Noreste**	Northeast
O.	**Oeste**	West
Ote.	**Oriente**	East
P.B.	**Piso Bajo**	Main Floor
Pte.	**Poniente**	West
S.	**Sur**	South
SA	**Sociedad anonima**	Inc.
SE	**Sureste**	Southeast
SO	**Suroeste**	Southwest
Sr., Sra., Srta.	**Señor, Señora, Señorita**	Sir, Madam, Miss

When mail should be sent

• Mail should be sent two weeks before you're expected arrival in a specific area. That's about how long it can take a letter to reach its destination in Mexico.

• Do not have mail sent to you during Christmas (from December 16 to January 6), during Easter, and late in May. During these times no one bothers with the mail. Mexicans simply accept this fact. After all, they're on holiday too!

How mail should be sent

● All mail should be sent *Airmail (correo aéreo)!* The stamps should indicate the amount of postage (don't use the D stamps).

Where mail should be sent

● If you're staying in a series of hotels, give your correspondents the exact address of each. Hotels will hold onto the mail until you arrive.

● If you're not staying in hotels, you can still have mail delivered to them. Be sure to tip the person at the front desk in this instance.

● You can also have mail sent to American Express offices wherever they're located in Mexico. If you have either an American Express credit card or American Express traveler's checks, this service is free of charge. If you don't, then there is a small fee. Expect long mail lines in the peak travel seasons in these offices. Your mail will be returned to sender if not collected within thirty days. Note that for a charge you can have mail forwarded from these offices.

● You can also have mail sent to post offices in large cities and smaller towns via General Delivery. This is called *Poste Restante* or *Lista de Correos.* You have to go to the post office to pick up your mail, which will be returned to sender if not collected within ten days. There's usually a small charge for this service per letter.

● If your mail is sent to *Lista de Correos,* your name will actually be posted on a list in the post office. This gives you notice that mail has been received. Here's an example of the format of mailing a letter to Mexico using this service:

John WHITMAN
Lista de Correos
Oaxaca, Oaxaca
México

- In this instance, Oaxaca is both a city and a state—which can often be the case in Mexico.

What's needed to pick up mail

- You have to have official identification to pick up mail. The passport is the very best because it has your picture and is the most reliable document available.

- If you want to pick up someone else's mail, you must have a permission slip from them and some form of identification. Post offices do not like this.

- If mail is addressed to a couple, the clerk has every right to ask that the couple be present to pick up the mail.

- If any fees are involved, you'll have to pay these before receiving the mail.

Sending mail home

- Send all letters and post cards by *correo aéreo* and mark this in bold letters somewhere on the mail.

- Never mail letters in a collection box on the street. These can be left for two or more weeks! Mail everything at a post office.

Saving money

- Aerograms are the least expensive way to write letters to the United States. You can buy these at the post office.

- Free post cards and stationery are often provided in hotels. Ask for them if they're not in your room.

Mexican mail idiosyncracies

- You've already picked up on a few by reading this section. The main one being that the post office is a zoo at Christmas and Easter time.

- Another is that posted hours are not taken as gospel. Employees come and go more or less on schedule depending upon their mood and the length of soccer games on the tube.

● Many post offices close for a little siesta. The length of the siesta varies according to the solar charts. Siestas are sacred, accept them.

TELEPHONING

It's not easy, and it's not impossible, using the telephone system in Mexico. The Mexican phone system is somewhat idiosyncratic, but you can make good use of it with a few hints.

Basic telephone vocabulary

call	*llamada*
call (to)	*llamar*
collect	*a cobrar*
Hello	*Hola, Bueno*
long distance	*larga distancia*
number	*número*
operator (international)	*operador (internacional)*
person (calling)	*de parte de*
person to person	*persona a persona*
station to station	*a quien contesta*
telephone	*teléfono*
telephone office	*oficina de teléfonos*
United States	*los Estados Unidos*

Mexicans and the telephone system

● In some areas you'll find that calls are filled with static. The Baja and off-shore islands fall into this category.

● Phones sometimes don't work at all—period.

● Mexicans do not like answering questions over the phone. You'll run into a special, noninformation lingo, which makes it difficult to accomplish much over the phone.

● Once you understand this, you go in person to get information on almost anything.

Local calls

- The simplest place to make a local call is from your hotel.

- If you have a phone in your room, you may be charged a small daily fee for its use. Or you may be charged on a per call basis. Ask if you're concerned about the cost of frequent local calls.

- If there's no phone in your room, you can often make local calls at the front desk. There may or may not be a charge for this service depending upon the hotel policy.

- You can also use public pay phones, as in the United States and Canada. These phones are for local calls only. Pay phones take 20-centavo *(veinte)*, 50-centavo *(cinquenta)*, and 1-peso coins. Keep some handy.

- Place the coin in the slot. It drops down when the other party answers. The first coin is good for three minutes. If you need more time, drop in additional coins.

Where to make long-distance calls

- You can make long-distance calls in most hotels, in the telephone offices of many towns and cities, at the airport, and at many booths displaying the sign *servicio de larga distancia.*

What will the charge be

There are five ways of making a call from Mexico with varying rates and added charges. Following is a chart giving you a typical com-

Type of call	Charge for first three minutes	Additional charge per minute	Additional charge per call
Direct dial day	$ 3.60	$ 1.20	49% tax
Direct dial night	$ 2.70	$ .90	49% tax
Collect	$ 6.30	$ 2.10	$ 2.00
Credit card	$ 6.30	$ 2.10	$ 2.78
Person to person	$ 11.04	$ 3.68	$ 2.78

parison in U.S. dollars (note that the actual charges vary by place and rate of exchange, so that this chart is just meant to give you an idea of *cost comparison*).

Miscellaneous charges and rip-offs

• The *hotel surcharge* is probably the single biggest rip-off in the travel business today. The hotel jacks up your phone bill by whatever amount it can get away with, calling it a service charge. You should always ask what this charge will be *before* making a long distance call. Note that you pay this charge even on a collect call!

• Another interesting charge: You pay a fee if no one answers. You pay a larger fee if someone refuses to accept your collect call. Try to work out an *exact* time to contact someone if you plan to call long distance from Mexico. But make sure that the other party knows that it may take several hours for you to reach him. For example, tell the person that you'll call Sunday evening between 9 P.M. and midnight.

• Finally, you pay a 15 percent VAT (Value Added Tax) on calls in Mexico.

Keeping the costs down

• There's a substantial discount on long-distance calls made on Sunday or from 8 P.M. to 4:30 A.M. Regulations change periodically, so inquire about current off-hours.

• Finally, if you'll be on the line for a long time, have the other party call you back station to station.

TELEGRAPHING

• You have to pay for telegrams in Mexico. They cannot be sent collect.

• An urgent telegram will be sent immediately, a regular telegram will be sent on the day its paid for, and a night letter goes out the next day at the latest.

- Night letters sometimes get through as fast as regular ones, but you can never be sure.

- The price you pay is related to the speed at which you want the telegram to get through.

Basic telegraph vocabulary

address	*dirección*
night letter	*carta nocturna, carta de noche*
regular	*ordinario*
telegram	*telegrama*
telegraph office	*officina de telégrafos*
urgent	*urgente*

NONVERBAL COMMUNICATION

People pick up on a lot more than you say. You don't even have to open your mouth, and they begin to have a reaction to you.

A relaxed attitude

- If you smile and seem relaxed around people, then they start to let their guard down. Mexicans pick up on your tension and fears.

- If you're impatient at a front desk or waiting in line, Mexicans tend to react negatively to you and make you wait a little longer. Patience is seen as a virtue, and the more your manner mirrors this quality, the better you'll be treated.

Simple gestures denoting respect

- A simple nod or bow goes over well as an acknowledgement, especially in rural areas.

- Shaking hands when meeting and leaving people means a lot. Most tourists aren't going to be shaking hands with every Mexican they meet, but if you have a good rapport with someone or appreciate a favor or had a good time bargaining, then shake that person's hand.

Things that say sex

- What says sex to one person may seem innocuous to an-other. In Mexico the following things say sex: bare skin, espe-cially breasts (says sex in a lot of places); tight-fitting clothes (look at how Mexican women dress); long, free-flowing hair (especially blond); lipstick, fingernail polish, and lots of makeup; and any overt flirting or drinking in public.

- Finally, a woman traveling alone says sex—no matter how unfair that may seem to you.

What doesn't say sex

- In Mexico men give men big hugs and kisses, and women do the same to women. Women holding each other's hands has no overt sexual connotation whatsoever.

POOR COMMUNICATION—CAUSING TROUBLE

Occasionally, what you say or do can cause some embarrassing moments in Mexico. Here's what to watch out for.

What not to do in Mexico

- It is very polite to admire things in the United States and Canada. In Mexico, this can cause trouble. If you admire something that belongs to someone else, he may give it to you. Imagine how guilty you'd feel if it were something personal or valuable?

- Machismo might be defined as a personal obsession with one's image of manliness. Many Mexican men fit the defini-tion. So lay off the horn, don't get into drinking bouts, accept any gifts graciously, and let lies lay—you can't win in a con-frontation with a macho.

- Women should never respond to any comments in the street. Even negative responses are seen as an open invitation to more harassment. Pretend the hissing, whistling, and open sexual invitations don't exist. You're above it all—the only attitude to have.

• Don't sit back and take abuse in Mexico. Get in there and push the way the Mexicans do—they'll admire you for it. If you don't speak, God doesn't hear. There are lots of people speaking at once in Mexico!

DOING THINGS

This section is devoted to special-interest activities, the fun things that draw over 5 million tourists to Mexico each year.

ARCHAEOLOGY

It is estimated that there are 11,000 archaeological sites in Mexico, many still unexplored and undiscovered. It is an archaeologist's paradise.

Major sites in the country

- The best-known and most publicized major sites are Chichén Itza (Mérida), Monte Albán (Oaxaca), Palenque (Villahermosa), and Uxmal (Mérida). The towns closest to these sites are in parentheses.

- The most impressive of these is Palenque. But it's isolated, requiring a long trek to get to.

- Monte Albán on the outskirts of Oaxaca has been closed occasionally by strikes, which can be frustrating since it and the market are the two main reasons to visit the city. Always ask in advance if the site is open before making a special trip to see it.

Not to be missed in Mexico City

● The Anthropology Museum in Mexico City is one of the best in the world. It is closed on Mondays, so plan your trip accordingly. It can easily be reached by subway or bus—just ask.

● Many visitors prefer starting on the second floor of this museum. Here you'll find a great deal about the culture and life-style of the many peoples who make up the overall population of Mexico.

● On the outskirts of Mexico City you'll find the Pirámides de Teotihuacán. These pyramids are very impressive and worth seeing. You can get to them by car (via tollway), tour, or public transportation. (Take the subway to the Indios Verdes metro stop. From there go to the Zona Arqueologico by bus.)

A lovely minor site

● Tulúm, south of Cancún and Cozumel, is a lesser sight, but it offers good snorkeling just off the ruins—a potent combination!

Gainesville, Florida

● Why mention Gainesville in a guide to Mexico? Because here you'll find the best reproductions of the art of Bonampak, a site which has been left to deteriorate over the years.

Fees

● All sites charge a small fee for parking (tip the attendant) and for entry. Fees drop on Sundays.

Hours

● Always get information locally on hours and days of closing. Try to arrive as early as possible to avoid the crowds.

Regulations

● If you're into photography, don't look too professional. You can't *legally* use tripods, flash, or movie cameras in archaeo-logical zones without special permits.

Clothes

● Wear comfortable shoes and a hat to protect you from the sun. Bring a swimsuit to Palenque, Tulúm, and Uxmal to take advantage of the clear pools or sea in those areas.

Sound and light shows

● Sound and light shows are given in English at many of the most spectacular ruins from October to May. Inquire ahead of time about exact hours. Bring warm clothes for performances during the winter—it can get quite chilly!

ART MUSEUMS (SEE SIGHTSEEING)

ART

● Check with the nearest Mexican Government Tourist Office about the courses offered in San Miguel de Allende—many famous writers and artists have taught there.

● Bring as many of your own supplies into the country as possible.

BALLET

The Ballet Folklórico de México is a *must* for all tourists.

Where to go

● The ballet is usually performed in the Palace of Fine Arts *(Palacio de las Bellas Artes)* in Mexico City.

● It is sometimes given in the National Auditorium in Chapultepec Park or at the Museo de la Ciudad near the zócalo in Mexico City.

• Performances similar to these take place in Acapulco and Cancún.

When

• There are three performances a week in Mexico City. Usually, these are on Wednesdays at 9:00 P.M., and on Sundays at 9:30 A.M. and 9:00 P.M.

About tickets

• Many tour companies and travel agencies sell tickets at inflated prices.

• You can get your own at the box office at the Palace of Fine Arts (Bellas Artes metro station).

• The office is open 10:30 A.M. to 1:00 P.M., and 4:00 P.M. to 7:00 P.M. Note the break for a siesta.

• It is usually easiest to get tickets for the Sunday morning performance (leaves you plenty of time for the Sunday afternoon bullfight).

• The price is very reasonable and varies by section. Pay extra to be on the main floor, close up.

• If you're hard up, settle for the highest seats in the house (bring binoculars). Skip these seats if you're prone to vertigo.

BEACHCOMBING

Some of the best beachcombing beaches are the ones isolated on the Baja facing the Pacific.

BEACHES

beach	*playa*
coconut	*coco*

coconut palm	*palmera*
current	*corriente*
it's cloudy	*esta nublado*
it's (very) hot	*hace (mucho) calor*
it's raining	*esta lloviendo*
sand	*arena*
shell	*concha*
sun	*sol*
tide (high) (low)	*marea (alta) (baja)*
undertow	*resaca*
water	*agua*
wind	*viento*
it's windy	*hace viento*

With 6,000 miles of coastline Mexico offers just about any kind of beach for any kind of personality.

- The water in the Pacific is not as clear or turquoise-colored as the water in the Gulf of Mexico or Caribbean.

- The water is poor around Tampico and Veracruz.

- The water is the calmest in the Gulf of Mexico and in the Sea of Cortez.

- The beaches on the Pacific have dark sand which gets extremely hot—wear sandals. (Remember Dudley Moore in the movie *10*).

- The white sands of the Caribbean stay cool—absolutely fantastic.

- There's tar on some of the beaches, another good reason to wear sandals. You can get it off with kerosene.

- Before you get into the water, ask the locals if it's safe!

BIRDING

Some of the best birding spots are Coba in the Yucatán (200 species a year pass through), Isla Contoy off Isla Mujeres, Isla Raza in the Bahía de los Angeles in the Baja, Rancho Liebre Barranca north of Mazatlán, and Río Lagartos (flamingo sanctuary).

- If you'll be traveling in the Baja, read Ann Zwinger's *A Desert Country Near the Sea.*

- Pick up one of the following field guides: *Audubon Water Bird Guide, A Field Guide to Mexican Birds, A Guide to Field Identification Birds of North America.*

- Bring a good, compact pair of field glasses (Steiner's are fine).

BULLFIGHT *(CORRIDA DE TOROS)*

Let's skip the cruelty debate and get right to the point—Mexicans love bullfights and so do a lot of tourists.

The best bullfights

- The best bullfights take place at the Plaza México in Mexico City. The stadium holds 50,000 avid fans and attracts the top matadors.

- The best matadors perform from December to March. Apprentices *(novilladas)* take over in the off-season—these fights are not recommended (poor bulls, poorer fights).

When

- Fights start at exactly 4:00 P.M. on Sunday—the one thing in Mexico that's always on time.

Tickets

- The best tickets are called *barrera,* the second-best *primer tendido.* You won't get these unless you have an "in" or a dynamite concierge (tip well).

- All travel books tell you to get tickets in the shade *(sombre)* and to avoid the sun *(sol).* Since Mexico City floats under a sea of smog, most of the time this advice is irrelevant.

- You can buy tickets at a steep price from tour operators and travel agencies. The extra money is probably worth it since tickets can be hard to come by, and the tour does provide transportation to the ring.

• However, you can get tickets at the ring from scalpers. And, if you're daring and willing to wait, you'll pick them up for face value just as the fight starts.

More bullfighting tips

• Bring binoculars! These will add immeasurably to the spectacle.

• Wear a hat, and if it's sunny (it can happen), bring sunglasses for the *sol* section.

• Bring a newspaper or rent a cushion at the stadium for fanny fatigue.

• Bring small bills and coins to pay for snacks and drinks.

• Don't bring valuables of any kind with you—this is a favored area for pickpockets.

• If you don't like a fight, leave. Showing disgust or getting upset is offensive to Mexicans who view bullfights as an art.

• Finally, most bullfights fall far short of art. If you see a great one, you'll know it.

CAMPING (SEE P. 216)

CLAMMING (SEE FISHING)

CLIMBING *(ALPINISMO)*

Although the sport is not well organized in Mexico, many climbers have found the volcanoes and ranges of the country fascinating.

• You're on your own if you get in trouble. Bear this in mind on all climbs.

• Some of the rock is extremely weathered and potentially dangerous, and much of the terrain is covered with dense jungle.

COCKFIGHTS *(PELEA DE GALLOS)*

In Mexico, sharp steel blades are sometimes added to the spurs to make cockfights even more deadly. Inquire locally if you're interested in seeing a fight, which is an excuse for heavy betting and heavier drinking. Be wary as a tourist in this situation.

DIVING (SEE SCUBA DIVING)

DRINKING (SEE P. 275)

DUNE BUGGIES

Californians have taken to the dunes near San Felipe in the Baja.

EXPLORATION

Much of Mexico remains to be mapped and explored. This is a highly specialized activity, and most experienced explorers recommend a guide, especially for remote, jungle areas.

FISHING

One of the primary attractions of Mexico for many tourists is its fabulous deep-sea, surf, and specialized fishing. It offers some of the finest fishing in the world.

Popular fish

Listed below are some of the many popular fish in Mexico. Names change by region in the country and can cause confusion, but the following list will help you communicate with charter boat captains and local fishermen.

albacore	albacore
amberjack	pez fuerte
ballyhoo, balao	escribano
barracuda	barracuda, picuda
bass (black)	lobina
bass (black sea)	cabrilla
black marlin	marlín negro
blue marlin	marlín azul
bonefish	macabí
bonita	bonito
catfish	bagre
corbina	curbina
dolphin, dorado	dorado, dolphin
grouper	cherna, mero, garropa
jack (crevalle)	jurel (toro)
jewfish	mero
lady fish	pez dama
mackerel (Spanish)	sierra
marlin	marlín
mojarra	mojarra
mullet	lisa
needlefish	picuda, aguja
parrotfish	perico, pez loro
pompano	palometa, pampano
porgy	mojarra
red snapper	huachinango, pargo rojo
roosterfish	pez gallo
sailfish	pez vela
sardine	sardina
seabass	mero
shark	tiburón
snapper	pargo
snook	robálo

striped marlin	*marlín rayado*
swordfish	*pez espada*
tarpon	*sábalo*
triggerfish	*pez puerco, bota*
trout (rainbow)	*trucha (arco iris)*
tuna (yellowfin)	*atún (cola amarilla)*
wahoo	*sierra golfina, peto*
white marlin	*marlín blanco*
yellowtail	*jurel*

Fishing licenses (permisos de pesca)

As in the United States and Canada, you're required to have a fishing license in Mexico. Anyone over 16 is required to have such a license in his possession while fishing. Anyone on a boat, whether fishing or not, is required to have a license.

• In theory, you can pick up a license from any of 140 offices of the Federal Department of Fisheries *(Departamento de Pesca)* in Mexico. In practice, it's much wiser to get a license before you get there.

• Licenses are good for three days, one month, three months, and one year. The cost varies with its validity.

• With the license you'll get information on seasons, limits, and laws, which include no fishing in reserves or national underwater parks.

• To get a license you must send a cashier's check or money order covering the exact amount to the following address (call just before sending the money to find out what the current charge is—the peso keeps fluctuating and so does the fee):

Mexican Department of Fisheries
  (Oficina Recaudadora de Pesca)
1010 Second Avenue, Suite 1605
San Diego, CA 92101
tel.: (619) 233-6956

Mexican Department of Fisheries
395 West Sixth Street, Suite 203
San Pedro, CA 90731
tel.: (213) 832-5628

• Be sure to include a self-addressed stamped envelope (SASE) with your check for the fishing license.

Boat permits

Follow a similar procedure to get a boat permit as you would for a fishing license. Start the process three weeks ahead of time.

- Call the San Diego office of the Mexican Department of Fisheries and ask what the fee will be for your boat.

- Send them a check for the exact amount of the fee in the form of a money order or cashier's check and be sure to include a SASE to cover return postage.

- Be sure that they have the registration number of your boat as proof that it really is yours.

- Mail the money, information, and SASE to the San Diego office listed above.

What not to fish for

Tourists are not allowed to take any of the fish or shellfish listed below. And they are *legally* not allowed to buy them directly from fishermen. In reality, the sale of these items is common.

abalone
coral
lobster
oysters
pismo clams
rock bass
sea fans
sea shells
shrimp
totuava
turtles

Fishing reports

If you would like current fishing reports and information on Mexico, consider joining the following club:

Mexico West Travel Club
2424 Newport Boulevard, Suite 91
Costa Mesa, CA 92627
tel.: (714) 662-7616

Deep-sea fishing tournaments

Most fishing tournaments take place in May and June which are two months with abundant deep-sea fishing. Here's where they take place.

Acapulco
Barra de Navidad
Cancún
Ciudad del Carmen
Cozumel
Guaymas
La Paz
Manzanillo
Mazatlán
Puerto Vallarta
Tampico
Veracruz

Best deep-sea fishing areas

• One of the finest fishing areas in the world is the stretch of water off the Baja south of La Paz to Cabo San Lucas. Special fishing camps have been attracting sportsmen to this area for years. These camps are listed on p. 212.

• Both Manzanillo and Mazatlán claim to be the "sailfish capital of the world." Mazatlán has a number of fleets from which to choose.

• If you have your own boat, some of the finest fishing areas are the ones none of the sports fishing fleets even service. The areas off the Baja and many fishing areas off the west coast to the south of Puerto Vallarta are superb.

Tips on deep-sea fishing

• If you want to go deep-sea fishing on a charter boat in December or during the spring break (Easter), you must reserve a boat far in advance.

• Most charters offer one-half or full-day fishing at set rates. These rates may be divided by a shared party.

• Although rates tend to be similar, they're rarely the same in any given location. In nonpeak seasons it is possible to get special, reduced rates for fishing trips. These are not advertised. You have to bargain directly at the pier.

• Write the tourist office nearest you for a list of charter boats operating in any one area (see p. 33).

• When striking a bargain with a captain or charter company, get the price in writing.

• Prices for full-day charters usually include a lunch, but rarely include drinks, license, or any extras.

• Prices for half-day and full-day charters usually include the boat, equipment, and bait. You should ask about the policy on lost or broken rods, reels, and lures.

• You may want to check out a boat before chartering it. Check to see whether it seems safe and has up-to-date safety equipment. From a fishing point of view check the rods and reels.

If fishing is all important

• In general, fish follow certain patterns each year. People have come up with fishing calendars to give a rough idea of what fish are in season when. Try to match your trip with the best time for catching the kind of fish you're after.

• Year in and year out certain boats have the most "luck" bringing in certain species of fish. Getting this information is difficult unless you're able to ask questions in person. Talk to other fishermen in the area for their advice on boats and captains. A good question: Who's the most sought-after captain for fishing tournaments?

• Some areas claim to have lots of good "big-game" fishing. When you check into the hotel, check the bulletin boards for pictures of fish caught that year. If they're not the kind of "big-game" fish you're after, consider moving on.

If you have your own boat

• You have to have a permit to cross the border into Mexico. To get this permit you must prove with a registration card that the boat is yours.

• Boats give you lots of freedom to try more remote areas, but watch tides and winds. Inquire locally about the safety of any area you intend to fish.

• Keep your boat and equipment as simple as possible to get the work done.

• In some areas, good fishing can be found right off the shore. For boaters these areas are the safest and simplest to fish. The southern area of the Baja and the southern part of the west coast of Mexico's mainland fall into this category.

• Inland fishing for bass is also very good in the dams and reservoirs of northern Mexico.

• You may have to get a launch permit in some towns before you can put your boat in the water. Inquire locally about regulations.

Surf fishing

• Bring all the fishing equipment you'll need with you into Mexico. It's extremely expensive and very difficult to find.

• Bring all the hooks, line, and lures you'll need as well. One of the best and most versatile lures is the Rapala in a variety of sizes. Most effective colors are white, white and blue, and white and red.

• Good live bait: chitons, clams, conch (endangered), fish, limpets, mussels, oysters, and worms.

• Shore or surf fishing can be fabulous in Mexico, but be sensitive to those areas where it's either outlawed or barely tolerated. For example, shore fishing on Cozumel has been described as the equivalent of hunting in a zoo.

● One of the best areas of shore fishing in Mexico is the area around Loreto in the Baja.

● When surf fishing, keep moving along the shoreline until you get action. Don't leave bait in one place for more than five minutes. No strike? Move another 50 yards down the shore and try again. Keep doing this until you find the fish.

Specialized fishing—tarpon, snook, and bonefish

Some fishermen could care less about sailfish and marlin. They're hooked on tarpon, snook, and bonefish—a triumvirate of smaller, but fierce fighters. If this interests you, contact:

World Wide Sportsman, Inc.
P. O. Drawer 787
Islamorada, FL 33036
tel.: (800) 327-2880
     (305) 664-4615
     (305) 238-9252 (Miami)

Tony Gonzales
Boca Paila
Calle 62 #489, Suite 18
Mérida, Yucatán
México

Bass fishing

Following are some contacts for anyone interested in bass fishing in inland Mexico:

Chapman's Executive Resorts, Inc.
P.O. Box 12163
El Paso, TX 79912
tel.: (915) 581-3580

Sunbelt Hunting and Travel, Inc.
P.O. Box 3009
Brownsville, TX 78520
tel.: (512) 546-9101

Fishing in the Baja

Tom Miller, author of the *Angler's Guide to Baja California,* runs a fishing service in the Baja and can arrange for boat permits and fishing licenses.

Mexico Angling Services, Ltd.
P.O. Box 6088
Huntington Beach, CA 92615
tel.: (714) 847-2252

Spearfishing

Some books tell you that spearfishing is illegal in Mexico. This is not true. You can use spear guns as long as they do *not* operate on compressed gas.

FESTIVALS

There are so many festivals in Mexico that a list fills a 200-page book *Fiestas in Mexico*. Every day of the year there's a major festival somewhere.

- Reservations are hard to make in towns with major festivals, such as during Carnival in Mazatlán. So plan ahead.

- Some hotels offer perfect views of festivals, and if you can make reservations in these, you have a ringside seat. For instance, the rooms at the Hotel Majestic or Gran Hotel overlooking the zócalo in Mexico City are in demand on the night of September 15.

- Certain towns are known for being the "best" in certain festivals. Holy Week in Taxco draws thousands of spectators. So if festivals are a major interest, study the options ahead of time and make reservations accordingly.

- Tourist offices (see p. 33) have lots of *free* information on festivals and a calendar of major events. Get these in advance.

FOSSILS

The best fossil hunting in Mexico is on the Baja.

GOLF

Golf is an aristocratic sport in Mexico with prices to match. Many courses are open to the public, but others are difficult to get into. Some courses only have nine holes and are indicated as such below.

The courses

Acapulco	Acapulco (9),
	Acapulco Princess (public),
	Pierre Marques (public)
Cancún	Pok-Ta-Pok (public)
Cuatla	Cocoyoc (9)
Cuernavaca	Cuernavaca (9),
	Tabachines
Guadalajara	Atlas,
	Country Club
	Santa Anita (public),
	Bosques de San Isidro,
Ixtapa	Palma Real (public)
Manzanillo	Club Santiago,
	El Palmar (public),
	Las Hadas (public)
Mazatlán	El Cid (9)
Mérida	La Ceiba
Mexico City	Acozac,
	Bellavista,
	Bosques de Lago,
	Campestre,
	Chapultepec,
	Chiluca,
	La Hacienda,
	México,
	Tlalpan,
	Vallescondido
Puerto Vallarta	Los Flamingos (public)
Valle de Bravo	Avandaro (public)

Getting into private clubs

- On weekdays some private clubs will let nonmembers play.

- If you have a letter of introduction from your club and if it is associated with the U.S. Golf Association, you can sometimes get into a private club.

- You can get into a private club if a member vouches for you.

- If you're staying in a fine hotel, the concierge can sometimes arrange for an entry to a private club. You won't know until you ask.

- Do not try to get into a private club on weekends, since restrictions at this time are tight.

Golfing tips in general

- Bring your own equipment and lots of spare balls. All sporting goods are ultraexpensive in Mexico.

- Golf carts are often scarce or "in the shop" being repaired. If you have to have a cart, check on availability far in advance.

- Want to make friends? Give extra balls away before returning home.

HANG GLIDING (PAPALOTES A LAS DELTA)

Not a big sport in Mexico, but growing. You have to bring all of your own equipment into the country, because none is available for rent locally (hang gliders don't rent out their gear).

- You should have credentials from a free flight club in the United States and Canada.

- The south winds from December to April are the best for hang gliding.

- Some good spots (states in parenthesis):

Acapulco (Guerrero)—The broadcast tower.
Cantamar (Baja)
Chapa de Mota (México)—Best June to September here.
Cumbres de Acutzingo (Puebla)
Guadalajara (Jalisco)—Tequila Hill.
Iguala (Guerrero)—The microwave (microonda) tower.
Jocotitlan (México)
Tapalpa (Jalisco)

Tulancingo (Hidalgo)—Best June to September here.
Valle de Bravo (México)

HIKING

You'll find some marked hiking trails in these locations:

Cuernavaca (Lagunas de Zempoala)
Ensenada (San Pedro Martir)
Mexico City (Desert of Lions, 15 miles west)
Mexicali (Constitución of 1857)
Toluca (Nevado de Toluca)

HORSE RACING

Horse races take place in Mexico City (Hipódromo de las Américas) and in Tijuana (Agua Caliente).

HUNTING

Bird shooting is excellent in Mexico for ducks and white-winged dove. The latter are very abundant. Most Mexicans cannot afford to hunt, which means that hunting is an aristocratic pastime in this country.

Basic tips

● Guides suggest that you bring your own guns into Mexico if possible. Although you can rent them in some camps, gun repair is difficult in Mexico and many rental guns are in poor condition.

● Prepare for a hunting trip far in advance since regulations on the importation of guns are strict.

● If you intend to bring game back to your area, check with customs on current regulations.

• Bring as much ammunition into Mexico as you're allowed to bring.

• Note that if you travel by plane, you will have to have the gun put in a case. Get the kind which will protect it even when checked—some airlines provide these cases at a reasonable price to customers.

Game birds and big game vocabulary

black bear	*oso negro*
deer	*venado*
desert sheep	*borrego cimarrón*
duck	*pato*
goose	*ganso*
morning dove	*paloma huilota*
mule deer	*venado burra*
pheasant	*gallo de montés, faisán de collar*
quail	*codorniz*
turkey	*guajolote silvestre*
white wing dove	*paloma de ala blanca*

Gun permits

You are not allowed to take a gun into Mexico without a special permit. Bringing a gun across the border without a permit is a serious offense. If you're caught, you'll be put in prison.

• Getting a gun permit involves high cost and lots of red tape. Contact the nearest Mexican Consulate for current regulations and fees. Do this as far in advance as possible—getting a permit can take a long time! Consulates are listed on p. 11.

• The following organizations also have information on hunting in Mexico and can help you with gun permits.

Chapman's Executive Resorts, Inc.
P.O. Box 12163
El Paso, TX 79912
tel.: (915) 581-3580

Sunbelt Hunting and Travel, Inc.
P.O. Box 3009
Brownsville, TX 78502
tel.: (512) 546-9101

Mexican Hunting Association, Inc.
3302 Josie Avenue
Long Beach, CA 90808
tel.: (213) 421-1619

Wildlife Advisory Services
P.O. Box 76132
Los Angeles, CA 90076
tel.: (213) 385-9311

Needed for hunting license and gun permit

You'll need both a hunting license and a gun permit to hunt in Mexico. Here are the requirements:

- You need a letter from the police in your town stating that you are a citizen in good standing in the community and that you have no criminal record.

- A certified copy of your birth certificate.

- Eight passport-size photos with your name signed on the back of each.

- Model, make, gauge, and serial number of the gun or guns you bring into the country.

- Personal information: weight, height, complexion, date of birth, color of eyes and hair, marital status, and sex.

Bag limits

Bag limits in Mexico are very liberal, partly because there are fewer hunters applying pressure. When you get your license, limits will be defined.

INDIAN CULTURE

- Your first stop should be the Archaeological Museum in Mexico City. The displays on the second floor will amaze you.

- Indian cultures thrived in Mexico and achieved greatness hundreds of years before the Europeans arrived on the scene. Many of these cultures are still alive. If you're willing to get off the beaten path, you'll find them for yourself.

JAI ALAI (FRONTÓN)

The best jai alai is in Tijuana. But you can also see it in Mexico City.

MARKETS *(MERCADOS)*

The best market in Mexico is the one you're closest to. They're all interesting, some are unbelievable in color and action.

- Here are favorites: Guadalajara's *San Juan de Díos,* Mexico City: *La Merced;* Oaxaca: *Juárez;* Puebla: *Tepeaca;* and the markets at San Cristóbal de las Casas and at Toluca (on Friday).

MUSEUMS (SEE SIGHTSEEING)

MUSIC

Guadalajara and Mexico City offer the most to music-lovers on a formal basis.

- *Mariachis:* These late-night entertainers are everywhere in Mexico, but one of the most famous areas is Garibaldi Plaza in Mexico City. Note that this area can get wild.

- You're expected to tip mariachis if they perform at your table anywhere in Mexico.

- *Happy hour:* This U.S. import is becoming very popular in Mexico in areas frequented by tourists. Normal happy hours are 4:00 P.M. to 8:00 P.M. The tradition is getting strong in the better hotels of Acapulco and Mexico City. What makes these happy hours stand out is the wide range of music.

NATURE

- *Turtle watching:* There are 9 miles of protected coast at Careyes. In March, April, and May nearly 300 turtles come to the Playa de los Tortugas to lay eggs. The same event takes place with caguama turtles in Kino Bay in May.

● *The Green Wave* (Ola Verde): Off the Manzanillo to Jiquilpan Highway at Cuyutlan, you can see the Green Wave in April and May. This giant wave breaks on the shore and shimmers green from the phosphorescent creatures in its curl.

● *Monarchs:* Two hours from Toluca in the town of Donato Guerrero you'll find the winter resting area for millions of monarch butterflies. They arrive in October and leave in March.

● *Sea lions:* One of the best places to see sea lions is on Isla Santa Margarita in the Bahía Magdalena on the Pacific Coast near El Medano northwest of La Paz in Baja California Sur.

NIGHT LIFE

Mexico comes alive at night when the temperatures drop and expectations rise.

Discos

● Most discos are closed on Sundays.

● The action starts very late in the average disco and runs into the early morning hours. If you arrive before 10:30 P.M., you'll just watch the help clean the floors.

● Discos can be extremely expensive with a high cover charge and steep price for drinks. Very few people "disco hop" under these conditions.

● Often, there's a minimum consumption requirement as a way of boosting sales.

● Drinks made from Mexican liquor will be 20 to 50 percent less than those made from imported booze.

● In some areas, reservations are necessary on the most popular nights.

NUDE BATHING

• Nude bathing is tolerated in part of the Yucatán, especially along the coast to the south of Tulúm. But remember that it is illegal in Mexico and highly offensive to many Mexicans.

• On beaches frequented primarily by foreigners, the sight of bare breasts is commonplace and doesn't seem to be ruffling official feathers as it did in the past. However, these safe havens are *limited* to resort areas (see p. 368 for cautionary advice).

PARASAILING

It's a thrill, dangling several hundred feet above the water and being buffeted by the wind like a kite. Give it a try.

• Prices are negotiable. You have to bargain, if you want to pay a fair price.

PHOTOGRAPHY

Mexico offers a visual feast for photographers. Be sure you bring enough film to record it! (I'm assuming that you have a 35-millimeter camera. If you have some other type, some of these tips won't apply to your outfit).

Equipment

• You're allowed one camera and one movie camera (up to 8 millimeters) into Mexico duty-free.

• You can bring additional lenses for these cameras. If you're serious about photography, bring a 50-millimeter lens, a wide-angle, and a good telephoto lens—but don't go overboard, try to keep it as light and compact as possible.

- A broad camera strap makes taking pictures easier and carrying cameras more comfortable.

- Be familiar with the workings of your equipment before you go to Mexico. Run a few rolls through the camera to make sure that things are working properly. It's very difficult to get cameras repaired in Mexico.

- Change all batteries and carry a few spares.

- Equip each lens with a Polaroid filter. Leave the filter on at all times (not only to improve photos but to protect the lens).

- Bring photographic lens tissue or liquid lens cleaner to clean lenses.

- Don't forget your instruction book if you're not completely familiar with your camera or haven't used it frequently in recent months.

Register your equipment

- Don't forget to register equipment to avoid problems coming back through customs (see p. 373).

Film

- You're allowed twelve rolls of film into Mexico duty-free. If you want to bring in more, remove the canisters from the boxes to show that they're not intended for resale.

- Film is very expensive in Mexico, so bring what you'll need. Figure one thirty-six-exposure roll for each day of shooting at the minimum.

- Avoid any film with "professional" printed on the label. These require refrigeration!

- Heat hurts all film, so keep it as cool as possible—often quite difficult in this hot country.

- Specify either slide or print film. Slide film allows you to view every photo before deciding which ones you want made into prints—a real savings.

- Get films with different ASAs. ASA is a measurement of light sensitivity. You can then use the appropriate film for specific light conditions. Kodachrome 25 is an excellent film for high-light conditions because it's color-saturated.

- Thirty-five millimeter film is easy to find in Mexico, but odd sizes are not.

Security inspections

- Don't have film in cameras when you go through security inspections at the airport. They may be opened. If you forget or can't help having film in the camera, ask the inspector not to open the back.

- The X-ray machines at airports can do damage to unexposed or undeveloped film, particularly those with ASAs over 400. Moreover, the effect is cumulative, so don't let the film go through these machines.

- Ask the inspector politely for a visual inspection at all check points. If you carry film in a separate case, this takes only seconds. In general, Mexican inspectors cooperate fully with this request and with a minimum of hassle.

- Don't put film in checked luggage, which can be subjected to high-level radiation. Even lead pouches are no guarantee that the film will not be harmed. Carry all film on board with you.

Protecting camera gear

- Dust in Mexico can be a problem—bring a plastic bag for each lens and camera to protect them, even if they're already enclosed in a leather carrying case.

- If you carry cameras in plain bags, potential thieves will be less likely to suspect that you're carrying them.

- Always zip up the bag—even if you're nearby. Leave nothing exposed to chance and sticky fingers.

- Hand carry all camera equipment onto a plane or bus. This way you won't lose it if you're luggage is lost or crushed.

• Wear a camera around your shoulder rather than around your neck in public places. A thief snatching at your camera can easily hurt your neck in his eagerness.

• Do not leave cameras in car trunks or glove compartments. Not only are they vulnerable to theft, but the heat of the closed compartment can damage the camera.

Photography etiquette

• In some areas, you must be especially sensitive about taking photos. Indians especially may resent any photos at all.

• In some remote villages photography is associated with witchcraft, something taken very seriously by many people in these areas. Photographers have been stoned to death in such areas.

• Do not take pictures of military installations or of the subway in Mexico City. Note too that certain restrictions apply for photography in archaeological zones (no tripods, no flash, and no movie cameras).

• You can often get good shots of people with a telephoto lens, and this can be done inconspicuously.

• However, if you're close to a person, don't sneak photos. If you want to take someone's picture, be forthright and friendly—it often works.

• Just lift the camera slowly, nod your head, and smile. If the person turns away or tosses his hand at you, don't take the photo. Or just say "please" as you lift the camera, to get a reaction.

• In the marketplace, an orange or tomato splatting against the side of your head or ricocheting off your shoulder is a good indication that photos are not tolerated.

• If you really want to get pictures in an area where this is tough to do, consider hiring a guide or an interpreter who can ask for photos as you go along. You may be asked for a small payment for some of the photos, which seems reasonable enough.

- Don't dawdle once you've taken a picture. Smile, shake hands, offer a gift—then go about your business.

Developing film

- Do it at home. It's the safest place to take care of film which may represent very special memories or a lot of effort if you take photography seriously.

RIDING *(EQUITACIÓN)*

A few recommended spots: The Meling Ranch in Ensenada, the Hacienda San Miguel Regla in Pachuca, Parras de la Fuente in Rincón del Monterro, Hotel Jurica in Querétaro, Rancho El Morillo in Saltillo, and Rancho El Atascadero in San Miguel de Allende. The latter is the best known and offers a riding school.

RODEO *(CHARREADA)*

Elegant rodeos take place in Guadalajara (the best spot), Mexico City, and Tijuana. They usually take place at noon on Sundays and are free.

ROMANCE

A good ration of passion can be found in many Club Meds for single travelers.

- Honeymooners take the plunge in the Acapulco Princess and Las Brisas (both in Acapulco), at the Villas Tacul in Cancún, and in Las Hadas at Manzanillo.

SAILING

- Remember to have a multiple-entry tourist card for yachting along the Mexican coast (see p. 11).

SCUBA DIVING *(BUCEO)*

The best scuba diving takes place off the island of Cozumel, which is famous for the Palancar Maracaibo, Santa Rosa, and San Francisco reefs. Nearly 50 percent of the people traveling to this island go diving.

- It is best to bring your own gear, and it helps to have a diving certificate (many outfits take you anyway). At least, bring your own regulator.

- The water ranges from 75 to 80 degrees Fahrenheit and reaches up to 250-foot visibility under ideal conditions.

- Other diving experiences include sinkholes and the craters of volcanoes for the adventurous.

SEX

Prostitution is legal in Mexico, and *La Zona* refers to the red-light district.

- Bordellos are accepted and even visited by more respectable citizens for an evening's entertainment, because here you'll find snacks, music, and humor—not to mention sex.

- Occasionally, girlfriends and even mothers come to cathouses to cavort—dancing, eating, and carrying on with the boys.

- There's one price of drinks for the customer, a higher price for the girl—a kind of built-in service fee.

- For full service the price varies by the size and standing of the community and is often related to bargaining skill and the degree of sobriety.

SHELLING

Seashells *(conchas)* can be a prize in Mexico. You'll find the best shelling in the Yucatán on Isla Holbox. Shells are also found in Progresso, Rio Lagartos, and San Felipe.

SIGHTSEEING

Mexico offers a fascinating blend of sights. Since these are often tourist-oriented, here are a few tips for the wary:

Local tour companies

- In every city or tourist town you'll find companies offering tours of the most popular sights. Such tours are well organized, but usually expensive.

- Prices for equivalent tours vary greatly, so comparison shop with competing companies.

- Many hotels have their own travel agency *(agencia de viaje)* which can set up a tour. Each time an agency is involved, the price rises.

- Sometimes, these agencies corner the market on tickets to popular events. You may be forced to use them.

- Mexico City makes a good base to explore a number of towns from Toluca to Taxco. Again, compare prices.

- Tip both the driver and the tour guide a dollar a day, if they are pleasant and competent.

Putting together your own local tour

- Generally, you can put together an equivalent tour for yourself, using local transportation, for a fraction of the cost of more organized tours.

● Many Mexicans discourage this by telling you that there is no way to get to the local sights without a tour. This is usually totally false. For example, you can get to all of the major sights in Mexico City using public transportation. You can get to the ruins of Monte Albán on a bus from the Hotel Meson del Angel. Getting this information can be tough, but persistence pays off.

● Cost is not the only big advantage of using public transportation. The other is freedom. You get to stay or leave an area when you feel like it, not at the command of a tour guide.

● For free information on suggested sights and routes, pick up brochures, maps, and detailed commentary from local tourist offices, from hotels, and from travel agencies.

● Good sightseeing suggestions are often listed in the yellow pages of local phone books. Free and detailed guides are often given away at better hotels and from tourist offices if you'll ask for them. Don't settle for a two-page pamphlet that tells you less than you already know.

● Allow plenty of time for an individual tour. Public transportation doesn't move along like a well-run tour.

Special sightseeing

● If you're a romantic and want to try a buggy ride, expect to pay in spades, not hearts.

● Whenever you're bargaining for a price for that "special" ride, get the price in writing or pay upfront.

Walking tours

● In Mexico City free walking tours are arranged. Call 512-6879 for information.

● Walking in the only practical way to get to know many of Mexico's most popular tourist towns.

● Always pick up booklets, pamphlets, and special maps designed for walking tours in the places you visit. These can point out places you might otherwise miss.

Hiring guides

- Guides can give you an entirely new perspective on a tourist attraction. Their prices are reasonable in most instances.

- Get a guide who can speak English fluently.

- At some sights you can join a group for a set price—usually just pennies. These arranged tours leave at a specific time.

- Or hire a private guide, either for a couple of hours or for a couple of days. For the latter arrangement you pay for all meals and lodgings.

- Don't "pick up" guides in the street or at tourist sights unless they can prove that they are licensed. A bonded, licensed guide carries a special permit with a photo.

- For information on getting a qualified guide contact:

Official Tour Guide Association
Serapio Rendon 62-6
Mexico City, D.F.
tel.: 566-0295

- Many guides get kickbacks from factory outlets and shops. Don't feel forced to buy things in shops they recommend.

- With any guide set the price firmly upfront.

- A tip is always in order and should be related to the guide's performance.

Sound and light shows

- At major archaeological sites, you can attend sound and light shows from mid-October to late May (sometimes into June). See p. 312.

When to go

- Before making a special trip to any tourist sight, find out the hours and days the sight is open.

- If you're traveling a long distance to see a specific site, call ahead to make sure it's open. Strikes and other "natural calamities" can shut sights down.

• Most museums and galleries close on Monday in Mexico. However, there are odd closing days as well.

• Most sights offer reduced admission on Sunday, a day which is usually very crowded.

• Holidays are also very crowded.

• Mid-week is usually the best and most relaxed time to visit most sights. Get to ruins at the earliest possible hour to avoid crowds and to get the best photos.

• The seasons may affect the beauty of natural sights. Some can be disappointing at the wrong time of year.

• The time of day can be important. For instance, the Sumidero Canyon is best visited in the early morning.

• The day itself can be crucial. Certain markets are best on certain days. Some are only open one day a week. Bullfights take place only on Sundays. *So plan sightseeing accordingly.*

Other sightseeing tips

• Always wear comfortable shoes. Leave high heels at home and settle for a snappy pair of tennis shoes.

• If someone opens up a secret little box or remote little room in a church or museum, that someone expects a nice little tip.

• There's always someone telling you that there are just *no* tickets for such and such. Show up to such and such and buy a ticket. They've got scalpers in Mexico too!

• If you're traveling by car, note that many sights have parking fees—even in the most remote areas.

• Hang onto your tickets when visiting tourist sights. They may be required for entry to a sight within a sight, or they may be necessary for spot inspections.

SLUMMING

This art requires risk, but can be fun. Don't argue, always tell everyone that Mexico is the best, avoid all fights, and buy drinks—but
beware, you're entering the world of the macho, and the rules here
are, well, foreign to foreigners.

SNORKELING

Going to Mexico without snorkeling is like going to the movies and
not eating candy or popcorn.

Where to go

- Akumal (fabulous), Cancún (good), Cozumel with its Chan-
canab Lagoon (tops), Isla Mujeres at Garrafon (beautiful), the
water off the ruins at Tulúm (drift lazily like a sea otter in the
current), and the National Park at Xelha—this is Mexican snorkeling at its best. All of these areas are in the Yucatán.

- Visibility in the Caribbean can reach 250 feet in the best of
conditions.

What to bring

- Bring a mask *(visor),* snorkle, and fins *(aletas)* if you can. If
you can't, skip the fins (bulky and heavy).

- In a few areas you can rent equipment. But you can snorkle
almost anywhere with just a mask and snorkle, and you want
to have good equipment—so bring your own. Fins help you
explore caves and push against strong currents. Rent these, if
necessary.

- Bring a t-shirt and possibly a leather glove for one hand (golf
gloves work great). You need to be able to push off from coral
in emergencies.

- Cover yourself with a water-resistant sunscreen on initial outings. You simply forget time when snorkeling in the Caribbean.

Safety

- Do not swim alone. This is a fundamental rule worldwide.

- Never go into water without asking the local Mexicans about its safety. Ask anywhere, in little restaurants, at the hotel, in local shops—but ask.

- Some areas have strong currents and deadly undertows—and you cannot detect these, even on a calm surface.

- Watch for warning flags in areas where these are posted. And if the sea looks rough, it probably is.

- Never swim at night. This is the time sharks like to feed.

- Look at but do not touch coral. Unless you're an expert, you cannot tell which varieties sting.

- Shy away from sea urchins *(erizos)*. Don't touch them, not even lightly. They'll sting you with their sharp spines.

Special tips

- If you're in a boat looking for a good place to snorkel, watch for dark blotches under the water. These are often rocks or coral, places where fish congregate. Turquoise water denotes sand—just so-so for snorkeling.

- Snorkelers with poor vision can have masks made with prescription lenses. Or they can wear contacts, but be sure the mask fits securely (if water seeps in, it doesn't fit).

- Try out a mask before going to Mexico. Buy the more expensive kind made of materials which will not deteriorate as fast as rubber.

- You'll get very thirsty snorkeling. Pack something to drink —a bottle of water or a six-pack of coke.

- Some beaches and seaside restaurants have fresh-water

showers. Wash the salt off your body and gear when you're through snorkeling.

● If your mask fogs up repeatedly, spit on the glass and rub saliva over the surface with your fingers. Rinse it off, and, presto, you have a no-fog solution.

SOCCER (*FÚTBOL*)

The best soccer is played in the Aztec Stadium in Mexico City.

SPAS

Write to the nearest Mexican Government Tourist Office for information on the many spas in Mexico. A detailed list will fill a book, or at least a long brochure.

● Hot water springs are common in the countryside and a good place to relax and clean up.

SPECTACLES

Two of the most famous are the high divers at La Quebrada in Acapulco (go to the terrace of the Hotel Mirador) and the Flying Indians of Papantla. If you can't quite make it to Papantla, see them in the Acapulco show.

STUDYING IN MEXICO

Both short- and long-term study holds great appeal for many people who want to learn Spanish or get to know Mexico well.

Visas

For long-term study you'll need a visa to go to Mexico. See p. 9 for information. If you'll be in Mexico for less than six months, forget about visas.

Information in the United States
The following organizations have lots of information aimed at student travelers.

Council on International Educational
 Exchange
205 East 42nd Street
New York, NY 10017
tel.: (212) 661-1414

Institute of International Education
809 United Nationa Plaza
New York, NY 10017
tel.: (212) 883-8200

Information in Canada

Canadian Federation of Students-
 Services
Association of Students Council
 Headquarters
44 St. George Street
Toronto, Canada M5S 2E4
tel.: (416) 979-2604

Other student offices: Travel CUTS (Canadian Federation of Students in Edmonton, Halifax, Montreal, Ottawa, Saskatoon, Vancouver, and Victoria).

Tips for study in Mexico

• If you're a serious language student, pick up the book *501 Verbs*. It's bulky and heavy, but the essence of the language.

• If you're given a room you really don't like, don't grin and bear it. Ask the administration to find a new place to stay for you. This is especially true when lodging is provided in private homes and not dormitories.

• Carry a good pocket dictionary, but note that these rarely have the kind of detailed listings that a serious student will need after more than an introductory course in the language.

• No one learns a language in ten weeks—no one! Patience, practice, and time—these are essential to master any language.

Don't be timid about making mistakes. You can only learn to speak by speaking.

● In some areas of Mexico even the Mexicans don't understand what's being said. So don't overreact to your inability to get the point across.

SUN

Mexico has the most reliable winter of any country in the world— and that says it all.

SURFING

Surfers guard their spots, but most say that the surfing is best in the Baja in the "Ensenada area" and also good in the "Playa Blanca area" and the "Puerto Escondido area" on the Mainland. Getting a pinpoint definition is like asking a fisherman where he catches his biggest trout.

SWIMMING

All beaches are public, but many pools are not. However, very few hotels restrict the use of a pool to guests only.

● Wash your feet and body before going into a pool at a private hotel. If you don't see where the shower is, ask.

● Feel free to order drinks and food poolside. Again, you don't have to be a guest in many hotels.

TENNIS *(TENIS)*

There are three great, and equally expensive, places to play tennis in Mexico: the Villa Vera in Acapulco, the Cuernavaca Racquet

Club in Cuernavaca, and the Guadalajara Racquet Club in Guadalajara. But there are dozens of other resorts throughout the country which offer fine facilities at a wide range of prices.

• Bring your own equipment to Mexico, including lots of extra balls. Any you don't use, you can either sell or give away at the end of your stay.

• Early morning and evening are the best times to play tennis in Mexico. For this reason it's often easiest to rent a court in the middle of the day.

• Some so-called private complexes open their courts at off-hours—ask to be sure. You'll have your best chance mid-week at noon.

WHALE WATCHING

From January through mid-March, whale watching is superb in the Scammon Lagoon near Guerrero Negro on the Baja California peninsula. Nearly 6,000 of the whales congregate here each year.

WHITE-WATER RAFTING

Most Mexicans consider life dangerous enough, but if you don't, try white-water rafting in the Mexcala south of Iguala.

WINDSURFING

Beginning to catch on in a few places and already running with the wind in the Loreto area and at the Rancho Buena Vista near La Paz.

21

SHOPPING

This chapter is devoted to shopping. You'll find information on unique handicraft stores, good buys, bargaining, shipping, and customs regulations.

Useful vocabulary

another color	*en otro color*
cheap	*barato*
cotton	*algodón*
expensive	*caro*
How much?	*¿Cuánto cúesta?*
large	*grande*
palm	*palma*
small	*pequeño*
wool	*lana*

COLORS

black	*negro*
blue (dark)	*azul (obscuro)*
brown	*café*
green (light)	*verde (claro)*
gray	*gris*
pink	*rosa*

purple	*morado*
red	*rojo*
white	*blanco*
yellow	*amarillo*

WHERE TO SHOP

You may be one of those people who enjoys shopping, who loves every minute spent in fashionable stores, street markets, and typical boutiques. If so, you will find Mexico a delight.

Comparison shop in the United States and Canada

• Since some articles you can buy in Mexico are also for sale north of the border, study prices before going to Mexico. Unless you do this, you will not know if you're really getting a bargain or a unique item.

• Unless an item in Mexico is much lower in price or of much higher quality than you can get at home, don't buy it. You'll lose on the currency exchange, you'll have to lug or mail it home, and you may even have to pay duty on it if you exceed your personal exemption. If you can't make a 40 to 50 percent saving, skip it.

Comparison shop in Mexico

Once you arrive in Mexico, try to get to one of the state-managed stores, selling authentic Mexican goods. There are two good reasons to do this: the products are thoroughly genuine, and they are chosen because of their high quality. Furthermore, the prices tend to be the highest you would expect to pay for any given item, so that if you know the price in one of these stores, you know the very *most* you should pay for anything from embroidered dresses and blouses to fascinating ceramics and candle holders.

Some of the state-managed stores are known under the title FONART *(Tiendas Artesanales del Fomento Nacional de Arte-sanias).* Others are found in regional folk art museums *(Museos de*

Arte Popular), civic centers, and art galleries. Ask locally for their location.

Department stores in Mexico City

Check out the Galería in the Zona Rosa, Liverpool, Palacio de Hierro, Paris Londres, and the huge complex Perisur at the end of Insurgentes Sur (don't miss this one).

Specialty shops

Once you've visited a FONART and some of the department stores, you'll enjoy comparison shopping in the many specialty shops and boutiques, especially in the Zona Rosa of Mexico City.

Artesans *(artesanos)*

If you've got the interest and time, you may want to locate the artesans who make goods sold in specialty shops. This can take a lot of legwork and patience, but many people enjoy the search.

- When you go to the artesan's home, studio, or shop, consider taking someone who speaks Spanish.

- You may be able to buy a truly unique piece from an artesan directly, the kind of piece that won't show up in shops or markets.

- All of this takes time, lots of it.

Duty-free shops *(tienda libre de impuestos)*

You'll find so-called duty-free shops in the airports of Acapulco, Guadalajara, Mazatlán, Mérida, Mexico City, Monterrey, and Puerto Vallarta. Prices are often higher in these shops than in many comparable specialty shops. The term duty-free is just hype.

Markets *(mercados)*

Mexico is famous for its fascinating and fabulous markets where everything from shiny onions to old shoe soles are sold. Guadalajara, Oaxaca, and Mexico City all have superb markets. The market in San Cristóbal de las Casas is very picturesque and colorful.

Factory outlets

Many tours and tour guides lead people to factory outlets, usually just retail shops offering the tour guides a kickback. Be wary.

Street vendors

You can't walk anywhere in Mexico without being hustled. It's just part of the culture.

- If you're not interested, just say no. A polite way of turning vendors off is to say that something is very nice, but that you don't want it. *Muy bonito, mas no lo quiero.* All right, this is "sparrow" Spanish, but who cares. It works.

- Some vendors offer some pretty good deals on some fairly decent items, but most offer junk at not-so-good prices.

WHEN TO SHOP

When you shop can make as much difference as where you shop.

Timing in shopping

- Some vendors are very superstitious about the first sale of the day. They don't want to lose out on it. You can often get the best price of the day if you're the first customer!

- One of the most pleasant times to shop is in the late evening —lots of action, nice temperature, and an easy-going pace.

- Hours of shops vary greatly, but tend to be from late morning to late evening with a break for a siesta or lunch.

- Shopping in certain towns is best at certain times of year. For instance, the pre-Christmas period is very good in Oaxaca because the peasants bring in many handmade goods at this time.

BARGAINING *(REGATEAR)*

It's actually improper for you to pay the asking price for goods when you shop at open markets, small owner-operated shops, antique shops, art galleries, and flea markets in Mexico. Bargaining is inappropriate only in state-managed and department stores.

Bargaining is not only accepted in most settings, it is also expected. If you're not used to bargaining, here's a chance for you to become an expert.

Basic bargaining

Bargaining is an attitude, a position, a style. The attitude is wariness; the position is: "I won't buy unless it's a fair price." The style is tough but breezy, with a good sense of humor.

- The basic rule of bargaining: He who cares least wins.

- Take your time and comparison shop first. When you've decided on what you really want, begin the bargaining game. Frivolous bargaining is unfair and a waste of the merchant's time.

- Ask for the price. Propose your own, undercutting the stated price by whatever you think you can get away with. Start with a fraction of what's asked (Mexicans sometimes ask six to ten times the real value).

- Tell the vendor that you'll have to shop around because you want to come up with the best price in town and are willing to spend the time to do it. Prices will often slide down on the spot.

- Let a missing person play the bad guy. "Oh, I think it's beautiful. But my husband (wife) would be very upset if I spent that much."

- Be complimentary but shrewd, saying, "It's one of the finest pieces I've seen, but I really think it's overpriced."

- Evoke the expert. "I've got someone who really knows about these things. I'd better ask his advice before I spend all that much." As a matter of fact, try to get yourself an expert.

- Use tour guides for information about what is authentic, but be wary because many of them get kickbacks from certain stores.

- Find a flaw. Almost everything has one, especially high-quality, handmade articles. I don't like this approach myself, but it does work. Try it only in desperation.

Advanced bargaining

• Play the add-on game. "I'll pay your price if you'll throw this extra item in." That so-called extra item may be exactly what you were after in the first place! This lets the vendor save face.

• Play the lump-sum game. "I'll pay you this much for this, that, and that." You play the lump-sum game after finding out the prices for the individual items. Naturally, you shave off a fair percentage for buying them as a group. This is another face-saving device (very important in Mexico).

• Take out the money and put it in front of the vendor. Tell him that this is your last offer. If he shakes his head, put the money back into your wallet and leave. Often, this will bring on a sale.

• Note that advanced bargaining is more difficult in areas where foreigners have been paying inflated prices for local goods. But don't believe it if someone tells you that you can't bargain in such and such a place.

Luxury-shop bargaining

• Some shops have a *precios fijos* (fixed prices) sign in the window. In short, you're expected to pay the full price. Non-sense! Try some polite bargaining anyway.

• Will the item soon be on sale?

• Is there a discount for paying cash?

• Will you give me a favorable rate of exchange for dollars? Some shops build in a discount by giving you more pesos per dollar than a bank.

Bargaining etiquette

• Treat the people working in a store or selling goods at a

market with a "hello" and "good-bye." This is minimum manners in a country where courtesy counts.

● If a vendor agrees to your price, it's considered poor form for you to walk away. A deal's a deal.

● Don't get frustrated or angry during bargaining. It must be considered a game.

● If the bargaining has been fun, or if you're very happy with a product, shake the vendor's hand. This is a warm, caring gesture.

SHOPPING PROBLEMS

● Never have anything made to order in Mexico. Your deposit may simply evaporate, or the item may be finished well after your departure.

● The Mexican market is glutted with cheap imitations of very fine products.

● If you're told upfront the price of a product, it's not considered deception if the item is vastly overpriced. It's strictly buyer beware!

● Make sure you get what you pay for. Some shopkeepers will switch items while packing them up (this is very rare).

● More common is asking a shop to ship you something and never getting it. If this happens, contact either of the following offices:

Instituto Nacional del Consumidor
Insurgentes Sur 1228
Colonia del Valle
Delegación Benito Juárez
Mexico 13100, D.F.
tel.: 568-8722

Procuraduria Federal del Consumidor
Dr. Carmona y Valle #11
Colonia de los Doctores
Delegación Cuauhtemoc
México 06720, D.F.
tel.: 761-3811

A GOOD-BUY GUIDE

Following are some items which generally cost less in Mexico than in the United States and Canada. Some prove quite expensive, but the quality of the work can be exceptional, making them unique in their own right.

What to buy in Mexico

abalone shell items
antiques
art
artifacts (copies
    only, not the real
    thing)
bark drawings
    (amatl)
baskets
blankets
blouses (beaded and
    embroidered)
brass
bronze
candles
ceramics
chess sets
clothes
copper
coral (black)
embroidery
furniture
glass
gold
guitars
hammocks
hats (straw and pan-
    ama)

Indian art
jewelry
Kahlua liqueur
lacquerware
leather
masks
mats
onyx
opals
paper flowers
papier-mâché
ponchos
pottery
sandals (huaraches)
serapes
shawls (rebozos)
shirts (guayaberas)
silver
table cloths
tin
toys
watches
weaving
wood animals
wood bird cages
wood bowls
wrought iron
yarn paintings

Tips on Mexican products

On some purchases in Mexico you have to be cautious. Following are a few tips when shopping:

- *Ceramics:* Unless a vessel is certified lead-free, do not use it for cooking or serving acidic foods. Glazed pottery, especially green-colored, should be used with caution.

- *Clothes:* Most clothes will shrink, so buy them on the large side and wash in cold water (let them drip dry).

- Many clothes will fall apart unless the seams are sewed when you get home. Mexicans assume you'll do this for yourself.

- Glossy ribbons will shrink, yarn embroidery will bleed, and some colors are not colorfast *(firme)*.

- Clothes are more expensive when handmade *(hecho al mano)*. The cotton thread used for embroidery normally does not bleed.

- Cotton *(algodón)* tends to be pure, while wool *(lana)* is often a blend. Polyester gives off a shine in the sun. To find out if something is 100 percent wool, say in Spanish: *"¿Cien por ciento lana?"*

- *Leather:* Make sure you're getting leather and not strips of leather glued to cardboard.

- *Sandals (huaraches):* Try both sandals on to make sure they fit. Buy them a little on the snug side because they'll stretch.

- Some people suggest soaking them in fresh water and then putting them on—this will make them shape to your feet.

- Don't expect sandals to be comfortable from the start. They take time to work in.

- *Silver:* Buy silver from a reputable shop, since most of the silver in the street is really alpaca, a very cheap imitation.

- Silver should be stamped sterling, or have a spread eagle mark, or bear the number .925 (92.5 percent pure). If it doesn't, buy the piece only for its beauty, not its silver content.

GETTING YOUR PURCHASE HOME

Here are a few suggestions on how to get your purchases home with the minimum of hassle and wasted time.

Take purchases with you

● Contrary to what many guides tell you, most shops are *not* experienced at handling shipping to the United States and Canada.

● It is always best to take any purchase with you *if* you have the ability to hand carry the item to the United States or Canada. In short, is it small enough to take on a bus, plane, or train, or to fit into a car or RV?

● If you ship an item that's worth more than $50 to the United States or more than $40 to Canada, you'll have to pay duty on it. It won't fall under your personal exemption which requires all goods to accompany you as you cross the border.

If stores ship it

● You are liable for duty unless it's a present to a friend or relative, and it's value is less than $50.

● Some stores dealing with tourists on a daily basis can handle shipping easily and efficiently, given the limitations of the Mexican mail service. In short, expect the package in two to three months even if it goes air mail.

● Pay to have all packages sent air mail. Get a receipt showing that you've paid for this.

● If insurance can be purchased, get it to cover the value of the product. You may have to send the package through a private company to get it insured.

Shipping packages through the mail yourself

● Many stores will suggest that you ship the package from

Mexico yourself. Wrong! You simply will not believe the amount of red tape and time involved. The store wants nothing to do with either. Never, *never* attempt to mail a package yourself.

Using a courier

● However, you could consider using a courier. Of course, you'll pay more for this service, but the extra cost might be worth it. In Mexico City contact:

Air Cargo Office
Liverpool 6
Zona Rosa
Mexico City
tel.: 592-0666

World Courier of Mexico
Reforma 390, 9th Floor
Mexico City
tel.: 553-8999

Unsolicited gifts

● You can send one gift a day to friends and relatives without paying duty.

● You are not allowed to send alcohol, perfume, or tobacco of any kind.

● The value of the gift must be under $50 for items sent to the United States and $40 for items sent to Canada.

Thank-you gifts to Mexicans

● Never send a thank-you gift from the United States or Canada to Mexico.

● It probably won't get there.

● If it does, it will be pure hell for the Mexican friend of yours to retrieve it.

● The Mexican will not be told what the package is or who it is from.

● The Mexican will have to pay a stiff duty on whatever is sent in.

● And finally, the whole process takes so much time and is so frustrating that no matter what the gift is, it isn't worth the hassle.

● If you want to thank someone, do it while you're still in Mexico!

22

TROUBLE-SHOOTING

Even in the best-planned trips, something is bound to go awry. Here's hoping that you never have to refer to this section!

LOSSES

No one wants to think about losing something while planning an enjoyable trip, but losses occur with such regularity that you should be forewarned with the following tips.

Lost passports

- If you lose your passport in the United States, report the loss immediately to the local branch of the Justice Department.

- If you lose your passport in Canada, report its loss to the nearest passport office. There is one in each province.

- If you lose your passport in Mexico, contact the nearest U.S. or Canadian consulate, or the Embassy in Mexico City.

- As a precaution, consider carrying two passport photos, a notarized copy of your birth certificate, a photocopy of the information in your passport, and a note listing your passport number to speed up the process of getting a new passport if the original is lost.

Lost tourist cards

- You can't leave Mexico without your tourist card (an exception follows later in the stolen car section), so guard it as if it were a passport.

- Make a photocopy *(fotocopia)* of it and use that for identification. Leave the *original* in a safe place.

- If you lose the original, report it to the police and appropriate consulate.

- A photocopy of the original will be invaluable in getting a new tourist card if you lose the first one.

Lost traveler's checks

- Report the loss immediately to the appropriate company. You'll need an exact list of the numbers of all checks for which you're making a claim.

- Some companies may reimburse you in pesos.

- You'll need identification to get money for a claim. The best is a passport.

- The following offices in Mexico City handle claims for lost or stolen traveler's checks (local branches will do the same):

American Express
Hamburgo 75
tel.: 525-8428

Bank of America
Reforma 116, 12th Floor
tel.: 591-0011 Ext. 121 or 125

Barclays Bank
Reforma 199, 8th Floor
tel.: 566-0605

First National City Bank
Reforma 390
tel.: 211-3030 Ext. 118

Wagon Lits Cook
Avenida Juarez 88
tel.: 518-1180

Lost credit cards

- The faster you report a lost or stolen credit card, the better for you. If you report a card before it's used fraudulently, you're not liable for any charges. In any event, your liability is usually limited to $50.

● Following are offices of major credit card companies who can handle the problem:

American Express Company Mexico, S.A.
Av. Patriotismo No. 635
tel.: 598-7122

BankAmericard (VISA)
Avenida Universidad No. 1200
tel.: 534-0034 Ext. 1261
    658-2188

Carte Blanche
Holbein No. 217 1st Floor
tel.: 598-0466 Ext. 29

Diner's Club
Insurgentes Sur No. 724, 2nd Floor
tel.: 543-7020, Ext. 272, International Dept.

Master Charge
Carnet
Dr. Andrade No. 60
tel.: 588-4422, 24-hour service

Lost luggage

It's frustrating to lose luggage. If you've followed the advice of never packing irreplaceable items in checked bags, you'll be relatively calm in your dealings with the airline. And that's the best way to be.

● Report the loss immediately to the airline representative. Be polite but vocal about the loss and note the representative's name.

● If the airline can't find your bags after checking the plane and baggage area, file a written notice immediately. Give a detailed list of the contents of the lost luggage. It helps if you've already made one out.

● Make sure you get a copy of the claim and do not surrender your claim checks, the only proof that you have that the airline has indeed lost your bags. If the airline insists on keeping a claim check, get a written receipt for it and the name of the person who takes it from you.

● Ask the airline to deliver your bags to your hotel in town if they are recovered shortly.

• You can also ask for emergency funds to handle necessities. In the United States you'll be given an overnight kit and enough money to buy odds and ends. Don't count on this in Mexico, but you can always ask.

• If the airline loses your bags permanently, you'll be paid a set amount by the airline. This is just a token amount in Mexico. In the United States and Canada the limit is now $1200.

• You may have to prove the value of articles in your baggage with *receipts*. Who can do that? And then a given amount will be taken off for the depreciated value.

• If you're concerned about this, take out baggage insurance ahead of time.

Dealing with damaged luggage

• If there is any sign of damage to your bag, check the contents immediately.

• If you find damaged goods, file a claim on the spot—not later. Corner an airline representative and get a copy of the claim form. You may be reimbursed for damage done to the bag and its contents.

• To collect money the airline has the right to collect your bag and its contents in return.

• A claim for *any* bag that is overpacked will be disqualified.

Stolen cars

• If your car or RV gets stolen (not just parts of it), report the theft to the police, your insurance company, and the consulate.

• The consulate is especially helpful in advising you how to handle this *delicate* situation, since there is always the suspicion that you sold the car!

• Furthermore, your tourist card has been stamped *con automóvil* which means you cannot leave Mexico without it—that is, without paying duty.

• Simple solution: Fly to a border town and walk across the

border with day visitors (tourist cards are not required for short stays within 14 miles of the border).

● Okay, the solution is *not* what you want to do, and it's definitely *not* what the Mexicans want you to do—this is a case of both sides not getting what they want. It's also illegal.

● The same approach may apply to a car crippled in a serious accident. But check on the insurance ramifications before abandoning a wrecked car in Mexico!

Robberies

● If you are robbed, report it to the police. If you follow this procedure and get a written copy of the report, you can get reimbursed for things from your insurance company.

● Also, report all thefts and problems to U.S. and Canadian consulates, since they keep statistics on such incidents.

● Do not expect to retrieve stolen goods. It is considered your responsibility to protect them in the first place.

ARRESTS

If you're arrested in Mexico, your rights are defined by local, not U.S. or Canadian law.

Mexican law

● The Mexican judicial system is based on Napoleonic law. You are presumed *guilty* until proven innocent.

● There is no trial by jury. A judge will decide your fate based on documents presented to him—similar to an arbitration. So no person should ever admit responsibility for anything in Mexico!

● You can be detained for seventy-two hours without being charged for any crime in particular.

● Although bail exists, it rarely is allowed—they assume (often quite rightly) that you'll split the minute you're free.

- Mexican law prevails in all cases, and foreign governments are powerless to do much about controversial cases.

- Note that there is presently an agreement for prisoner exchange between Mexico and the United States.

If you're arrested

- Call the nearest embassy or consulate immediately. This call is guaranteed by international law.

- Although the consulate has no power to get you released, it can provide many vital services.

- Once in jail, don't pay anyone for a "quick release." This is just a con.

- Don't hire a lawyer or pay out any "bribes," until you've talked to the embassy or consulate. They have detailed information on local scams.

- You are entitled to have an oral translation of any document you sign.

- Don't have money sent to you in jail. Checks and money orders are commonly cashed—fraudulently. Have the consulate or embassy help you with transfer of funds.

Drunken driving is illegal

If you get arrested for drunk driving, you may be in deep trouble.

- If you have been drinking, you're liable for criminal charges. Since "drinking" is a vague term meaning anything from a glass of wine to a total stupor, don't drink at all before driving.

- Bribe your way out of the situation, before you are arrested. It is sometimes possible.

- In short, take a taxi if you've had too much to drink.

Car accidents

Yes, accidents do happen. Even minor ones can cause serious disruption of your trip. Here's advice to smooth over the bumps.

MINOR ACCIDENTS

If you have a minor accident *(accidente)* and no other car is involved, take off. Running off the road, nailing a wandering goat or burro, missing a corner and hitting a sign—these qualify as minor accidents. If the police get involved, you've got trouble.

• If you have a fender-bender, follow the Mexican's lead. If he wants to exchange information, fine. If he splits, do the same. Remain totally polite and calm—never get into an argument! Try to avoid any police involvement.

SERIOUS ACCIDENTS

If you're involved in a serious accident and if you're at fault, you can be open to criminal charges.

• Be prepared for lengthy questions and a detailed report. Note that these reports can be used in court. Do not admit to anything.

• You're at a disadvantage in Mexico because of the language barrier.

• All people involved in an accident are detained automatically. The police try to determine responsibility for the accident, which will in turn determine the settlement.

• In practice the police often split responsibility for an accident so that both insurance companies have to pay up.

• Contact your insurance company as soon as possible after an accident. Good insurance will keep your stay with the police short and sweet (or a little less bitter).

IF YOU SEE AN ACCIDENT . . .

• If you see an accident, don't stop unless you feel you can give first aid *before* police arrive on the scene.

• Most Mexicans advise tourists not to stop at all since they can be blamed for an accident in which they were not even involved.

• This is a very difficult decision, but you can get into very deep trouble at the scene of an accident, including a suit for medical malpractice.

TRAFFIC VIOLATIONS

● The police generally leave traffic to the survival of the fittest. Mexicans routinely disobey signs and speed laws.

● If you're pulled over for a traffic ticket, you're in a situation where the police are milking the tourists and the cows. When requested for a certain amount, hand the cop less than what was asked for—that will often do the trick.

Drug dealing

● Do not use drugs in Mexico—it's not worth the risk, even though you can't help smelling the stuff everywhere.

● If you're carrying small amounts (less than 100 grams) of marijuana, you'll be booted out of the country. Note that you can still be tossed in the slammer for this amount, but a "gentleman's agreement" exists unofficially to make minor drug offenses minor.

● If you're jailed for dealing in drugs, God help you. Sentences served in Mexican jails are best described as *intolerable*.

● People are paranoid about drugs in Mexico. That's why no one picks up hitchhikers. In Mexico you're presumed guilty, if even by association. Furthermore, the same people who sell drugs often play a double role as police informant. It's a bad scene. Skip it.

Exporting artifacts is illegal

Although it's legal to take antiques out of the country, it is illegal to take out any genuine artifacts, such as items from archaeological sites.

Nudity is illegal

● As far as Mexicans are concerned, it's never hot enough to take it all off. Nudity is illegal, which baffles Europeans who consider skinny dipping and nude bathing as an innocuous sport.

● In the most popular beach areas you can get away with the barest of essentials. Women can even go topless and nearly bottomless *if* they're surrounded by other foreigners doing the same thing.

● On a few beaches nudity is more or less tolerated, as at El Mirador, roughly a mile south of the ruins of Tulúm. But keep clothes handy, just in case of a surprise raid.

● Inland, it's extremely offensive to be caught nude. If you're hiking and want to clean up, keep something on. And men and women should not wash together in the altogether.

● Women should note that nude bathing may attract admiring Mexico machos, especially in remote areas. The situation can turn hot, especially if they've been drinking. Be alert.

Prostitution is legal

It doesn't have to make sense, it's just the way it is. Sex between consenting adults for pleasure or pay is just plain okay.

THE POLICE

The police in Mexico can be a problem. Wariness is certainly advisable. Bandits posing as police—that's another scare in the system.

Police inspections

● Military and police inspections are normally routine and usually do not include body searches. They're most common along the coast and near borders.

● Mexico does have secret police. They are most common in areas with drug smuggling, as in Cabo San Lucas where the ferry lands from Mazatlán.

Bribes

● Bribes *(mordidas)* are also a fact of life, but most tourists rarely find themselves in a bribe situation.

• If you are asked for a bribe, sometimes the best thing is to ignore the request. If the person is persistent or going to cause more trouble than it's worth, pay up as if it were a tip.

• Don't go to Mexico expecting to pay bribes. You can cover yourself in most situations so that you don't have to.

• However, if you're in a tight spot, use a bribe to get out of it. The upfront cost of a bribe can be worth it.

IF TROUBLE STRIKES

The addresses below are of the consulates and embassies of the United States and Canada in Mexico. These offices can help in virtually any trouble situation. Don't hesitate to ask for help—that's their job!

There are consular agents in Acapulco, Cancún, Durango, Mulege, Oaxaca, Puerto Vallarta, San Luis Potosí, Tampico, and Veracruz. They are to be used only in emergencies. For their telephone number and address call the U.S. Embassy in Mexico City.

U.S. Embassy

U.S. Embassy
Paseo de la Reforma 305
México 5, D.F.
tel.: (905) 553-3333

U.S. Consulates and Consulates General

Consulate General
924 Avenida Lopez Mateos
Ciudad Juárez, Chihuahua
tel.: (161) 34 048

Consulate General
Progreso 175
Guadalajara, Jalisco
tel.: (36) 25 29 28

Consulate
Isssteson Building, 3rd Floor
Miguel Hidalgo y Costillo No. 15
Hermosillo, Sonora
tel.: (621) 38 922

Consulate
Avenida Primera No. 232
Matamoros, Tamaulipas
tel.: (891) 25 250

Consulate
Circunvalación No. 6
Mazatlán, Sinoloa
tel.: (678) 12 905

Consulate
Paseo Montejo 453, Apartado Postal
130
Mérida, Yucatán
tel.: (992) 55 409

Consulate General
Avenida Constitución 411 Poniente
Monterrey, Nuevo León
tel.: (83) 43 06 50

Consulate
Avenida Allende 3330
Nuevo Laredo, Tamaulipas
tel.: (871) 40 512

Consulate General
Calle Tapachula 96
Tijuana, Baja California Norte
tel.: (706) 86 10 01

Canadian Embassy

Canadian Embassy
Schiller 529
Colonia Polanco
México, D.F.
tel.: (905) 254-3288

Canadian Consulates

Honorary Consul for Canada
Hotel Club del Sol, Mezzanine
Costera Miguel Aleman/Reyes Catolicos
Acapulco, Guerrero
tel.: (748) 46 356

Honorary Consul for Canada
Avenida Albatros 52
Mazatlán, Sinoloa
tel.: (678) 37 320

Honorary Consul for Canada
Calle 1-F #249 (x 36)
Fracc. Campestre
Mérida, Yucatán
tel.: (992) 70 460

Honorary Vice-Consul for Canada
German Gedovius No. 5, Office 201
Condominio del Parque
Río Tijuana, Baja California Norte
tel.: (706) 84 04 61

TOURIST PROBLEMS

Mexico has set up a system to deal with tourist complaints, no matter what they are. The following office handles these:

Orientación, Información y Quejas
Secretaría de Turismo
Mazaryk 172
Colonia Polanco
México, D.F. 11587
tel.: 250-4618 or 250-8555 ext. 10

CUSTOMS

In this chapter you'll find hints on clearing customs both in the United States and Canada.

DUTIES AND U.S. CUSTOMS

The brochure "Know Before You Go" gives detailed information on customs procedures. Since regulations change frequently, get it from any local customs office or from U.S. Customs Service, P.O. Box 7407, Washington, DC 20044, tel.: (202) 566-8195.

Personal exemption

● You are allowed to bring back from Mexico $400 worth of goods without paying 1¢ of duty. This personal exemption applies to each member of a family regardless of age.

● Anyone over twenty-one can bring in 1 liter of alcohol, 100 cigars, and 100 cigarettes without paying duty.

● All goods must accompany you to be exempt from duty.

● All personal articles which went into Mexico with you are allowed back into the United States without duty. However, you should have receipts or a registration slip for anything of great value.

Registration

● You must register all valuable articles with the U.S. Customs Service before going abroad. If you don't, you may have to pay duty when you return even though you didn't purchase the items in Mexico.

● To register items, you must take them in person to the nearest office of the U.S. Customs Service, many of which are located in major airports. You will receive a small white registration slip to prove that the articles were not purchased abroad.

Duty-free articles

● Many products from Mexico can be imported free of any duty. These articles need not be part of your personal exemption. For a list of exempt products, ask for "GSP and the Traveler," available free from U.S. Customs Service, P.O. Box 7407, Washington, DC 20044, or from any local branch office.

● Here are some of the more popular duty-free articles which can be brought in from Mexico:

antiques (not pre-Hispanic)	jewelry
art	lamps
basketry	leather goods (not luggage)
books	musical instruments
candles	onyx
candle holders	papier-mâché pieces
ceramic articles	picture frames
furniture (of any material)	piñatas
headware (not caps)	saddles and harnesses
household articles	wood products

Not allowed into the United States:

animals and animal products	birds (except pets)
archaeological finds	bullion
artifacts	Cambodian imports

Cuban imports
Decca and Columbia records
eggs (unless cooked)
fruits (except for bananas, blackberries, cactus fruits, dates, dewberries, grapes, lychees, melons, papayas, pineapples, and strawberries)
gold coins
hazardous materials (drugs, toxic substances, absinthe, and liquor-filled candy)
livestock
lottery tickets
meats and meat products
medals
monkeys, primates
narcotics
North Korean products
nuts (except acorns, almonds, cocoa beans, chestnuts, coconut, peanuts, pecans, pine nuts, tamarind beans, walnuts, and, waternuts)
plants and plant products
pornography
prison products
products made from animals on the endangered species list (particularly conch and tortoise shell)
poultry (unless cooked)
seditious literature
snails
soil
trademarked items (scrape off the trademark)
uncured hides
vegetables (specifically Irish potatoes, okra, sweet potatoes, and yams)
Vietnamese products

Oral declarations

• Coming back into the United States from Mexico, you must declare the total value of your purchases there. If you are under $400 per person, you can make an oral declaration.

• A head of household can make a declaration for the whole family—you need fill out only one form.

Written declarations

• If you've gone over your $400 personal exemption, you have to fill out a written declaration of all items.

• Anything related to business must be declared.

• You are required to make a written declaration if asked by a customs inspector to do so.

Possible snags in customs

• If you buy any prescription or over-the-counter drugs in Mexico, you must declare them. If they contain narcotics, you should carry a prescription for them.

• Although it is not illegal to carry large sums of money, it must be declared. If you've got more than $10,000, you must fill out a form with customs.

• If an official catches you bringing in something that you haven't declared, admit the mistake immediately. Just say that you forgot about it. Avoid confrontations and arguments.

• If an official breaks an item while searching bags, file a U.S. Government form SF9-5 with the regional customs office in the state where the damage takes place. You'll be reimbursed.

Custom inspection tips

• Have your registration slip at hand for valuable articles that you took from the United States, or you'll have to pay duty on them if you're over the $400 personal exemption.

• Have all your sales receipts handy to prove the actual cost of things purchased in Mexico. Note that customs officials know values almost to the cent. Don't try to get by with doctored sales receipts. Furthermore, the new allowances and duties seem liberal and appropriate.

• Put all purchased items in one spot, so that it's easy to check them over. The official may feel the corners of your bags, but often he'll take your statement at face value.

• *Never* carry bags or items for someone else through customs—you don't know what's in them. What would you do if they found something illegal?

• A customs official may ask you to empty your pockets, and very rarely he or she may ask for a body search.

• If it makes you feel better, you're expected to be slightly nervous going through an inspection. But don't make jokes, jabber, or volunteer information. Answer all questions as politely and briefly as possible.

U.S. Customs regulations on packages shipped separately

● You can send any personal article home without paying duty, as long as it was purchased in the United States. Mark the package "American Goods Returned."

● You can send a friend or relative one duty-free gift per day just as long as its fair retail value is less than $50. Mark the package "Unsolicted Gift—Value Less Than $50." Clearly state on the package what the gift is.

● You can also send many separate gifts in one large package, as long as each gift is individually wrapped and marked with the name of the recipient. The nature of every gift within the large package must be marked on the outside.

● You must pay duty on all items you send to your home, but not on those gifts sent to friends. Many travelers arrange to send items to friends, who will hold them for their return.

Problems with customs

● If you have a problem with customs or think that a duty seems unreasonable, take up your complaint with the following person:

Assistant Commissioner
Office of Inspection and Control
U.S. Customs Service
Washington, DC 20229
tel.: (202) 566-8195

U.S. state liquor regulations

● Each state in the United States has its own regulations on the amount of liquor which can be imported from Mexico. This ranges from no restrictions to no liquor at all.

● If you intend to import liquor, write for the pamphlet summarizing local liquor laws published by the following organization:

Distilled Spirits Council of the
  United States, Inc.
1250 I Street Northwest, Suite 900
Washington, DC 20005
tel.: (202) 628-3544

CANADIAN CUSTOMS

• Canada allows a personal exemption on goods purchased abroad. Once each year, you're allowed to bring in $300 worth of goods duty-free *if* you stayed in Mexico for a week or longer.

• Smaller exemptions are allowed for shorter stays.

• After a one-week stay in Mexico you're also allowed to import 40 ounces of alcohol, 50 cigars, 200 cigarettes, and 2 pounds of tobacco.

• Make sure that you register all valuables with customs before going to Mexico. You'll fill out form Y-38 which applies only to items with serial numbers.

• If an item has no serial number, you must have a bill of sale or an appraisal with photo (signed and dated) to prove that the product was of Canadian origin. It's much easier to leave valuable things at home!

• You're not allowed to import alligators, cacti, cats (wild), crocodiles, falcons, ivory, monkeys, orchids, otters, and sea turtles—or the products made from these endangered species.

• You're allowed to send gifts to friends and relatives as long as the value is less than $40. Check locally for current restrictions and regulations since they change frequently.

THE TEN COMMANDMENTS

Be realistic in your expectations. Mexico is a developing country.

Never assume anything. If something can go wrong, it might.

Be wary of all information—prices; bus, train, and plane schedules; telephone numbers and addresses.

Don't be too quick to take "no" for an answer. You can frequently turn "no" into "yes."

If your record's spinning on 45, slow it down to 33. The pace in Mexico is not going to speed up for you.

"One who does not speak, God does not hear." If you want it, ask for it.

Accept Mexico as is—poverty and all. Mexicans appreciate this basic courtesy.

Don't lay your standards on the Mexicans. They aren't going to change, so why bother?

Even if you're angry, pretend you're not. Anger is bad form in Mexico and counterproductive.

If Mexicans don't do or use it, it will be expensive. If saving money really counts, travel in Mexico like a Mexican.

INDEX